THE ULTIMATE INSIDER'S GUIDE TO INTELLECTUAL PROPERTY

To Dr. Andersen:

Congratulations and welcome to the Trademark Factory® family. Be Legendary — It's Worth It!

ANDREI MINCOV

THE ULTIMATE INSIDER'S GUIDE TO INTELLECTUAL PROPERTY

WHEN TO SEE AN IP LAWYER AND ASK EDUCATED QUESTIONS ABOUT COPYRIGHT, TRADEMARKS, PATENTS, TRADE SECRETS, INDUSTRIAL DESIGNS, CONTRACTS, AND OTHER WAYS OF *PROTECTING YOUR IDEAS AND COVERING YOUR ASSETS*®

PRAISE FOR
THE ULTIMATE
INSIDER'S GUIDE TO
INTELLECTUAL PROPERTY

Thinking about IP? Get this book! The first chapter alone could save you thousands in legal fees.

Greg Smith
Co-Founder, Lawyer and CEO of Thinkific.com

This book demystifies intellectual property and explains when you need to protect it—without scaring or overwhelming you with legalese. If you use the internet to generate leads or deliver your services online, make sure you read this book and learn how to protect your assets!

Matt Astifan
Founder of Web Friendly

Without question, Andrei Mincov is one of the country's foremost experts in intellectual property. With this book you will learn proven and practical step-by-step strategies for using IP as a tool that can take your business to the next level.

Darren Jacklin
World-Class Professional Speaker, Corporate Trainer,
Angel Investor, www.DarrenJacklin.com

If you have any questions about trademarks, copyright, patents or anything to do with intellectual property, Andrei has it all covered in this book. This is the ultimate guide to everything you need to know to protect your brand.

Melonie Dodaro
Founder of TopDogSocialMedia.com, Author of The LinkedIn Code

As someone who has been practicing and teaching sports, media and entertainment law for several decades, I can't stress enough the importance of intellectual property for modern businesses. Neglecting IP is a sure recipe for failure. Make sure you read this book, it will deliver information that every business owner needs to know. As an added bonus, it's actually interesting to read.

Joe Weiler
Professor of Law at University of British Columbia

Most entrepreneurs and companies start worrying about IP protection when it's already too late. Andrei's book provides a bird's eye view on the entire intellectual property landscape—see which parts apply to your business, then act to secure, grow and multiply the assets.

Igor Faletski
CEO of Mobify

Andrei Mincov takes a complex subject and makes it simple to understand for anyone who is mystified about intellectual property matters. I strongly recommend it for entrepreneurs—it's a quick read and it provides an excellent introduction to the world of IP.

Mike Volker
Director of Simon Fraser University Innovation Office,
Angel Investor in 100+ Tech Startups

The Ultimate Insider's Guide to Intellectual Property /
When to See an IP Lawyer and Ask Educated Questions
about Copyright, Trademarks, Patents, Trade Secrets,
Industrial Designs, Contracts, and Other Ways of
Protecting Your Ideas and Covering Your Assets® /
Mincov, Andrei

ISBN-13: 978-0-9912964-3-9
ISBN-10: 0991296435

Cover design: Andrei Mincov
Interior layout concept and design: Andrei Mincov
Cover photograph: Pollux Chung

Published by Expert Author Publishing
www.expertauthorpublishing.com

Canadian Address: 1265 Charter Hill Drive, Coquitlam, BC V3E 1P1
Phone: (604) 941-3041 Fax: (604) 944-7993

US Address: 1300 Boblett Street, Unit A-218, Blaine, WA 98230
Phone: (866) 492-6623 Fax: (250) 493-6603

ALSO BY ANDREI MINCOV

From Faceless to Legendary:
The Ultimate Insider's Guide to Intellectual Property
for Bars, Cafes, and Restaurants

http://FacelessToLegendary.Com/Restaurants

From Faceless to Legendary:
The Ultimate Insider's Guide to Intellectual Property
for Coaches, Mentors, Trainers, and Consultants

http://FacelessToLegendary.Com/Coaches

GET ALL THE HELP YOU CAN GET

Order your free trademark search:
http://freeTMsearch.com

Get your brands trademarked:
http://TrademarkFactory.com

Watch cartoons explaining trademarks in plain English:
http://TrademarkCartoons.com

Buy contract templates related to intellectual property:
http://NiceContracts.com

Order Intellectual Property Strategy Review consultation:
http://IPStrategyReview.com

To my father, Mark Minkov, who made me.
I miss you.

To my wife, Emilia Mincov, who misses me
even when I'm in the next room.

TABLE OF CONTENTS

ABOUT THIS BOOK

WHY THIS BOOK?

The purpose of this book is to equip you with enough knowledge about intellectual property to enable you to timely identify situations when you need to see an IP lawyer and ask educated questions. Questions that will give you answers that you can actually use rather than leave you frustrated from having to respond to a 15-page legal opinion with a one-line email that goes: "*So what does it all mean and what should I do?*"

This book is for you if you are a business owner who is tired of being intimidated by the legal mumbo jumbo that typically surrounds intellectual property and if you want to finally have some clarity about IP in order to have meaningful conversations with investors, partners, competitors, employees, and—yes—lawyers.

Intellectual property, commonly abbreviated as IP, surrounds us everywhere. If you look around, you will see thousands of examples of what is or once was intellectual property. Let's start with this book. The text that you are reading now is my intellectual property. The design of the cover of this book is intellectual property. My photograph on the cover of this book is intellectual property.

I typed this book using software that someone had written, using a computer that someone had invented.

Chances are that you are dressed in clothes that someone has designed, sitting on a couch that someone has contrived, in a house designed by someone from materials that someone has invented, heated and lighted by means invented by someone else. All of this is intellectual property.

Maybe you're reading this book with some music in the background.

That music is intellectual property. The musical instruments used to perform this music have been invented by someone. The equipment used to record these performances has been invented by someone. The device you are using to play that music has also been invented by someone. All of this is intellectual property.

Maybe you have just downloaded a movie you're going to watch later tonight. That movie is intellectual property. The software you used to download that movie is also intellectual property.

Someone has written the apps you use on your phone. Someone has invented something that made your phone possible. Even the telephony itself has once been invented by someone. And while we're at it, the GPS system and the satellites that allow you to find your way around have all been invented by someone. Yes, all of this is also intellectual property.

Love it or hate it, you shop based on your loyalty to or knowledge of brands. You google stuff using brands as keywords. Speaking of googling, the Google search engine is also intellectual property, along with all trade secrets that are behind their algorithm.

The money you use has been designed by someone. The national anthem you proudly sing has been composed by someone.

Look around you! Unless you've been living in a cave for the last decade (in which case, how did you get hold of this book?), pretty much everything that surrounds you is intellectual property. And no, the lake that you drive to, the park you bike to, or the sky you look at through your window are not good counter-examples because—you guessed it!—the car, the bike and the window have all been invented and designed by someone and are embodiments of intellectual property.

Some of this intellectual property was or is being commercialized, some of it was or is being given away, some of it was or is being stolen, and some of it was or is being neglected.

Remember, just because someone lets you use something for free does not mean that it is no longer their property, their *intellectual* property.

What owners do with their intellectual property is up to them. Or at least it *should* be up to them.

And because intellectual property is everywhere, it is crucial that you understand how it works. Not only because it will allow you to better see the opportunities to build a sustainable competitive advantage, but also because you need to know what *others* can do to *your* business if you improperly use *their* IP.

This is what this book is about.

You see, business owners make two major mistakes when it comes to dealing with intellectual property lawyers. Either they go and see a lawyer when they don't need to, and so they get frustrated with having to pay for something that is of little value to them. Or they don't go and see a lawyer until they can no longer be helped and need to be saved— at which point, it is often too late.

Business owners make these mistakes because they don't know what they don't know and because they are afraid to see a lawyer due to the less than stellar reputation of the legal profession.

WHO IS THIS BOOK NOT FOR?

While dealing with a very specialized topic, this book will be useful to a great many people.

However, let me say who this book is NOT for.

This book is not for you if you are a lawyer looking for a bucketload of footnotes and legal citations. There are many great thick books on different areas of intellectual property, and I've used my share of them in my practice. The purpose of this book is not to replace such books or even compete with them. This book is designed to be as non-lawyer reader friendly as possible. If anything, this book can be a springboard for reading those other books after you have mastered enough to honestly say: *"Oh, I finally seem to be getting it."*

This book is not for you if you believe that you are entitled to other people's work—for free. If you think the world owes you something, if you think that you have a right to listen to the last album by your favourite band or watch the latest movie, if you think that the government has an obligation to restrict the rights of creators in order to ensure the benefits to consumers, you will see very little respect for your beliefs in this book. There are lawyers out there who publish books for people like you. I am not one of them.

This book is not for you if you have just been sued and are looking for an inexpensive way to become a do-it-yourself IP litigator. This book is not for you if you are hiring an employee tomorrow and need to draft a proper IP assignment clause. This book is not for you if you are an investor who is looking for a comprehensive manual on how to conduct an IP due diligence. While this book will answer many questions, it will not replace legal advice.

HOW IS THIS BOOK STRUCTURED?

We'll start with me telling you who I am, how I got to be an IP lawyer and what makes me qualified to write this book.

Then, in Part I of this book, I will share with you 10 Big Secrets about intellectual property (and about law in general) that will answer most of your specific questions and "what ifs."

You have probably looked at the list in the Table of Contents, but these 10 Big Secrets are so important that I'm going to list them here again:

1. IP is just an umbrella term for several areas of law.
2. Focus on IP coming IN and IP going OUT.

3.   IP is not just about the money.

4.   IP is just a tool.

5.   Judges look for better stories, not better law.

6.   IP is just about risk management.

7.   IP is only as good as your ability to defend it.

8.   IP is only as good as your business.

9.   IP is strong. Contracts are stronger.

10.   Paying does not mean buying.

These 10 Big Secrets are so important that I will be referencing them throughout this book. Many paragraphs of this book will have a reference to at least one of these Big Secrets. I'm doing this for a simple reason—you need to be able to absorb legal information *in context*.

For example, you will see a   next to the paragraph where I tell you that you should store drafts of your works. This references Big Secret #5 and reminds you that keeping drafts will allow you to create "the better story" which will help convince the judge that you are the good guy.

Another example: you will see   (Big Secret #4) next to the paragraph where I explain the reasons for registering trademarks. This reminds you to check if these reasons for registering trademarks meet your overall strategy, because IP is only a means to an end (a tool), not the end itself.

In Part II of the book, you will learn important information about different areas of IP—copyright, trademarks, patents, industrial designs, trade secrets and contracts. Again, the purpose is not to teach you everything I know about these areas. This would make it into a book that I say it is not. The idea is to condense what you need to know into a digestible chapter that you can read in one go. This way you will have enough information to filter out what is irrelevant to your business and start asking the right questions while you focus on what *is relevant.*

For example, you will not find a definitive answer to the question whether your particular trademark is registrable. What you will learn is that not all trademarks are registrable, that registration has specific benefits, and, most importantly, how to find out whether registration is even desirable in your case. Equipped with this knowledge, you can go and see an IP lawyer with a short list of specific questions, be prepared to address your lawyer's concerns, and walk away with conclusive, actionable answers.

In Part III of the book, we will put everything together. This isn't just a summary of what you've learned in the book. Part III will look at how to apply the information to your particular business. This is where you will answer the question, *"When is the right time for me to see an IP lawyer?"*

In the Appendix, you will find a table listing different parameters of different laws pertaining to intellectual property. This is your quick reference guide if you are looking for specific legal information. For example, *"What is the term of protection for industrial designs? What are the requirements for patentability? What are the possible defences in a copyright infringement lawsuit?"*

I made some valuable additional materials available to readers of this book in electronic form. Please go to ***http://ipbook.ca/more*** to download them.

BORING, BUT NECESSARY, NOTES AND DISCLAIMERS

1. This book is not, it is not written as, is not designed to be, and should not be considered legal advice. I have made every effort to make sure this book contains accurate and authoritative information about the subject matter covered. However, no warran-

ties or guarantees are made that the information is or remains accurate or updated. This book is published for information purposes only. If you need legal advice, specific business advice, or require other assistance, seek the services of a competent professional. Neither I nor Trademark Factory International Inc. assume any responsibility or liability of any kind for whatever decisions you purportedly make as a result of something you read in this book. Even if you think your situation is the same as a situation described in this book, do not assume that you can rely on this book as legal advice.

I wrote this book while I was a lawyer and the owner of Mincov Law Corporation. As you will learn from this book, in 2015, I voluntarily gave up my lawyer license in Canada, to be able to scale up Trademark Factory® and offer guaranteed flat-fee trademarking services to entrepreneurs and businesses around the world. This book should not be taken as a claim or representation that I am authorized to practice law in your or in any jurisdiction.

Just in case, I need to say it again. If you require legal advice, seek legal advice from a lawyer who will have the benefit of being able to hear your story and ask you the necessary questions before providing an opinion. I would like to believe that this book will help you choose Trademark Factory International Inc. as your No. 1 destination for trademarking and intellectual property strategy review. Having said that, Trademark Factory International Inc. is not a law firm; we don't provide legal services outside of trademarking. There will be times when you should seek legal advice from other firms.

2.   This book contains legal information about patents. For the purposes of full disclosure, I am not a patent agent, in Canada or

elsewhere. I have the knowledge about how the patent system works and am happy to share this information with you, but I have never filed a patent application, nor do I intend to. This book is designed to teach you to recognize situations when you need to have a patent professional help you draft your patent application. It is designed to teach you to recognize situations when you need to conduct a patent search in order to avoid getting sued by your competition. However, this book is not designed to teach you how to draft your own patent applications.

3. The legal information in this book is primarily based on the laws of Canada. While most of it is relevant to you, wherever you are, some specifics may not apply to you.

4. The opinions expressed in this book are those of the author. Some of these opinions are critical of the current state of the law in Canada. When you read that something should or should not be one way or the other, do not assume that this is the law or that it is a prevalent opinion of the majority of Canadian lawyers, or—indeed—that it is an opinion of anybody other than myself. I attempted to reasonably separate my opinions from statements.

    For example, when I say that it is very unfortunate that Canada now has a copyright exception for parodies, the "*Canada has a copyright exception for parodies*" part is a statement of fact, while the "*it is very unfortunate*" part is my opinion. If you cannot separate one from the other, you definitely should not read this book. Several times throughout this book, I make an analogy between infringement of IP rights and rape. If you are easily offended by such analogies, do not read this book.

5. To anyone who is sensitive to issues relating to gender or political-correctness, my use of "he", "him" or "his" in this book

when referring to a person who may be either a he or a she is for convenience only. I find it awkward to say "he or she", "him or her", "his or her", "the person" or "they" when referring to a single person. Trust me, I don't hate women. I don't think women are any less (or more) deserving because they are women. If you are still going to be upset, I suggest you close this book and find yourself a better way to spend a few hours of your life.

6. Throughout this book, I mention various trademarks that I do not own. This does not constitute "use" of these trademarks in the legal sense because I am not offering any products or services under these identifiers. However, you should know that these marks are trademarks of their respective owners.

    Trademark Factory International Inc. owns, among others, the following trademarks:

    TRADEMARK FACTORY ®

    PROTECTING YOUR IDEAS AND COVERING YOUR ASSETS ®

    IF IT'S REMARKABLE, IT'S TRADEMARKABLE ®

    IF IT'S WORTH PROMOTING, IT'S WORTH PROTECTING ™

    TRIPLE PEACE-OF-MIND GUARANTEE ™

    FROM FACELESS TO LEGENDARY ™

    IPSR ™

    IPSR QUADRANT ™

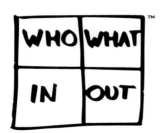

7.   In this book, you will see offers from Trademark Factory International Inc. You don't have to wait until you complete this book to take advantage of these opportunities. To find more information about the services provided by Trademark Factory International Inc., visit our websites at:

http://TrademarkFactory.com

http://IPStrategyReview.com

http://NiceContracts.com

ABOUT THE AUTHOR

I was an intellectual property lawyer for most of my life.

I'm fortunate not only to love the work that I do, but also to know exactly *why* I love it.

Let me tell you my story.

This story will probably feel pretty long to those of you who are simply looking for answers to your legal questions, so feel free to move on to the next part. I won't take offense.

If, however, you are curious to learn how I got to be what I am, you will learn many things about me that I've never shared with anyone. Things that define who I am today, why I do what I do, and how I treat my customers. These things are important when you are choosing an IP lawyer to help you, aren't they?

Born in Moscow, Russia a few years before the final whimper of the socialist Evil Empire, I became an IP lawyer when my father Mark Minkov, a famous Russian composer who had written music for over 100 movies and a countless number of hit songs, heard his music on the radio advertising an event organized by Samsung. The problem was that nobody had asked his permission to use his music. So he called the radio station and told them that they couldn't just take his music and use it however they pleased. They told him to sit down, shut up, and be grateful because they were doing him a favour by making him even more famous.

Believe it or not, he didn't like this very much. As it often happens in Hollywood movies, he told them, *"I'll see you in court!"* and hung up. He was yet to figure out who would represent him in court.

You see, Russia had just adopted its first post-Soviet *Copyright Act* that gave authors the exclusive right to control how their works could be used by others. There were a handful of renowned Soviet-era specialists in the field of intellectual property, but their number was minuscule compared to the number of authors who were in need of their services.

At that time, I was in my second year of university majoring in international law. Russia does not divide education into undergraduate and graduate studies. After 10 to 12 years of secondary school, one may attend a university, usually for 4 to 6 years. I was in my second year and, honestly, becoming a lawyer didn't really appeal to me at that time.

When my father asked me whether I could help him take this matter to court, I literally had no idea about copyright, civil procedure, or what to do in a courtroom. I still wonder what part of his request was just a test to see if I would chicken out. But I didn't throw in the towel. I said, *"Sure, let's do it!"*

Now it was my turn to figure out what to do. I asked around, read a ton of literature and found a couple of samples (and, just so you understand—you could not simply google "Copyright Lawsuit Papers". Back then, there WAS NO Google!). I finally managed to draft my very first statement of claim alleging that the radio station had infringed my father's copyright.

Then, I had to deliver the statement of claim to the judge (the process is completely different in Canada). So after sitting in line for a few hours, I finally got to see a real judge for the first time in my life. In Russia, you don't have to be called to the bar, or even have graduated from a law school, to represent clients in court. That's not to say that people weren't surprised to know that I was still a student, but no law prevented me from doing what I set out to do.

So I get to meet the judge who took my statement of claim and read all 5 or so pages while I was sitting across from her, in awe of her years of experience dealing with complexities of the Law.

She asked me a few questions to make sure she properly understood the claim and set the date of a preliminary hearing with the defendant in attendance. Before I left, I decided to build some rapport with the judge, so I asked her a probing question, "*So, there must be a lot of copyright cases coming in with all the piracy out there?*" She responded right away, "*Yes, there are so many of them, I should probably finally read the Copyright Act.*"

It was like going to a heart surgeon and asking him, "*So you must be busy these days?*" and to be told, "*Yes, there are so many patients, I should probably finally learn where the bloody heart is…*"

This was my first encounter with the Russian legal system in the 1990s.

The next thing I remember was the first day of trial. It was 8 in the morning, my dad was driving the car to the courthouse and my mom was in the back seat. I was in the passenger seat, wearing my best jeans and my best denim shirt, my rock-star down-to-my-mid-back hair carefully arranged into a ponytail, with a briefcase holding the courtroom speech I had been writing until 4 in the morning.

The closer we got to the courthouse, the more I felt my hands shaking and my knees trembling. A feeling of absolute horror. Like every good mother, my mom had a solution. She asked my dad to pull over, rushed out to a convenience store, came back with a small bottle of vodka, gave it to me and said, "*Here, have a drink, son!*" It was the only time I ever had a drink before trial. Then, it just brought me back to my senses.

I got to the courtroom and ripped the radio station's lawyer to shreds. I felt like a protagonist from a Chuck Norris film knocking out his opponent in the early minutes of the film. On a technicality, the other side's lawyer managed to get an adjournment (that's when the judge tells you that you're done for today and should come again on a different day).

The next day, instead of one lawyer, the radio station was represented by three. On our side, it was still me, wearing a different shirt this time. I might have been wearing the same pair of jeans. I don't really remember. I proceeded to deliver a number of knockout punches until the judge told us that she had heard enough to make a decision.

She solemnly announced that the radio station did not infringe on my dad's copyright.

I was absolutely devastated.

This is how Roy Jones Jr. must have felt when he was cheated out of the gold at the 1988 Olympics in Seoul.

When I got to read the full decision, I could not believe the nonsense I was reading. I am the first to admit when an opponent has a valid argument, but what I was reading was incomprehensible. Essentially, the judgment confirmed that the radio station had infringed my father's copyright, and because of that, it did not infringe on the copyright and so it did not have to pay.

Given that that judge was later dishonourably fired from the court, I would not be surprised if she had been driven by more than her misunderstanding of the law when she awarded the case to the radio station. Yes, that's another way of saying that I think they bought the judge.

I remember this as if it was yesterday. I was sitting in my room with that decision in my hands, feeling horrible. My dad came in my room and asked, *"So what are you going to do now?"*

I muttered, *"I really have no idea. I've done all that I thought needed to be done and I don't know how I could have done it any better."* He looked at me and said, *"We both know that we are in the right. We both know you did a good job. If you're not going to appeal this, you should just quit law school and find yourself another profession."*

We filed an appeal—which we lost, but at that point I refused to give up. We appealed the case even higher and it eventually made its way all the way up to the court just below the Supreme Court of Russia—this time I won. This was the best legal education I've ever received in my life.

Since that very first case, I have been hooked on intellectual property law.

During the two years it took me to win this first case, I learned so much about copyright and became so passionate about it that when my university offered me the opportunity to stay for another three years and do my PhD in law, I said that I would only be interested in doing it if I was allowed to write my dissertation on issues of intellectual property. I used that dissertation, which covered all international treaties in the field of IP, as the basis for my first book, *International Protection of Intellectual Property.*

Just shortly out of law school, I was made the CEO of a music publishing company founded by my father, mother, and myself on one side, and a recording company on the other side. It was a recording company that we had caught selling unauthorized copies of my dad's greatest hits. In the process of forcing them to pay, my dad and the recording company's president became the best of friends.

I had zero experience in running a business, and the business was crawling, but I was also the one who was responsible for drafting all sorts of agreements with authors and users of their work, so it was a priceless experience—both on the drafting and litigation side. When the global markets collapsed in 1998, we could no longer collect royalties because users had more important things to do, such as saving their own skin. I decided that the best thing to do was to dissolve the music publishing company for lack of capital or cash flow. This was one of the dumbest things I've ever done in my life, and I've blamed myself for it mercilessly for many years. If I had known what I was doing and persevered, the passive income it would be generating today would have been enormous.

In 2003, 9 years into practice, I joined the Moscow office of Baker & McKenzie, the largest international law firm on the planet. This was the first time I had to work in a real law office. The firm principals and I both had our doubts whether I'd be able to work in a large firm environment. I had to buy my very first suit and tie. I even had to cut my hair. I still keep my cut-off ponytail along with before and after photographs in my office. To my amazement and to the amazement of everyone at B&M, a glove could not have fit any better. I soon became the go-to person for all matters involving copyright and domain names.

While I was working for Baker & McKenzie, I used to take the quality of work I was involved in for granted. Now that I think about it, this is where the bulk of my diverse experience in IP came from. When I had to compile a list of my former clients and representative matters for my firm's website several years ago, I was so impressed with the list that I called my former IP principal in Moscow to thank him for the opportunity to work on those files. Indeed, I have helped hundreds of creators and businesses, including composers; designers; book writers, such as J.K. Rowling; film directors; singers; artists; individual software developers; movie producers; film companies ranging from small ones to Dreamworks; software companies ranging from one-man startups to Apple, Microsoft, and Sun; recording companies; electronics manufacturers, including Sony and Motorola; car companies, such as Porsche and Ford; apparel companies, such as Columbia Sportswear; perfumery and skincare companies, such as Amway, L'Oreal, and Mary Kay; and a countless number of other clients, big and small.

In 2006, my wife Emilia, our then 6-month-old daughter Masha, and I went on a brief vacation to Prague. We were blown away by how quickly the Czech Republic had developed into a civilized country after the era of Soviet serfdom. Despite 20 years of transformative changes, Russia was nowhere near achieving the same result, and it wasn't even moving in that direction.

I caught my first thought, "*How can some godforsaken tiny strip of land now live like a normal country, while the allegedly great Russian empire was still a very hostile place to be?*" Immediately, a new thought followed, that the greatness of a country is not measured in the number of millions of people killed in various wars to protect its territory, its minerals, oil, theatres and museums; it is about whether people treat each other like decent human beings instead of a means to a collective end.

Once we realized this, we decided that we had to get out of Russia, and that it was probably our last opportunity to actually do it. For years after my first trip outside of Russia (which happened to be to the U.S.), I had dreamed of living there, but I was too afraid to make the move. The more successful my career became in Russia, the harder it was for me to face the reality that I would need to start over from scratch in a new country. After the Prague visit, I said to myself, "*If I don't do it now, I will never be able to do it, and I will always regret that I never even tried.*"

Out of all the countries where English is an official language (which was a necessary condition if I wanted to re-launch my legal career in a new country), Canada offered the most transparent immigration system. So the decision was made.

Everyone seemed to be using my father's music, so I continued to help him protect and defend his copyrights. In fact, by the time I left Russia, there was not a single federal TV channel in Russia that I had not sued for infringing my dad's copyrights. I won every time, and I only had to do it once per channel. Subsequently, all that was necessary was for me to pick up the phone and say, "*We got you again, here's the bill.*"

When I shared my idea of moving to Canada with the then managing partner at Baker & McKenzie, who is a Canadian, she asked me, "*Do you know that you would need to go back to law school?*" At first, I thought it was a joke meant to make me stay. Then I realized that she was not kidding. She suggested that I apply to Canadian law schools from Russia. This was priceless advice that I will be forever grateful for.

In 2007, we landed in Vancouver airport, and a new chapter of my life began.

I made myself a promise to be open-minded towards other areas of law while at Canadian law school. I wanted to make sure that my focus on intellectual property was not merely an accident. No such luck. While my marks were great all around (in fact, during my last year I finished first in class in half my courses and in the top 10 in the remaining ones—not bad for an ESL student), the only times my eyes lit up were when the subject had to do with IP.

We loved our new home and were extremely happy about the move. There was only one thing that did not really click in our minds. We moved to Canada based on the assumption that it was a capitalist country. We experienced a very traumatic cognitive dissonance to find out that the ideals of capitalism were not universally recognized in Canada, to put it mildly.

Assumptions are a terrible thing. You don't give them up easily. You attempt to explain reality as if your assumptions are true, even if everything around you suggests that they are not. Having come from a country that was devastated by socialism, I could not believe that anyone in their right mind would seriously offer to repeat the brutal experiment in North America—voluntarily. I was seeking answers.

The answers came in the form of two books that happened to be the thickest books I've ever read in my life, *Atlas Shrugged* and *Fountainhead* by Ayn Rand. I always thought that a life-changing book was nothing but a cliché. These two books proved me wrong. I will never forget how I found myself in an empty bathtub at 5 in the morning—two hours after I had drained the water, unable to put the book down and get out. I had goose bumps all over—and not just because I was freezing. I finally found the answers I was seeking. I finally realized why I could not reconcile my assumptions with reality. In the words of Ms. Rand herself, "Contradictions do not exist. Whenever you think that you are facing a contradiction, check your premises. You will find that one of them is wrong." So I did.

This is when I realized that politically I had a mission to defend freedom, capitalism, and individual rights. I started reading all sorts of literature, and obtained a much better understanding of the subject, the tactics of collectivists, and the reasons why they are bound to lead to bloodshed. It was not unusual for me to read Frederic Bastiat and Karl Marx, Friedrich Hayek and Ayn Rand, Saul Alinsky and Glenn Beck almost simultaneously in the spare time I had between law school and family.

The more books by Ayn Rand I read, the more childhood memories came back to me. One of them will probably haunt me forever. I still vividly remember getting on a bus with my mom to go to my music lessons. I was probably around 11. I came up with this theory I referred to as *rational egoism*, and I was trying to convince my mom of its merits. Basically, the idea was that everything people do, they do for their own sake. That even when parents genuinely love their children and wish them all the best, they do so because they, the parents, feel good when people they care about (their kids) are happy. As it turned out some 25 years later, the theory I developed was almost word-for-word Ayn Rand's vision of selfishness.

I have finally realized what the *real* reason for my immigration was. Seven years later, now that I have become a Canadian citizen, I know *why* I wanted to immigrate and what it is that I wanted to immigrate to. I wanted to go to a place where individual rights are respected regardless of whether it benefits the "community" or "society as a whole." I wanted to go to a place that does not live by the utopian principle of "to each according to his needs, from each according to his abilities." I wanted to be surrounded by free people, equal under the law, who did not have to, in the famously sinister words of Bernard Shaw, "justify their existence [by the weight they pull] in the social boat." I wanted to be in a place where people and companies are free to compete without the state giving out privileges to the "more equal" ones.

My mom told me shortly before I left Russia, "*Remember, everywhere you go, you take your crap with you.*" She was right. But she missed a very important point. Sometimes, you don't know what you're carrying until you make the move.

One of my favourite quotes is from the Rocky VI movie where Rocky talks to his son about life. He says, "*It ain't about how hard you hit, it's about how hard you can GET hit and keep moving forward, how much you can take and keep moving forward. That's how winning is done. Now if you know what you're worth, then go out and get what you're worth, but you gotta be willing to take the hits and not pointing fingers saying you ain't where you wanna be because of him, of her, or anybody. Cowards do that, and that ain't you! You're better than that!*"

I've always had ambitious goals and equally compelling excuses why those goals could not be achieved. I would blame a lack of public respect for intellectual property, a despotic regime in Russia, stupid judges, inadequate court awards for infringement of copyright, corrupt lawmakers, and corrupt law enforcement officials. When I caught myself on the verge of complaining about the same problems in Canada and in the world at large, I realized that while these issues may really be the cause of the world's predicament, I could no longer let my happiness remain hostage to such issues. Just because Russia (or Canada) has idiotic copyright laws does not mean that I cannot help creators protect their rights. Just as it does not mean that I should passively await the miraculous moment when everything somehow fixes itself.

In 2011, after 3 more years of law school and a year of articling with a Canadian law firm, the Law Society of British Columbia graciously allowed me to call myself a lawyer again. What was missing was a long line-up of law firms competing with each other for the opportunity to make me an offer of employment. Let me rephrase that, nobody wanted to hire me. I kept thinking about the line from the first Rambo movie when he said, "*Back there I could fly a gunship, I could drive a tank, I was in charge of million-dollar equipment, back here I can't even hold a job parking cars!*"

Right about that time, I came across Robert Kiyosaki's book *Rich Dad, Poor Dad*, where he convincingly demonstrated the difference between the insecurity of employment income and the unlimited potential of running one's own business.

This also made me remember one of the posters for my favourite band, W.A.S.P., that I've had on my wall for years. It was a picture of Blackie Lawless holding a "*Who Dares Wins*" sign. Indeed, it is amazing how easily most of us give up our childhood dreams, how easily we put up with people around us providing all the right reasons why we should take an easy road lest we fail.

It wasn't until then that I realized that I didn't fail as the CEO of the music publishing company because I was no good at being an entrepreneur. I failed because I didn't have a slightest clue how to run a company. Thinking back, I would have been a miracle if, in fact, the entire thing worked out!

So, I took a leap of faith and started my own law firm in 2011. I couldn't think of a better name, so I called it simply—Mincov Law Corporation.

Very soon I discovered that not being hired by other firms was a blessing in disguise, because it allowed me to do what I love to do best— practice law in the field of intellectual property and grow everyday by learning how to be an entrepreneur. I can honestly say that the last few years have been the most exciting years of my life.

I kept looking for ways to grow my business in a way that would make the competition irrelevant. Through endless marketing trials and errors, my firm was slowly but surely gaining popularity among Canadian startups.

Remember the movie *Back To The Future*, where Dr. Emmett Brown exclaims, "I finally invented something that works!"? This is how I felt in 2013 when I came up with the idea of the **Trademark Factory**®, a service that provides a one-of-a-kind way to register trademarks. This was a game changer, not only because it crystallizes the unique selling proposition of my firm, but also because it allowed me to fuse all the different things I like doing into a single activity. I protect intellectual property, I run a business, I deal with brilliant people, I speak a foreign language, and I write computer code that works!

In 2015, I sacrificed my Canadian lawyer license in order to be able to deliver guaranteed flat-fee trademarking services to clients around the world. Because of many arbitrary regulations, I simply could not do what my clients wanted me to do while remaining a lawyer. Thus, I voluntarily gave up my lawyer license, renamed my firm to Trademark Factory International Inc., and our sole focus as a business is now trademarking.

Why should you care about any of this?

Because if you become my client, it won't be because IP happens to be the only way I can make a living. It will be because I deeply care about intellectual property and the ability of those who create it to protect their right to decide how their property should be used. This is also the reason I don't take cases when I would be required to justify deliberate unauthorized use of somebody else's works.

You see, one of the reasons I love doing what I do so much is that I have the privilege of dealing with brilliant people all the time. My clients create what millions of people around the world want to use, listen to, play, watch, or steal. I have profound admiration for what people have created. Without the creative genius of all these individuals, our lives would have been truly miserable. I admire my clients' accomplishments and because of that, I thoroughly enjoy the moments when I realize that I came up with an outside-the-box legal solution that helps them achieve their goals.

I strongly believe that creators deserve to have a say in how their creations are used. I strongly believe that they deserve not to have their rights and property stolen from them.

These are the reasons I do what I do and this is why I love doing it!

Now that you've gotten to know me a little bit, let's get started with the real reason you're holding this book in your hands.

Time to learn about intellectual property!

PART I

TEN BIG SECRETS ABOUT INTELLECTUAL PROPERTY (AND ABOUT LAW IN GENERAL)

This part of the book has the least to do with specifics of intellectual property—yet I claim that this is where you will find the most valuable information.

The information you'll find here will probably answer close to eighty percent of the questions you may ever want to ask a lawyer. In fact, this information is useful even if your questions have nothing to do with intellectual property. If you teach yourself to always look through the prism of these 10 Big Secrets, you will be able to narrow the focus of your questions about the law that remain unanswered, while dramatically improving your understanding of the answers you do receive.

Without a laser focus, you are inviting excessive fees in exchange for a sea of legalese grandiloquence you cannot comprehend.

In fact, there are only two ways to understand a complex subject. First, you can study it thoroughly and become an expert. For example, you study addition, subtraction, multiplication and division first, then pre-algebra and algebra, before becoming capable of understanding calculus.

The other way to understand a complex subject is by reducing it to an understanding of what it is, what it is for, when you need it, how you know you need it, and what you do about it. For example, you reduce your understanding of the mechanics of an automobile to the knowledge that if you press the gas pedal it will move forward, and if you have smoke coming out of your hood, you should get your car fixed.

Lawyers are notorious for attempting to convince mere mortals that they are the gatekeepers to some higher knowledge. By artificially complicating things (and even the language) surrounding laws, lawyers have created an atmosphere that prevents people from even attempting to understand these laws, let alone master them. For a perfect example, try reading a few pages from Canada's *Income Tax Act*.

Often, discouraged by their failure to understand the incomprehensible, business owners tend to avoid dealing with the subject altogether, until they really have to.

The purpose of this part is to equip you with enough context to give you the confidence to make important decisions without having to completely rely on others to tell you what to do, and to overcome the urge to stick your head in the sand until you can no longer evade the harsh reality.

WHAT DOES THAT MEAN?

When I was starting Mincov Law Corporation, I had virtually no idea how the tax system works in Canada. That is despite getting a B+ in my Tax I class.

I still remember the combined feeling of awe and frustration that I had during my first conversations with bookkeepers, accountants and financial planners.

I felt like I was the target of a grimy conspiracy where I was expected to sit with an intelligent face and make it appear as if *I* was the one making decisions. They would ask me, "*Do you want it this way or that way?*", as if I had the capacity to understand the consequences of either option. They would throw long words at me pretending to expect that I should know their meaning.

All I wanted was to get out of the room and get someone to do something so that I would never have to think about this again.

Then, one of my clients who happened to be a tax specialist sat down with me and walked me through the basics—in a language I could understand.

No, I did not become a tax guru. I still can't read the Income Tax Act, but I vividly remember the overflowing pride that I felt walking out of the next meeting I had with my accountant where not only could I ask meaningful questions and understand her answers, I could in fact engage in an argument about the strategy.

This part of the book is designed to do the same for you when it comes to dealing with intellectual property matters.

> It will give you the context to apply the specifics of the next part of this book to your life and your business and to get rid of that sense of intimidation that most business owners have when they feel they need to talk to a lawyer.

The information contained in this part answers most of the questions people ask me. Sometimes, I even get the urge to simply print 10 big signs with these 10 Big Secrets and silently raise them in front of my clients. If I did this, I would save a lot of breath during my consultations.

It is important to recognize that this is *not* a list of Frequently Asked Questions. These are the answers to questions that nobody asks. However, I believe that if business owners were equipped with this knowledge, they would feel a lot more confident about talking to their lawyers.

You see, very seldom does a business owner knowingly choose a catastrophically wrong option when the owner has full knowledge about all the options available to him. Most of the problems happen when the business owner makes a decision without knowing much about the issue at hand.

Obviously, we don't know what we don't know, and so business owners often feel intimidated because they don't have a way of telling whether doing something their lawyer suggests is necessary or simply nice-to-have. Business owners don't know whether their lawyer's recommendations are the result of the lawyer trying to cover his ass by offering an unnecessary and outrageously expensive bulletproof solution or whether it's safe to ignore such recommendations.

Lawyers, like doctors, are terrified of being sued by their clients for failure to cross all the t's and dot all the i's. On the one hand, the desire to offer the perfect solution is commendable, but, on the other hand, business owners do not always need a perfect solution to deal with their situation.

Usually, all you need is a good-enough solution, and, from the legal perspective, that good-enough solution may be very different from the perfect solution. In practice, a good-enough solution is more often than not the same as the perfect solution because nobody ever gets to test which one actually works better. After all, the 80/20 principle (according to which, roughly 80% of all effects come from 20% of the causes) applies to law and lawyers as well.

IS MY CONTRACT WORTH THE COST?

The vast majority of contracts never see the light of a courtroom.

So really most of the time, clients don't know if the contracts that they pay thousands of dollars for are any good.

This is the classic case of whether a tree that falls in a forest makes a sound when there is no one to hear it.

On a practical level, a contract that never gets tested is substantially better than a contract that is proven to be good through a 3-year litigation.

It's like having a fire insurance policy: you don't get upset if your house did not burn down just because you have a policy.

You may find this hard to believe but even the largest and most profitable companies have budgets. There will always be things that the business does not have a budget for. There are always things that an IP lawyer may suggest that the business is not willing to implement. The scale may be different but the problems and the approach needed are still the same.

Just to be clear, my goal here is not to convince you to spend more money on lawyers, or on me, in particular. The idea is to give you the ammunition to tell whether given a specific situation you should:

- do nothing;
- do something without getting lawyers involved; or
- see a lawyer.

Without understanding when to contact a lawyer, you run the risk of having to choose between the option of wasting limited resources on unnecessary services and the option of missing something very important for your business.

So, without further ado, let's go to the ten big ideas about intellectual property and the law in general, or as I like to call them—10 Big Secrets that other lawyers don't want you to know.

IP IS JUST AN UMBRELLA TERM FOR SEVERAL AREAS OF LAW

Up to this point, I've mentioned "intellectual property" 44 times and "IP" 32 times. So what exactly do these terms mean?

While "intellectual property" sounds like a legal term, in fact it is not. Intellectual property is merely an umbrella term for a number of different areas of law, each with its separate subject matter, rules, requirements, and scope.

These areas of law are copyright and neighbouring rights, trademarks, patents, industrial designs, and trade secrets. Contracts and contractual rights also play an important role in how intellectual property is used, so they should also be included under the same umbrella.

Intellectual property is a convenient term that refers to a set of exclusive rights recognized by governments in respect of various intangible assets created by the human mind.

According to the Convention Establishing the World Intellectual Property Organization, intellectual property includes the rights "relating to:

- literary, artistic and scientific works,
- performances of performing artists, phonograms, and broadcasts,
- inventions in all fields of human endeavour,
- scientific discoveries,
- industrial designs,
- trademarks, service marks, and commercial names and designations,
- protection against unfair competition,

and all other rights resulting from intellectual activity in the industrial, scientific, literary, or artistic fields."

All of these rights may be grouped into two categories:

- the rights to use your own intellectual property without interference from others; and
- the rights to prevent others from using your intellectual property.

Importantly, like all proper rights, intellectual property rights are not about granting you the royal permission to use your own IP. For example, the right to life is not about your right to live, it is about your right to stop others from killing you; your right to property is not about your right to own an iPhone, it is about your right to stop others from stealing your iPhone.

Similarly, the focus of intellectual property is on granting you the monopoly to use your IP in a way that would allow you to control its use by others, including preventing everybody else from using your IP without your permission. This is about getting a competitive advantage over everyone else who is not smart, creative, talented or industrious enough to have come up with whatever you came up with.

The only obligation your intellectual property rights impose on others is the obligation to not use it without your permission. Just because you own a copyright or a patent is not sufficient to force others to buy your products or listen to your music. But it is sufficient to prevent others from copying your invention and from sharing your music against your wishes.

The reasoning behind intellectual property is simple: you have invested time, talent, money, and effort to create something that did not exist before, so you should be able to preserve an advantage over everyone else who may be willing to parasitically copy what you have created.

Different types of IP provide different scope of protection to different types of things you may create, and we will discuss them all in this book.

You may have noticed that I mentioned that intellectual property is about rights recognized by governments. This is important because intellectual property rights are independent from country to country. While there are several international treaties that facilitate international protection of IP, you have a separate set of rights protected under the laws of each specific country.

So, what is so important about this Big Secret that I placed it at No. 1?

Make sure you understand these key points as you keep reading this book:

- There is no single unified law that uniformly regulates all aspects of intellectual property;

- Intellectual property is not about letting you use what you have created;

- Intellectual property is not about forcing others to use what you have created;

- Intellectual property is about giving you the right to prevent others from using what you have created; and

- Intellectual property is protected on a per-country level.

FOCUS ON BOTH
IP COMING IN
AND IP GOING OUT

I hear it all the time. A business owner says, "You know what, we really don't have anything to protect, so we don't think that we should be talking to a lawyer."

This is one of the biggest mistakes you can possibly make. Just because you are not interested in protecting your own stuff, does not mean that you can safely ignore the intellectual property rights owned by others. Maybe you think your property isn't valuable, maybe you just want to give it away, or maybe you simply want to save costs. That's all fine and dandy. However, it's still important for you to understand that intellectual property is a double-edged sword.

Remember that I told you that "intellectual property" is not really a legal term? Let me take it one step further.

While there are many technical aspects about the various types of intellectual property (which you will learn in Part II of this book) you should think of intellectual property as comprised of two parts: intellectual property that comes IN your door and intellectual property that goes OUT your door—in that particular order.

IP COMING IN YOUR DOOR

Intellectual property coming IN your door is what you create, what you have other people create for you, what you buy from other people, and what you steal from other people. *And no, I'm not saying you should steal from other people*, but if you're using someone else's images on your company's website without the owner's permission, that's *still* intellectual property coming IN your door, albeit stolen.

Anything that you have created or you use can be viewed as coming IN your door, regardless of whether it comes in legally or illegally. Once you have a good understanding of what is coming IN your door, you can begin to look at how to build an effective intellectual property strategy.

IP GOING OUT YOUR DOOR

This one is even simpler to understand because this is what most people think about when they hear the words "intellectual property". This is what is commonly thought of as your "million dollar idea." But it's not only that. IP going OUT your door is, in fact, any intellectual property that you are selling or giving away.

It also includes any intellectual property that you are afraid that other people might steal from you. The important thing to remember is that the stuff going OUT your door may be based on other people's stuff that came IN your door, not just the stuff you created from scratch.

IT'S ABOUT MORE THAN PROTECTING YOUR OWN IP

Intellectual property is not only about you protecting your stuff from others; it's also about making sure that others can't use *their* intellectual property against you.

If somebody else's IP comes IN your door, by definition, it is going OUT of their door.

Just because you've managed to survive the early stages of your business without any attacks, doesn't necessarily mean that the same thing will continue to happen as your business grows. If nobody is after you for unauthorized use of their IP, this may mean several things:

- you're too small for them to notice what you're doing;
- you're too small for them to care about what you're doing;
- they don't think that you have enough money for them to bother;
- they genuinely don't care about their IP going OUT their door; or
- they are genuinely happy that you are using their IP.

Unless you know for sure that they are happy with you using their IP (in which case, make sure you get them to confirm it in writing), you want to make sure that you have the right to use their IP to build anything that is critically important for your business.

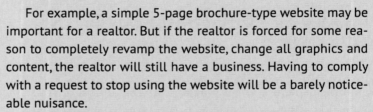

IT'S ALL RELATIVE...

The same types of IP can mean different things to different businesses.

For example, a simple 5-page brochure-type website may be important for a realtor. But if the realtor is forced for some reason to completely revamp the website, change all graphics and content, the realtor will still have a business. Having to comply with a request to stop using the website will be a barely noticeable nuisance.

On the other hand, if Google or Facebook are forced to completely change the code behind their websites, it will be a complete disaster from which they are not likely to recover. This is because their website is not a fancy addition to their business—it is their business.

If someone else's IP coming IN your door is critical for your business, make sure it cannot be taken away from you.

BUT I'M JUST GIVING IT AWAY

Even if you want to give your stuff away, you *still* have to worry about intellectual property. You still need to make sure that you are not violating any intellectual property rights of other people. Just because you're giving your stuff away does not mean that the owners whose material you are using are also willing to give it away for free.

People often assume, "*Well, if we are going to be giving our stuff away, it means everybody else is going to be happy if we do the same thing with their stuff.*" Not true.

SHARING IS FUN...

In 2000, Metallica sued Napster for unauthorized sharing of their music.

At that time, Metallica's drummer, Lars Ulrich, took part in an anti-Napster commercial (***http://www.youtube.com/watch?v=aQcOx5E9jOc***), where he famously said: "Sharing is only fun when it's not your stuff."

Regardless of whether you agree with him, or whether he still agrees with himself, there will be those who think this way. And if they catch you using their stuff without permission, even if you're giving it away, your business will be in for a lot of pain.

This becomes an even bigger problem if you or your business is starting to make money (even if you are giving your product away for free), because every dollar you make increases the risks of you being sued.

BIG MONEY BRINGS BIG LAWSUITS

With the rare exception of plaintiffs who will pay anything to prove their point, no one is interested in bringing a lawsuit against someone who doesn't have any money. But everything changes as soon as you are seen as a business with deep pockets. People will start coming out of the woodwork taking a hard look at your business to see if you are using their intellectual property improperly and suddenly remember all the tiny bits and pieces of their IP that you might have used while you were building your empire. You can be viewed as a potential source of income by people who are looking to make a quick buck.

People won't bother taking you to court if there is a chance that they will have to pay for it out of their own pocket, but it's a different story once you start to hit the big time. Once lawyers recognize that you have deep pockets, they will be more than willing to bring a case against you on a contingency basis.

CONTINGENCY-BASED LAWSUITS

What does on a contingency basis mean? It means that a plaintiff (the person suing) doesn't have to worry about figuring out how to pay the lawyer. The lawyer will get a percentage of whatever the other side pays, if the other side pays. If the other side does not pay, the plaintiff pays nothing, and the lawyer gets nothing.

What does this mean for you? Two things, really.

First of all, this means that lawyers only take cases on contingency when they think that there is a high likelihood that they would be able to get enough money for the plaintiff that would more than cover the value of their time.

Secondly, and probably the most important, if someone can easily prove that you've done something wrong and you have a lot of money, lawyers will be lining up around the block to sue you into oblivion, and plaintiffs won't have to worry about paying for the expensive litigation—because you'll pay for it.

A LAWYER COSTS HOW MUCH?

Let's do some math. For example, the lawyer's hourly rate is $400, and the lawyer expects to spend 200 hours on your file. The lawyer also thinks that the chances he can make the other side pay a substantial amount are 70%. You are prepared to pay the lawyer 25% of what the other side pays.

The lawyer would only take the case on a contingency basis if he is confident that he can make the other side pay at least $460,000:

$400 x 200 = $80,000 in fees that the lawyer would make if he was charging an hourly rate.

$80,000 is 25% of $320,000. The plaintiff would need to be paid at least $320,000 to make up for the lawyer's fees.

$320,000 is 70% of about $460,000. There is a risk of 30% that the lawyer gets nothing (in the lawyer's own estimation), so the lawyer would be willing to offset that risk.

If the lawyer does not think that the other side is going to shell out $460,000 or more, the lawyer will ask the plaintiff to just pay the hourly rate. An $80,000 bird in the hand, so to speak.

THE BOTTOM LINE

So, even if you don't care about protecting your own intellectual property, you still need to be concerned about the intellectual property of others that you may be bringing IN your door—to ensure that you protect your pockets.

Understanding intellectual property rights will allow you to make intelligent decisions regarding the use of other people's intellectual property.

This is exactly what this book is for. Keep reading.

IP IS NOT JUST ABOUT MONEY

One of the common misconceptions about intellectual property is that it is only about money. Now, don't get me wrong, money is very important, but intellectual property is primarily about *control*.

Intellectual property is about having the right to say, "*You can't do that because it's mine!*" This reason alone is sufficient for you to prevent others from using your intellectual property.

Often, advocates of piracy claim that piracy does not really hurt the artists. They allege piracy actually promotes public interest in the artists, so eventually they make more money. I'm not even going to argue whether this is true or not. Let's assume that it is.

I claim that it is improper, immoral, and just plain evil to force your views upon others, *even* if it benefits them in the long run—even if they eventually agree with you. The only exceptions are children and people who are deemed to be incompetent. In other words, those who are legally unfit to make decisions on their own. This usually does not apply to musicians, writers, software programmers, film companies, inventors, and research centers.

It's one thing to convince and demonstrate the superiority of one model over another. It's quite another to force the decision upon someone.

This goes back to the story I told you about my very first copyright case. The radio station that used my father's music without authorization suggested that my father was supposed to be grateful to them for making him even more popular. The reason he became furious was not that the ratio station's statement was false. That was irrelevant. The reason for his fury was that somebody made the decision *for* him, without asking first.

In the midst of Metallica's battle with Napster, Lars Ulrich said, *"All we want as an artist is a choice. There's nothing to argue about. Nobody has the right to do with our music whatever they want. We do. We're saying, as much as the next band wants to work with Napster, we have the right not to."* This is yet another confirmation that IP is about control, not just money.

FAILED BUSINESS MODELS

Here's a short passage from an article I wrote on this subject, *Failed Business Models of the Past, Eh?*

"Crusaders should not expect to be embraced and to have their views that they attempt to forcefully impose on their victims celebrated. Unless the sole interest of new model missionaries is in the mere sadistic process of the forceful imposition of their ideas unto those who resist them, there are only two interrelated ways to efficiently reach the objective of conversion: to let the "old" models fail without any external pressure, simply by allowing them to rot by themselves, unable to provide something useful enough to keep them afloat; and to recruit new adepts by demonstrating the superiority of new models, without any violation of terms established by those who prefer to keep running the old models. This is the only way to have a controlled experiment, the only way to objectively prove that one system is better than the other."

The full article is available at:

http://mincovlaw.com/blog-post/failed_business_models_of_the_past

The other side of this coin is that often you can get the required permission to use someone's works *simply by asking*. In many cases, the ability to say *yes* or *no* is all that an IP owner needs to satisfy his desire for a demonstration of respect that he thinks he deserves. In fact, it may be all that he seeks.

Countless times I have been involved in litigation where IP owners would have gladly granted the permission to use their IP for free if only they were given the courtesy of having been asked for permission.

The logic goes, "If you had asked before you used my work, I would have let you use it for free, but since you didn't, I'm going to use everything available to me to make your life miserable, and this or that provision of this or that law happens to be a great way for me to achieve it."

YOU DIDN'T ASK AND NOW IT'S GOING TO COST YOU!

My father was always amazed with makers of TV programs who asked permission to use his songs after they had already used them.

In fact, he had four going rates for the license fees that he charged: a regular rate when they asked permission before using the music in a program, a double rate when they asked permission after they included the music in the program which had not yet aired, a triple rate for cases when they didn't ask permission until after the program was aired, and a quadruple rate for cases when we caught them using his music before they figured out that they had to ask permission.

The reason he could charge double when they asked him after they used the music but before the program was aired was because he'd always tell them, "Look, I never asked you to use my music in your program. I'll understand if you decide to remove it from your program if it's too expensive." In fact they just painted themselves into the corner where they had to redo something they'd already done or pay more.

But guess what, my dad always preferred to deal with those who qualified for the regular rate.

Why?

Because IP is not just about the money.

SO WHAT DOES THIS MEAN TO YOU?

If you need to use someone else's IP, show them some respect by asking them first. This may save you a lot of money and aggravation.

If you own the IP, don't buy the argument that since you didn't lose a lot of money (or the infringers didn't make a lot of money), then it's OK for them to use your stuff. While they might not have stolen your money, they stole your ability to control how your work is used, which is very valuable.

Oh yeah, and to those people who tell you that if you want to retain control over the use of your works, you should keep them to yourself, tell them to use the same argument to explain to rape victims how they should have simply stayed home if they had the audacity to wish to not be raped. It makes just about as much sense.

The only purpose of having laws about intellectual property is to allow creators and IP owners to reveal their works to the world without fear of being screwed. If these laws only covered IP that had not been made public, there would have been no need for these laws, because it is impossible to use something that is unavailable.

IP IS JUST A TOOL

Often, people will call me asking if they should register their trademarks or patent their inventions. This is an impossible question to answer without having more information.

This is like asking someone, *"Do I need a handsaw?"* The answer would depend on what you're planning to achieve using the handsaw, wouldn't it?

Intellectual property is a means to an end, not an end in and of itself. It's a tool, and like any other tool, deciding if you need it depends on the job.

BE WARY OF A LAWYER'S ADVICE

Getting a lawyer's advice can be a good idea (and you will have a much *better* idea when to see a lawyer and how to ask educated questions after you've finished reading this book), but you should always keep one very important thing in mind. Lawyers want to protect themselves from lawsuits just like you do.

Just like doctors, lawyers are trained that first and foremost they must do no harm. If you register your trademark and later realize that you don't need it, you can't blame the lawyer for giving you bad advice, since having a registered trademark is almost never worse than not having a registered trademark. On the other hand, if the lawyer tells you that you don't need to register your trademark and you run into a problem with a competitor because you didn't register it, then you can turn your wrath towards the lawyer, sue him for professional negligence (legal malpractice), and have him compensate you for everything you've lost as the result of his bad advice.

This is why you will almost never hear a lawyer categorically tell you not to do something that might turn out to be beneficial for you. On top of that, if the lawyer is going to be paid for doing the work, the lawyer has an additional incentive to suggest that you take a variety of steps that might turn out to be beneficial. As a result, you may get a lot of recommendations to do things you may not need.

Just to make it clear, I am not trying to paint a picture of a conspiracy of evil lawyers who are all trying to sell you what you don't need in order to squeeze the last penny out of your business. I don't think that's the case, and neither should you.

The thing is, a lawyer can't and won't make strategic decisions for you. On the other hand, you can't make a meaningful decision without having some workable criteria for making the decision. Whether you think all lawyers are crooks or all lawyers are angels is not going to help you make the right decision.

Liking and trusting a particular lawyer is also a poor solution. Most disappointments start with an exclamation, *"But I trusted you!"*

So how do you make decisions about IP?

You need to clearly understand your business strategy. What is it that you are trying to achieve, and how does your lawyer's advice fit with your strategy? More specifically, how does the lawyer's advice get you closer to realizing your business strategy?

And yes, you have to have a bit more of a specific strategy than simply deciding that you want to *"make a ton of money and do cool stuff."*

INTELLECTUAL PROPERTY STRATEGY REVIEW

One of the most valuable services that I have developed is the Intellectual Property Strategy Review (IPSR). The important thing about the IPSR is that it is not a sales pitch for my other services. It focuses on *your* business, not mine. The focus is not on whether you *can* get something protected, but whether you *should*. This approach has saved my clients tens of thousands of dollars.

Essentially, it's a 90-minute consultation during which we will discuss your business and determine which strategies would make sense from the legal, business, PR, and economic points of view. It's not a typical consultation, since most of the time, *I* will be asking *you* questions, not the other way around. Then we'll be looking for the answers together.

Knowing if you can protect your IP (and if yes, how to do it) is one of the most important steps any business should take as early as possible. Imagine if Coca-Cola Company founders said, *"Let's wait till we sell the first hundred thousand bottles and then we'll hire the best lawyers to deal with trademarking and protecting the recipe's secret."* They wouldn't have gone very far, would they?

I'm a big fan of lean startups, agile development, and bootstrapping. But don't mistake these strategies of building your business by continuously testing the market with "build first, think later". Choosing to be lean and agile is *also* a strategy, and you need to clearly understand what exactly those terms mean in practical terms.

One tool that I created and use to help my clients decide what they should and should not be doing, and when, is the Intellectual Property Strategy Review Quadrant (IPSR Quadrant™):

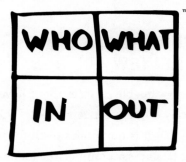

It has four areas (hence the name *quadrant*): WHO, WHAT, IN, and OUT.

WHO deals with the structure of your business.

WHAT deals with what your business does, what it sells, how it sells it, how your customers find your business, and what your long-term and exit strategies are.

You probably noticed that the first two quadrants do not actually deal with intellectual property but deal with ways at looking at the business as a whole.

Only then, at the third step, will we discuss the intellectual property that comes IN your door. This step will allow you to see which actions are critical to your business in order to protect it from attacks of right holders and competitors.

Finally, OUT deals with the intellectual property going OUT your door. This step will let you determine if you should be using your IP as a tool to provide your business with a competitive advantage.

During sessions with clients where we've filled out the IPSR Quadrant, I've witnessed many eye-opening moments. Often, business owners have never asked themselves (let alone thought about the answers to) my questions.

Normally, I don't make the questions I ask during the IPSR available to the public. But I will share most of them with you in this book. I know that you can keep a secret.

When you go through these questions with me in person, I can help you interpret your answers into a cohesive strategy. But since I promised that this book will equip you with enough knowledge about intellectual property to enable you to timely identify situations when you need to see an IP lawyer and to be able to ask educated questions, here is your introduction to the wonderful world of the Intellectual Property Strategy Review.

QUADRANT 1: WHO

The first thing we need to figure out is how your business is organized. To do this, we need the answers to a number of questions.

- What is the legal form of your business?
    - ✓ Is the business a sole proprietorship?
    - ✓ Is the business a partnership?
    - ✓ If it's a partnership, is there a written partnership agreement?

    ✓ Is the business a corporation?

    ✓ If it's a corporation, is there a written shareholders' agreement?

    ✓ Most importantly, do you know *why* you chose one form and not the other?

PARTNERSHIPS

Partnerships come and partnerships go. Someone's your partner today and your enemy tomorrow.

I always tell my clients that the worst disputes *always* start with the best friendships.

When partnerships start off, everybody is your best friend—you like each other and are excited about the new venture. Each partner wants to work with the other, and brings unique experiences to the table.

Unfortunately, as things develop either too slowly, too quickly, or just unexpectedly, problems can arise.

The worst type of partnerships is the one where you don't have a written agreement with the other partners. This is because the law usually prescribes various default terms that govern the relationships between partners, unless they agree otherwise in writing.

A partnership is not a separate legal entity. All partners are personally responsible for everything that the partnership does.

Moreover, unless you have a written agreement that says otherwise, every partner in a partnership is responsible for the business actions of all other partners. For example, if your partner, without asking you, takes out a few business loans on behalf of the partnership and disappears in the Bahamas, you will be personally responsible for these loans. If your partner decides to sell the partnership's intellectual property, then there is nothing you can do about it except to try and get some of the money from the partner. To the extent that IP belongs to the partnership, that is, to all the partners, any one of the partners has the right to dispose of it.

A partnership *can* be a manageable form of running a joint project, provided that there is a written agreement between the participating parties that clearly delineates who can and should do what and who owns what before, during and after the partnership is formed and dissolved. However, very rarely it is the best form of running a business.

In most situations, a corporation is the preferred legal form of running a business. Don't take this as tax advice from me, but what convinced *me* to incorporate my business before I made a dime with it, was that I don't have to dump the money I make into the government pension plan. Because I don't take out my income as an employee, I have a lot more flexibility in regards to taxes.

PARTNERSHIP DANGER

A long time ago, a friend, who is also an intellectual property lawyer, was a founding partner of an intellectual property law firm that grew into a large and successful business. Years later, she decided that she'd had enough and wanted to leave the partnership. If only it was that easy!

What used to be a friendship is now a total mess. It's taken the partners several years to figure everything out.

Now, think about this! All these partners are experienced lawyers and even though they're supposed to know how to deal with these situations, it still took them several years to unwind this thing. It cost everybody a lot of money, a lot of nerves, and a lot of emotions.

I can guarantee that if YOUR partnership falls through, you won't be as well equipped to deal with it as they were. If they had so much trouble, imagine what you will go through trying to dissolve a partnership without losing your shirt.

ADVANCED PLANNING

But even beyond the actual legal form of your business, you should discuss and agree with the other founders or partners about how the business is going to operate.

A successful partnership requires much more than simply agreeing that you will share profits and costs equally. You need to think about various scenarios—both good and bad—and plan how you are going to handle them.

Some of the things you will need to think about include:

- When and how does the money get split?
- How do we go about hiring people? Who decides which person gets hired?
- How do we decide if a loan is necessary?
- What if a partner wants out?
- How and when do we bring in more partners?
- How do we advertise? How much money do we spend on advertising?
- How do we decide if someone wants to buy us out?
- How do we make decisions that affect our business?
- Who is responsible for the debts? How is liability shared?
- Who owns the intellectual property?
- Who owns the physical property?

You will save yourself a lot of dollars and nerves if you think about all these issues well in advance, and consult a lawyer to make sure that your arrangement is properly documented.

The desire to avoid or at least deal with potential horror scenarios is the reason you have written agreements. You hope that you can sign them and put them aside to never have to look at them again. But lawyers, just like the investigator in the movie *The Firm,* get paid to be suspicious when they've got nothing to be suspicious about. This is why lawyers often have a reputation as deal-killers—we are trained to come up with all sorts of crazy what-ifs and what-thens.

DIVIDING ASSETS

You need to figure out what happens if your partnership falls apart, particularly who gets control of the assets. In some respects, figuring out the split of physical assets is fairly easy, but it can be a lot harder when it comes to intellectual property. This is because there are two sides to intellectual property, as you have learned: it's not just money, it's also control.

In legal terms, this means that joint ownership of intellectual property involves not only the splitting of profits that the IP earns for the partners, but also deciding who will have the right to use and let others use the IP.

Essentially, you would need to decide who will have the right to control the use of the IP if one of the partners leaves the partnership or if the partnership dissolves completely (which is often the same thing).

Here are some possible solutions:

- Some partners assign (that is, outright sell) their share of the IP to the other partners (for royalties or a lump sum);
- Some partners license (that is, provide a permission for others to use) their share of the IP to the other partners (for royalties or a lump sum);
- The IP can be split, so that some partners can only use and allow others to use some of the IP, while some other partners can only use and allow others to use some other IP;
- The IP continues to be jointly owned and its use requires the consent of all partners;
- The IP continues to be jointly owned but some partners grant the other partners the power of attorney to act on their behalf in respect of the use of the IP.

The decisions you make are completely up to you and your partners. There are no right or wrong answers, just answers that you all agree to. You can write a contract that deals with these issues any way you want. What you do need to ensure is that everything is clearly spelt out and dealt with before success comes or problems arise.

Remember, even if you're entering into a partnership with your best friend, make sure you think about what will happen if you become enemies. It's much easier to figure out solutions to problems when you are on speaking terms than when you hate each other. Even if you don't want to see a lawyer, there are piles of templates on the Web that you can look at to get some idea of what to consider when setting up a partnership.

Money can make people act strangely and if they see you making millions of dollars, they will want their piece of the pie. Even your ex-partners who left the project before you hit gold could be the source of aggravation because they will suddenly remember, *"You know what, you're now a multimillion-dollar business which wouldn't exist if I didn't create this IP for you, and I actually own it and you don't."*

As a business owner, you need to think about these situations before they arise. It's easier to deal with this possible situation when someone first comes to work for you and you aren't making any money than it is when you're making millions.

A PARTNERSHIP GONE MAD

This discussion about partnerships reminds me of a case I took on while I was practicing law in Russia. It was probably the most bizarre partnership agreement I had ever been involved in.

Two good friends, a film producer and a director whom I was representing, agreed to make a movie together. The director had somehow managed to get the film producer to agree to a contract where the director retained the copyright in the film.

During the making of the film, the two friends had a major falling out and their friendship turned to hate.

At some point, the director sent the producer a letter that, in addition to explaining to the producer what a dirtbag the producer was, stated that the director, as the owner of copyright in the film, forbade the producer any use of the film, including licensing it to theatres and TV channels.

The film producer disagreed with the director's assessment of his human qualities, suggested that if there was a dirtbag among them, then it was the director, and reminded the director that the only physical copy of the film was owned by and remained in the possession of the producer.

The director wrote back, sincerely surprised that the producer could not see what was obvious to the director, that there was no question about the producer being a dirtbag, and reminded the producer that if the producer attempted or purported to attempt to use the film, the director would sue the producer and whoever would end up using the film.

The producer responded, *"Great. You can use your copyright as much as you want, but we're not going to give you access to the physical film. We're actually going to burn it and see how much you can accomplish with your copyright!"*

The director called me, yelling hysterically that the producer was about to burn the only copy of the film.

I realized that we didn't have the time to litigate over the ownership of copyright or who was the worst human being. I came up with the idea for the two of them to enter into a partnership agreement to save whatever little was left of the project.

This was a very long document. The entire four pages were dedicated to what would qualify as "mutual consent" which would be required for most of the things that could occur in the final stages of making and distributing the film (the description of which took another 8 pages).

Miraculously, we worked out an agreement, and they finished and released the movie—which promptly tanked, but at least they had an agreement that gave them a chance to release the film.

So you've figured out the legal form of your business. There are more issues that should be addressed during the *WHO* stage of IPSR.

– What is your personal status in the business?

  ✓ Are you the owner?

  ✓ Are you a co-owner?

  ✓ Are you a co-founder?

  ✓ Are you a partner?

  ✓ Are you an employee?

– What is your company name?

  ✓ Have you checked if it's unique?

  ✓ Did you conduct a trademark search to check if the name is not someone's registered trademark?

  ✓ Did you get a NUANS (Newly Upgraded Automated Name Search) report to confirm that the name had not been registered as a trade name in other provinces?

  ✓ If your business is not incorporated, did you register your company name as a DBA (*doing business as...*) name?

  ✓ Did you conduct a domain name search to make sure the name is not used by a competitor?

  ✓ Did you conduct a **DOMAINSBOT.COM** search to check for similar domain names?

  ✓ Did you use **TMFDOMAINS.COM** to register domain names that are identical or so similar to your company name that most people would associate them with your business?

✓ Did you conduct a **NAMECHK.COM** search to check if your name is not taken on various social media platforms?

✓ Did you register your name on some of the bigger social media sites, such as YouTube, Facebook, Twitter, Yelp, and LinkedIn?

✓ Do you understand the difference between a trade name and a trademark?

TRADE NAME VS. TRADEMARK

A trade name is the name you use to refer to your company, whereas a trademark is used to refer to your products and services.

For example, "Microsoft Corporation" is a trade name, but "Microsoft Word" or "Microsoft Windows" are trademarks. A trade name can also be part of the trademark and sometimes they are the same thing.

A trade name may only be protected as a trademark if you *USE* it *AS* a trademark. You will learn what "using as a trademark" means in Part II of this book.

It is important to realize that just because you have a trade name does not mean you have a trademark. A trade name does not give you the same protection as a trademark.

Simply incorporating the business or registering a DBA (*doing business as...*) name is not enough. All this does is prevent your competitors from registering an identical or similar name as their corporate name. However, this registration does nothing outside the province where your business is registered. It also does very little to protect you against competitors who might use your brand without using it as part of their corporate name or their DBA name.

QUADRANT 2: WHAT

The second quadrant deals with what the business actually does and how it does it. There are a number of questions that need to be answered in this section as well.

- What does the business do?
- What products does the business sell or make?
- What services does the business offer?
- Is the business involved in permitting others to use any of its intellectual property (licensing)?
- What is the market for the business's products and services?
- Do the business's products and services target a specific geographical area?
- Is there a specific category of buyers for the business's products and services?
- What are the marketing strategies?
- How do customers find the business?
- Do they find the business online?
- Do they find the business in the Yellow Pages?
- Do they find the business through word of mouth?
- Do they find the business by using Google search?
- What keywords do they use to find the business online?
- Do they find the business simply because they bumped into it on the street?
- What is the business owner's exit strategy?
- How long has the business been operating?
- How long will the business be operating?
- What is it that you're trying to achieve in 3 years, in 5 years, in 10 years?

Some of these questions are quite easy to figure out but some of them, particularly the questions regarding how people find you, can be important for considering trademarks.

If most people find you online or some other method by using a particular name or tagline, then this is an indication that you have developed a valuable asset that needs to be protected.

ONLINE ANALYTICS

Make sure you use the statistical tools that allow you to check who your online visitors are, where they came from, what they searched for, and what pages they visited.

The most popular tools are Google Analytics and Statcounter.

If you see that most people find you by using generic keywords, "Vancouver plumber", "Canadian trademark lawyer", or "SEO services", then there is less of a need to protect your trademarks.

On the other hand, if most people find you using your business name, the name of your products or services, it is a sure sign that you have developed something that must be protected ASAP.

If the vast majority of your customers find you through word of mouth, for example, because you've been networking or you're the company next to the bank, then maybe you can afford to be less concerned about trademarks.

In addition to these questions, we also need to take a look at your competitors. You will need to figure out who your competitors are and how easy it is for other companies to recreate the product or services that you provide.

Some questions we would look at include:

- How easy is it to reproduce what the business does?

- Is your product unique, or is it something generic?

- Why would people buy from you?

- Do you do the same thing as everybody else, only better?
- Have you invented something absolutely unique?
- Have you improved an existing product?

We also need to evaluate what it would mean for your business if a competitor decided to copy your product or service. For some businesses, this doesn't matter whereas for others it would cause a big problem. For example, if you were making pizza and another pizza restaurant opened up, this would not likely be a problem. A problem would arise if the other company started using your company name.

QUADRANT 3: IN

If you remember, in a previous chapter, we described intellectual property as falling into two different categories—what's coming IN your door and what's going OUT your door. Quadrant 3 deals with IP coming IN your door, while quadrant 4 deals with intellectual property going OUT your door.

In order to figure out the intellectual property that is coming IN your door, you need to look at everything you use to deliver your product or service. This could include software you use or even your website, particularly if it was created by someone else. You need to look at everything you use to run your business. This includes equipment, data collection methods, or anything else that has to deal with the internal operations of your business, the making of your products, or the delivering of your services. Anything that you create, have other people create, buy from people, or even steal from other people, to the extent that it falls under one or the other form of intellectual property, should go in this quadrant as IP going IN.

You also need to look at how you handle material that was created by contractors and employees. Just because the person who created the material is an employee does not necessarily mean that you automatically own the material. Even if you do, there are still things you need to be aware of. The way this works is treated differently from country to country so you need to ensure that you take this into account as well. You need to make sure that you have written contracts with all your employees stating that you own the intellectual property that they create.

If the business is a separate legal entity (a corporation), then even if it has a single owner, yourself, it is important to distinguish what IP is owned by the business, and what IP is owned by you as an individual.

I usually recommend that clients make a three-column table to list this information:

Object	Who created	Dependency in %. (0–100)
Website	Mary Smith	40
Marketing materials	John Jacobson	20
Photos used on the website	Silvia Whatsherface	5

The first column will list every bit of IP coming IN your door, the second column will indicate who created each object, and in the third column you will specify on a scale of 0–100 how important that particular object is to your business:

0   = you can stop using it immediately with no impact on the business

100 = your business will be gone if you can no longer use it.

The usual items to go to the first column include:

- website, including text, images, HTML code, and scripts;
- marketing materials;
- images and designs;
- photos;
- articles;
- social media posts;
- software;
- business confidential information;
- logos and slogans;
- music;
- inventions;
- internal manuals; and
- user-generated content.

When you indicate who created the item, be as specific as you can. If it was created by your employees, try to list them by names. If the item was jointly created, try to list each person who contributed to the creation of it. If you license the work from others, specify the source. For example, if you use images from a stock photos website, write down the name of the author (if available), and the website that claims to own the right to license the images to you.

Very few of the items on your list will be rated at 100, but some may be. Most would be between 20 and 80. Remember the example with a realtor's website and Facebook? To the realtor, the website is probably 20. To Facebook, their website is 90+.

Check if your images and text are unique using online tools such as:

- Google Image Search;
- TinEye;
- Copyscape;
- Duplichecker; and
- Plagiarisma.

Also, you need to make sure that for every item that ranks higher than 40%, you have a written agreement that you either own the material or are able to use it. You need to be able to state: *"We own this because of this and this and that"*, or *"We have the right to use it because of this and this and that."*

If you have a website that is set up to let visitors leave comments or, even more important, upload files, make sure that you have proper Privacy Policy and Terms of Use clearly visible on your website.

Feel free to download the template for this table (as well as many other goodies) at ***http://ipbook.ca/more*** .

QUADRANT 4: OUT

This final quadrant looks at intellectual property going OUT your door. As you have learned, this includes any intellectual property that you sell or give away. It also includes the IP that you are afraid others may copy or steal from you.

Intellectual property going OUT is typically the only reason business owners see a lawyer. As you see, this part is only one fourth of the entire IPSR, and the last one, at that.

You need to answer the following questions:

- If you are making some of your IP available through your website, do you have meaningful Terms and Conditions specifying that you retain all rights to that IP and are only providing a limited license to use this IP?

- If you are in the business of licensing out or selling your IP, are you using proper license and assignment agreements?

- What are your systems for enforcing licensing terms?

- If you are or are planning to become a franchisor, does your franchising agreement meet all requirements in the province where your franchises are operating?

- Does your franchising agreement properly address all issues relating to intellectual property?

- Have you considered licensing instead of franchising?

- Do you know the difference between the two?

- Have you protected your trademarks?

- Have you protected your inventions?

- How are you protecting your trade secrets?

- How are you protecting the musical, literary and artistic works that are created in your business?

I will not focus too much on this part of the quadrant at this point, because in order for you to properly answer these questions, you need to have a better grasp of the various areas of IP. This is what you will acquire after you read Part II of this book.

The primary purpose of the IPSR Quadrant is to identify the

gaps in your strategy—the things you have not given any thought to.

When you see these gaps, you can make a meaningful decision whether, when and how they should be filled. When you complete the IPSR Quadrant, you will have a good understanding of how your business runs and the things that you need to take care of. It will help you develop not only your business strategy but also your intellectual property strategy.

Order IPSR from: ***http://IPStrategyReview.com*** .

JUDGES LOOK FOR BETTER STORIES, NOT BETTER LAW

To assess and improve your chances in a legal dispute, you need to understand how a judge's mind works.

Judges have seen and heard it all. They are no longer surprised to realize that some people sometimes say things that are not entirely truthful. To take it one step further, it is not uncommon for most parties to attempt to enhance their version of the events.

It is the judge's job to decide which of the parties is more believable. When that is accomplished, the judge's job is to decide which laws to apply in a particular situation and then—*how* to apply them.

Forget the theatrics. Don't expect the other side to start beating their head against the wall wailing how sorry they are to have done you wrong. This will not happen. Do not be surprised that the other side will have their own version of what actually happened. The most common comment from inexperienced litigants is, "*How can they get away with all these lies?!*" It is especially amusing when these comments come from the opposing parties at the same time. Often, both parties actually believe that their version of the story is true.

First impressions matter. You want to be the one that the judge thinks of as the good guy, and you want your opponent to be the one that the judge thinks of as the bad guy. Because when the judge goes home to his wife, he wants to feel good that justice was served, and both parties got what they deserved. To accomplish this, the judge will apply the right law the right way in order to confirm the conclusion that he has already arrived at—good guy wins, bad guy loses.

How do you become the good guy? By having the better story. You don't need a perfect story; you don't need a good story. You need the *better* story.

I ONLY NEED TO OUTRUN YOU

There are many variations of this story. Below are the two versions I really like.

1. Many folks will say that the .22 calibre is no good for self-protection because it has no stopping power. Have you heard about the woman who was out hiking and managed to stop a vicious grizzly bear attack with a mere .22-calibre pistol? As the massive bear charged her and her boyfriend, the woman calmly unholstered her pistol, took careful aim, shot the boyfriend in the kneecap, and fled.

> 2.   Two guys were out in the woods when suddenly
>   they were charged by a grizzly. As the bear is gain-
>   ing on them, one man stops and begins to put on a
>   pair of running shoes. The second man stops beside
>   him and says, *"Are you crazy? The bear is too fast for*
>   *us. You don't think those running shoes will help you*
>   *outrun the bear, do you?"* The first man replies, *"Don't*
>   *need to. All I have to do is outrun you."*
>
> When you are in court, you don't need to be the judge's role
> model in order to win. What you need is to be at least slightly
> less awful compared to the other side.

Because intellectual property deals with intangible matters, there is always a lot of room for subjective interpretation of the facts.

For example, in a copyright infringement case, the judge typically has to decide between two different stories:

- Did the defendant, with utmost disregard for the law, take advantage of this vulnerable copyright owner whose only source of income is his creativity; or

- Is this shady person, who claims to be the copyright owner, trying to take advantage of this well-respected defendant by trying to squeeze money from the defendant's deep pockets, based on a technicality?

In a case involving a non-disclosure agreement, the two different stories are:

- The vulnerable inventor trusted the work of his life to this mean corporation that benefited greatly from what the inventor had confided in it; or

- The corporation has been working to develop its

invention for decades, and now this opportunist is trying to extort money from it because he told them his "big secret" which was nothing more than 2+2=4.

In a case involving a non-compete clause in an employment agreement, the two stories are:

- The virtuous ex-employee is now forced to die of starvation because if the agreement is to be followed literally, the ex-employee can't work for anyone, ever; or

- The deceitful ex-employee was paid handsomely in exchange for his promise that he would not join a competing venture the day after he quit.

These situations cover the same set of facts, but you see how a different interpretation of these facts, based on who is the good guy and who is the bad guy, may lead to completely different results.

WHY IS THIS IMPORTANT?

The Canadian and U.S. courts are not as formalistic as some of the courts in other countries governed by civil law, so every single time you are thinking about going to court in North America, you should think about the story. Think about how you are going to convince the judge that you are the party that needs to be helped.

If the judge thinks you're a jerk, then even if the law is 100 percent on your side, the judge will do everything possible to ensure that even if you do win, the amount you get will be so small that it's not worth your time.

On the other hand, if the judge thinks the other party is a jerk, then even if you're 100 percent in the wrong, the judge will try to help you out. The judge will do everything possible to ensure that even if you lose, the amount you have to pay will be so little that you can still walk away with a sigh of relief and a smile on your face.

Stories are important. That's why you always need to think how your story will look to the judge. Whatever you do, think how it fits the story that you are trying to create. If the judge thinks you're the good guy, the judge will help as much as possible; if the judge thinks you're the bad guy, the judge will do the exact opposite.

HOW TO HAVE A GOOD STORY

The important thing is to always run your business in a way that allows you to have the better story. Even if you are doing something wrong, a good story in the courtroom will make things go much easier on you.

Many website owners will add a disclaimer to their website stating that, *"We don't intend to infringe other people's rights."* Legally, this disclaimer is meaningless. But if you have facts to back up the story that you're doing your best to cooperate with IP owners in rare cases when indeed, by mistake, you end up having their unauthorized IP on your website, such a disclaimer will certainly contribute to a good story.

If you can show the judge that you've done a lot of things to make sure that everyone is happy with what you're doing and that you are prepared to take other steps to make sure that they become even happier, then the judge will be more inclined to view your case favourably.

Showing the judge that you're a good person who is interested in doing the right thing will do a lot more for you in court than being a jerk with an agreement with all the i's dotted and the t's crossed (although a good agreement will always help as well).

A TALE OF TWO STORIES

I once had a client who had been a programmer for a software development company. The company and the programmer had signed an agreement but it was not very clear regarding who owned what and how the software could be used by the employer.

The programmer and the company had a falling out and the programmer decided to quit. The company then refused to pay him what he was due. The programmer asked me if we could use the uncertainty of the agreement as the leverage to make the former employer pay.

I still remember what I told the programmer:

"It's going to be two stories.

Your story is going to be that you're a victim of this unscrupulous employer who's trying to take advantage of the little guy who's doing his best to make ends meet and who spent the best years of his life creating the crucial lines of code for the employer.

Their story is going to be exactly the opposite. They're a small business that's trying to finally make it. They were relying on you, they trusted you with the most important project of their lives, and you're now trying to take advantage of them because of a small technicality in the agreement, so you're the bad guy and they're the good guys."

It really doesn't matter what the agreement says, what the employment law says, or what the copyright law says about who's right and who's wrong. What matters is who the judge is going to see as the good guy (the victim), and who the judge is going to see as the bad guy (the bully).

In this particular case, we sent a cease-and-desist letter to the former employer demanding that they remove the code written by the programmer from their software and pay the amounts due. The assumption was that it would be very difficult for them to change the code and that they'd be easy to convince. However, they hired someone else to rewrite the software from scratch, and removed my client's code. This way, while—from the legal perspective—everything remained the same (we could still sue them for infringement that occurred in the past), everything changed in terms of the story. While there was some moral satisfaction about forcing the former employer to change their software, not only did we lose the leverage of being able to take away the code, we no longer had a story that the company was taking advantage of the little guy. Now we had our guy making demands from a company that was not even using his code.

This is yet another confirmation that you don't need a good story, you need the better story. My client's story didn't change. It just suddenly stopped being the better story because when the former employer stopped using my client's code, they created an even better story.

You need to always pay attention to your story so that you can present yourself in the best possible light. Remember, the story is more important than the law when it comes to intellectual property cases.

IP IS ALL ABOUT
RISK MANAGEMENT

Most business owners don't need to have (and certainly don't want to pay for) the ultimate comprehensive 100-percent bullet-proof opinion about what's right and what's wrong.

Let me give you an unrelated example. If I'm speeding, I don't need a six-page legal memo to tell me that what I'm doing is illegal. I already know that. What I do need to know are the odds of getting caught and the consequences of getting caught. Now, I'm not advocating that you should run out and break the law. What I am saying is that you need to be aware of the risks associated with your behaviour.

The risk is usually the other side of a reward, however illusive or subjective that reward might be. The real question is not whether bad consequences are bad, it's whether the reward is worth the risk and if there are effective ways of minimizing the risk while maximizing the chances of success.

This is risk management 101.

Whether it involves speeding or intellectual property rights, it still boils down to risk management.

If you know that the cost of lowering the risk is greater than the worst consequences of that risk, it does not make a lot of sense to invest in the costly reduction of that risk.

MILTON FRIEDMAN EXPLAINS
FORD PINTO SITUATION

Milton Friedman, the great free-market economist, once answered a question about a faulty part of a Ford Pinto car which, under certain circumstances, could lead to fatalities. The cost of fixing the flawed part was $13 per car. But Ford estimated in an internal memo that the defect would cost about 200 lives a year, and that the cost of each life, in terms of how much they would have to pay to compensate for the deaths, would be around $200,000. They did their math and established that the cost of fixing the part was greater than the cost of paying compensation, so they didn't fix the part. The student who was asking the question was furious with the idea that one could weigh lives and dollars and calculate their risks like this.

Milton Friedman's response was brilliant. With the air of infinite boredom, he asked the student, *"Well, let me ask you, let's suppose it would have cost a billion dollars per [life saved], should Ford have put the part there nonetheless?"*

When the student could not find words to answer, Friedman continued, *"Nobody can accept the principle that an infinite value should be put on an individual life... You cannot accept a situation when a million people should starve in order to provide one*

> *person with a car that is completely safe!.. So you're just arguing whether Ford used $200,000 as the right number or not... Suppose it would have been $200,000,000 per life saved. What should Ford have done?..*"
>
> He continued, "*Every one of us separately in this room could at a cost reduce his risk of dying tomorrow: you don't have to walk across the street! The question is whether you are willing to pay for it...*"
>
> If you have not seen this video, watch it at:
> *http://www.youtube.com/watch?v=EYW5I96h-9w*

Just as we cannot accept the principle that an infinite value should be put on an individual life, we cannot accept the principle that an infinite value should be put on having 100% of our business affairs 100% legal 100% of the time. We all do our own math about what is justified and what isn't. But the important thing is that it always, *always*, boils down to risk management. And whoever is selling you the 100% solution for 100% of the issues 100% of the time, is doing you a disservice because the cost of that solution usually greatly exceeds its benefits vis-à-vis the worst consequences of only having a 90% solution that covers 90% of the issues 90% of the time.

Intellectual property is no different, and it is unreasonable to invest an infinite amount in order to ensure that 100% of your IP coming IN is 100% legal 100% of the time and that 100% of your IP going OUT is properly protected and defended 100% of the time. Now, I'm not implying that you should start pirating other people's stuff and use it in your business. What I'm saying is that we all have limited resources, and the resources you spend on something will be unavailable for something else. As a business owner, you have an obligation to your business to make the most efficient use of its resources.

Risk management is precisely about calculating whether investing in reducing a certain risk will have a better return than investing the same amount elsewhere.

GETTING CAUGHT

Every lottery involves risk. It's not really a lottery if every ticket pays more than you spend on it. Likewise, there's no risk if no matter what you do, there are no consequences to your actions.

Personally, I don't believe in risk without consequences.

While I openly tell my clients that there may be situations when their money is better spent on things other than ensuring 100% compliance with 100% of the laws 100% of the time, I also tell them that there is a risk involved in not being 100% compliant with 100% of the laws 100% of the time.

The corollary from that is that I expect the client to make a decision as to what degree of risk is acceptable and then deal with the consequences if the risk materializes.

I became an IP lawyer fighting for my father's copyrights, which shaped my principles when it comes to intellectual property infringements.

I refuse to represent anyone who would require me to imply that using someone else's IP without permission is OK. I might agree to help you negotiate the numbers, but I would not tell the IP owner or, even worse, a judge, that, in my opinion, infringement should be left without a consequence.

Now, this does not mean that if you have a valid defence and your use of the IP does not really infringe anyone's IP that I won't help. But I refuse to engage in lawyerly trickery to get you off the hook after you deliberately chose to take the risk.

When I was just starting my firm in Canada, I had a request from someone who received a letter from Getty Images alleging unlawful use of images that they own. It turns out my potential client found the photos on Google and just posted them on his website without checking if he had the right to do it, which he didn't. Getty Images owned the copyright in the photographs, so they sent him a strong cease-and-desist letter requesting a substantial sum of money.

This is what I told him and what I have told many others who ran into similar problems: *"Look, you took the risk and they caught you. Now you have to pay the price. You have two options. You can promptly take the image down and pay what is demanded of you. Or you can promptly take the image down and hope that they will not make an example of you by taking you to court. This will also be your decision, depending on your risk aversion. But if they do decide to take you to court, do not expect me to help you figure out how to prove that you should not be made to pay. Because they are right, and you are wrong."*

You thought that lawyers take every case, regardless of how they feel towards the accused? I didn't.

FIGURING OUT YOUR RISK

If you've decided to use some content that is not yours, there are three questions you should ask.

- If somebody finds out about it, what are the chances they will do something about it?

- If they decide to do something about it, what are the chances that they will win?

- If they win, what's the worst thing that can happen to me?

If you realize that the chances of getting caught are high and the potential consequences are very serious, you will probably stop using that content without asking permission.

If both the consequences and the risk are small, then, while what you're doing may still not be perfectly legal, it wouldn't be the first thing you would fix in your business. There are always other important things to be done first.

Again, I'm not advocating infringement of others' IP. And I certainly am not encouraging that you violate the law. However, from a practical perspective, I understand that seldom will you be able to have everything perfect at all times, and IP is no exception.

RISK MANAGEMENT AND LAWYERS

Now, if you ask a lawyer about intellectual property, the proper response would be, "*Yes, you need to get all those licenses and permissions for it to be perfectly legal.*"

Why do lawyers say this? Like I've said a number of times already, lawyers also need to protect themselves from lawsuits. As you've learned from this chapter, just because something is perfectly legal doesn't necessarily mean that it's perfectly advisable in your particular situation. Sometimes people whose rights you may be infringing simply don't care.

THE MATH OF LEGAL RISK MANAGEMENT

Let's say you are planning to enter into an important deal. How do you decide if you should hire a team of 10 expensive lawyers to draft a 100-page contract, hire a reasonably priced lawyer to draft a 15-page agreement, use a free sample you downloaded from the internet, or have no agreement at all?

The only way to decide this is through the prism of risk management.

To simplify things, there are 4 questions you should ask yourself:

1. What are you risking if the deal falls through without a contract?

2.   What is the likelihood of the deal falling through without a contract?

3.   What are you risking if the deal falls through with a contract?

4.   What is the likelihood of the deal falling through with a contract?

Let's say, if you have no contract, there is a 20% risk that you will lose $200,000 if the deal falls through. On the other hand, there is a 5% risk that you will lose $100,000 if things go sideways even if you have a contract (there is never a 0% risk or 100% certainty).

Here's the simplified math: without the contract you are betting $40,000, while with a contract you are only betting $5,000. The difference is $35,000. Depending on your risk aversion, any expenditure that is less than $35,000 would therefore be reasonable to reduce the risk.

Similarly, let's say you are caught using someone else's IP without permission. You need to ask yourself 4 similar questions:

1.   What are you risking if they really take you to court and you represent yourself?

2.   What is the likelihood of them taking you to court and the worst consequences materializing?

3.   What are you risking if they take you to court and you have a lawyer represent you?

4.   What is the likelihood of them taking you to court and the worst consequences materializing, even if you have a lawyer?

Let's assume that the most you would pay out if you are taken to court and represent yourself is $25,000, and the chance of that is 30%. On the other hand, the most you would pay out if you are taken to court and have a lawyer represent you (including the lawyer's fees) would be $40,000, with a 20% chance of losing.

In this example, if you represent yourself, the risk-adjusted amount is $7,500, while the risk-adjusted amount of being represented by a lawyer is $8,000, which makes little sense.

However, if they have *already* taken you to court, then the percentages will change: now that the lawsuit is already in the court system, the risk that you, when defending yourself without a lawyer, will have to pay out $25,000 has increased from 30% to 60%. On the other hand, the risk that you would have to pay out $40,000, while represented by a lawyer, has increased from 20% to 25%.

In this second example, if you represent yourself, the risk-adjusted amount is $15,000, while the risk-adjusted amount of being represented by a lawyer is $10,000. In this situation, the numbers suggest that you should have a lawyer represent you.

In reality, of course, there are more variables to this equation, but the principle remains the same.

MANAGING CONSEQUENCES

When you get caught using someone's intellectual property without permission, you need to deal with the consequences. And the first thing you need to do is answer these questions:

- What do I do now?
- Do I just take it down and wait to see what they do?
- Do I simply pay them what they're asking me to pay?
- What are the odds that they're going to use me as an example and take me to court?
- If they do take me to court, how much money will the judge award them?
- Will it be worth it for them to take me to court?
- Will it be worth it for me to try and defend myself in court?

Figuring out the answers to these questions still largely falls under risk management. Unless the amounts at stake are significant, in most cases, nobody is going to take you to court. But…they may. That's the risk you take.

Whenever you set up a business, the main question you need to address is, *"What is it that I need to do to make sure that if somebody comes after me, my business still survives?"* You don't have to be 100 percent bulletproof because that is going to take a lot of money, but you need to protect the foundations of your business. This is why it is crucial that you understand your IP strategy.

But remember this about the law, and intellectual property law in particular, it's always about figuring out if the potential reward is worth the cost of getting there.

It's your risk. Manage it responsibly.

IP IS ONLY AS GOOD AS YOUR ABILITY TO DEFEND IT

I often hear complaints that intellectual property rights are only as good as your ability to defend them.

But that's the nature of any true rights! A right is the enforceable ability of someone to prevent everyone else from violating it. True rights are always negative, in the sense that they allow you to prevent others from violating them. True rights are never about getting stuff at someone else's expense.

BUT IP RIGHTS ARE GRANTED
BY THE GOVERNMENT!

The fact that intellectual property rights are government-granted monopolies has led to a common misconception that IP rights are positive rather than negative rights.

I've even heard allegations that the government gives something to IP owners at the expense of the public.

But those who say that have gotten it totally backwards.

This assumes, as Ayn Rand mockingly wrote in *Atlas Shrugged*, that "*money is made by the man who invents a motor at the expense of those who did not invent it... by the intelligent at the expense of the fools... by the able at the expense of the incompetent... by the ambitious at the expense of the lazy...*"

The author who composed a piece of music is not depriving anyone of anything by not allowing the public to use his music against his wish.

Otherwise, to go back to my rape analogy, you could also say that beautiful women are viciously depriving men of carnal pleasures by exercising their government-given right to not be raped.

The public cannot be deprived of something that is not theirs. The song written by a composer, the drawing created by a painter, or the code written by a programmer are not the public's to distribute. The only reason the public has a fighting chance of enjoying the song, the drawing, or the code is because the composer, the painter, and the programmer had created and decided to allow the public, on certain conditions, to enjoy them.

IP laws protect the composer's, the artist's, and the programmer's ability to enforce the conditions upon which they made their song, drawing, or code available to the public.

Your freedom of speech is not worth very much if you never say anything contradictory. Your right to property is useless if you give out your possessions to anyone who so requests.

Here's another example. If you buy a gym membership but never go to the gym, it is unlikely that you would be greatly satisfied with the results. A gym can be a great tool in order to get fit, but only if you use it. At the same time, there is no law that says that you are required to have a gym membership to exercise.

The same can be said of IP rights.

On the one hand, you are not required to protect your IP from others in order to be able to use it. Just because you are not policing your music, drawings, or software does not mean that you no longer have the right to use them. In other words, intellectual property is not about giving you permission to use your own works, trademarks, and inventions.

On the other hand, just because you own the copyright in your music does not necessarily mean that nobody would ever attempt to use it without your permission.

Rights, and intellectual property rights are no exception, give you ammunition against anyone who would dare attempt to take your rights away from you. In case of intellectual property rights, the ammunition is very strong. But you still have to use it!

Of course, if you are not planning on defending your rights, you probably should not be investing in the protection of your IP. All your trademarks, patents, copyrights, and trade secrets are not going to be very valuable if you don't use them to stop others from using your IP to take away your competitive advantage.

This is yet another reason why I say that IP is a tool. If you buy the best handsaw in the world and let it rust in your tool shed without ever using it, don't expect any value out of it.

IP IS ONLY AS GOOD
AS YOUR BUSINESS

Some intellectual property is only as good as the business that it is attached to. If you have a business that sells an innovative product that nobody wants to buy, then your IP is not going to be very valuable in most cases.

For example, registering a trademark will not miraculously create value for a struggling business. It's the combination of business success and how you protect your trademarks that makes trademarks valuable.

THERE IS AN EXCEPTION TO EVERY RULE

In early 2013, the Eastman Kodak Company, which has been struggling since the advent of digital cameras, sold and licensed its approximately 1,100 digital imaging and processing patents to Apple, Google, and Facebook for net proceeds of $527 million.

Since 2001, the Polaroid Corporation has gone through several bankruptcies and auctions of its assets, which primarily included its company name, intellectual property, and photography collection, with amounts paid ranging from tens to hundreds of millions.

In all honesty, these two outcomes, however flashy, are not very good examples of an exception to the rule because they show two things:

1. A company that once had a significant share of the market will have built up so much goodwill that it remains a desirable target for investors despite it losing its business edge;

2. A company that has invested in building its IP assets through a sophisticated IP strategy could still make a lot of money even when it is no longer capable of selling its products.

It's very unlikely that anyone would have been interested in buying these companies' assets if they had never achieved what they did in their glorious past.

3 TYPES OF BUSINESSES

All businesses fall into three basic categories.

BUSINESSES THAT FAIL

This is a business that fails because it offers something that nobody wants to buy. For this type of business, every penny spent on lawyers is a wasted penny.

The money this business spends on protecting its intellectual property often never generates any returns. Similarly, if this business infringes on someone's intellectual property, no one is really going to care because there's no money to be made.

Nobody bets on a horse *knowing* that it will come in last. Yet, there is *always* a horse that comes in last, and there are always people who will bet on it. If only they'd known that the horse would come in last, they wouldn't bother betting on it.

Likewise, nobody builds a business in anticipation that it will fail as a result of its inability to offer people something they want to buy. They wouldn't bother building the business if they'd known it was going to fail.

This means that you won't know whether you've wasted your money on a failing business until you've built it.

Lean and agile strategies serve the purpose of not putting too much into building a failing business of this kind. However, you must be very careful not to confuse lean and agile with reckless. You don't have to test the market at the expense of neglecting the foundations of your business.

BUSINESSES BUILT ON BAD FOUNDATIONS

As mentioned before, if your business isn't doing well, most people won't worry about what you're doing, but once a business begins to grow quickly, it will become a target for former employees, former partners, competitors, and other opportunists. The sharks will begin to gather waiting to attack.

If the business hasn't taken the proper steps to protect itself in the beginning, these gold diggers will probe every facet of the business that may not be perfect to see if they can get a piece of the pie. In fact, it's not uncommon for your competitors to sponsor potential plaintiffs and draw their attention to the fact that you may be using their intellectual property without proper permission.

A business that relies on other people's stuff without getting the proper documentation is taking an extremely high risk. This business will eventually be destroyed simply because when the company is no longer allowed to use the intellectual property needed by the business, there is really nothing left.

Bad foundations do not just relate to intellectual property. They can also relate to how the business was set up and how contractual issues (like the ones mentioned in previous sections) have been resolved during the early stages of the company.

The result is the same: the business grows having neglected to build strong foundations, it attracts sharks, the sharks attack and the business dies. It's a very sad story. Don't be a part of it.

BUSINESSES BUILT ON GOOD FOUNDATIONS

A healthy business requires a good foundation which will allow it to overcome the scenario described above. I know that this is somewhat circular logic, but a business built on good foundations is a business that can withstand and survive these attacks.

The same things will happen: the business will grow, it will attract sharks, sharks will attack, but this time they will break their teeth against the iron vault that you have built around your treasure chest.

Think of McDonald's. Because it is such a successful company, it gets sued all the time. I won't even go into the discussion about whether the award of $2.86 million was reasonable for failure to make sure that a customer didn't spill hot coffee over herself. People sue McDonald's for forcing employees to receive their wages through a payroll card; for pouring hot coffee that's too hot; for losing their voice as a result of swallowing glass in a sandwich; for targeting children with its advertising and toys; for firing employees over putting too many chocolate sprinkles on a McFlurry; and all sorts of other nonsense.

However, despite the never ending avalanche of complaints and lawsuits, McDonald's has done two things right:

1. It is generating enough profits to survive these attacks, which result in losses that are relatively small compared to the profits; and

2. It is built on such a solid foundation that nobody has found a way to destroy the business with more serious allegations.

There is no question that if McDonald's had not been built properly, the anti-capitalists and nanny-staters would have destroyed this glorious company long ago.

Two very important elements of a good foundation are:

- a comprehensive agreement between the business's founders that thoroughly details their relationships as the business grows and matures; and

- a solid IP strategy that guarantees that the business maximizes its competitive advantages and protects itself from losing the right to do what it does.

MORE MONEY, MORE RISK

It's a fact of business life that the more money you have, the more interested people will be in taking some of that money away from you. We have already discussed this in the chapter that dealt with risk management.

Do you know what is the first thing that a litigation lawyer will ask a client? It's *"How much money does the other side have?"*

If the other side has no money, then the next question the lawyer is going to ask is, *"Well, how are you going to pay for my services?"*

As we've discussed in the chapter that dealt with the need to focus on both IP coming IN and IP going OUT, most plaintiffs try to find a lawyer who will take their case on a contingency basis.

The moment your business becomes profitable, it also becomes a target for anyone who wants a piece of your pie.

The statistics show that close to 97% of all lawsuits filed in Canada settle before trial. This means that the parties at some point figured out that it was cheaper for them to find an out-of-court resolution than it was to go through the whole battle in a courtroom. People will sue you even if they are not planning to take the case to trial. You will see people suing you in the hope that you will just pay them off so that they go away.

The weaker your foundations, the higher settlements you will end up paying because of the threat of losing it all in the courtroom. On the other hand, if you have everything lined up properly, you will be able to withstand the pressure.

Another important negative side of litigation, especially for small businesses, is that it distracts you from doing the most important thing—running your business. McDonald's can hire hundreds of lawyers around the world and only keep track of their legal budgets. A small business will be living and breathing each and every dispute around each and every little issue, simply because everything is so personal to its owners.

Our resources are limited. When we pour our heart and soul into trying to prove to a judge that we are the good guys, and the other side are the bad guys, we are no longer capable of giving our business 100% of what it requires from us and the business suffers.

The weaker the foundations, the more distracted you'll be, thus contributing to the demise of what could have been your empire.

THE MORAL OF THE STORY

The takeaway from this is that unless you are *planning* to be a business that fails, you must build good foundations for your business.

No, it does not mean wasting early money you don't have on buying things you don't need. It means just that you need to invest in strong foundations without which you'd have no business.

And the most important step to building strong foundations is to have perfect clarity into what is involved in building these foundations. That's what this book is going to help you with—at least from the perspective of intellectual property.

IP IS STRONG—
CONTRACTS
ARE STRONGER

This is a point I keep bringing up to my clients. You cannot be successful in your business unless you fully understand this Big Secret.

A contract is an arrangement between two or more parties that documents an agreement to exchange certain mutual promises.

These promises are supposed to change the status quo by:

- granting certain rights to parties who didn't have these rights before;

- by taking away certain rights from parties who did

have these rights before;

- by creating certain obligations for parties who didn't have these obligations before; and

- by relieving parties from certain obligations that they previously had.

For example, when you bought a new iPhone with service,

- you became the owner of the phone;

- the seller passed the ownership of the phone to you;

- you passed the ownership of a certain sum of money to the seller;

- you undertook an obligation to pay monthly fees to your service provider;

- your service provider undertook an obligation to provide you with services.

Before you bought the iPhone with service,

- you did not own the phone;

- the seller owned the phone;

- the seller had no obligation to provide you with the phone;

- you had no obligation to pay the seller;

- you had no obligation to pay the service provider; and

- the service provider had no obligation to provide you with services.

This may sound obvious, but is absolutely critical for you to understand that contracts can create and destroy rights and obligations, overriding default provisions contained in most laws.

The law says that you can't take the property of others without permission. This is theft. But once you have a contract with the seller pursuant to which they give you the phone, and you give them the money, this has now become a contractual relationship. They just lost their right to accuse you of theft since you gave them your money in exchange for the phone. You didn't steal their phone. They didn't steal your money.

Why is this important in terms of intellectual property? Because no matter what steps you have taken to protect your IP, if you sign a bad contract that deals with your intellectual property, you may be in for a big surprise about how the status quo has just changed. Oh, and sometimes you will be deemed to have entered into a contract without signing anything. Simply because you did something, such as responding *"OK"* by email or clicking the *"I ACCEPT"* button, may mean you have entered into a contract with someone.

INTELLECTUAL PROPERTY GIVES, CONTRACTS TAKE AWAY

I had a client who was a book writer. He was paranoid about registering his copyrights. He was writing a book, and for some unknown reason, he thought it was a good idea to obtain a new copyright registration certificate every single time he finished writing a new chapter. By the time he had finished the whole thing, he had a big stack of copyright certificates.

Ironically, a few days after he had received the final registration certificate for the entire book, he met with a publisher in a restaurant. The publisher told the writer how much he loved the book and that he really-really-really wanted to publish it. He even brought a standard agreement with him. *"Here, see, it says that you will be paid a hefty 30% of the publisher's revenue from each book sold. This is way more than the usual practice, but this book is amazing, and I want to make sure I get this deal."*

The writer could not contain his smile. Life has just gotten better. Finally someone has recognized his superior ability to write great books. And here he was, just a few days after typing the last paragraph of the last chapter, signing an amazing contract with this charming publisher. He signed.

And waited.

And waited some more.

A year later, the writer found out that a film company was making a movie based on his book.

He called the movie company and inquired how come nobody told him that a movie would be made based on his book, and more importantly where was his money?! The movie company told the writer that they had purchased all necessary rights from the publisher and that they were very sorry but they had no obligation to pay anything.

Then he called the publisher. The publisher told him that according to the contract, the writer had assigned all of his rights in the book in exchange for 30% of the publisher's revenue from each book sold. But you see, the publisher had no revenue from books sold because the publisher never published any books. In fact, the publisher never intended to publish the book. The publisher merely resold the rights to the movie company. The publisher was, of course, very sorry, but he had no obligation to pay the writer. Not until some books were sold.

This is when the writer came to see me. He brought with him all of his copyright certificates, carrying them as if he was holding a priceless treasure, or at least a priceless treasure map. Matter-of-factly, he also produced the copy of his agreement with the publisher—as if it was a meaningless piece of paper.

When I read the contract and told him that his registration certificates on which he spent well over a thousand dollars were worthless, it was a tough pill to swallow. He just could not fathom how a simple contract could override his copyrights.

But this is the nature of contracts. This is their very purpose—

to change the status quo by creating and destroying rights.
By signing the agreement:
- the writer passed the ownership of copyright to the publisher;
- the publisher obtained the ownership of the copyright in the book, including the right to sublicense and resell these rights;
- the publisher undertook an obligation to pay the writer 30% of the publisher's revenue from book sales; and
- the writer obtained the right to claim 30% of the publisher's revenue from book sales.

The transfer of copyright rendered copyright registrations in the writer's name worthless. And failure of the writer to foresee that he was giving away his rights for free destroyed his ability to make any money off the book he tried so hard to protect.

The moral of the story: be very careful about allowing others to use your IP—whether you do it through a written agreement or not.

BUT I DIDN'T READ IT!

As long as you were given a reasonable *opportunity* to read the contract before you signed it, you're stuck.

Everyone knows that virtually no one reads standard agreements.

People achieve record speed reading times when they are presented with online terms and conditions which they must accept by scrolling the entire document from top to bottom.

Unless the contract contains some extremely unusual provisions (such as your obligation to jump off the top of the Trump Tower in exchange for the privilege of temporarily leaving your car in their underground parkade), your failure to read the contract is your problem, and no one else's.

Again, whether or not you read them, contracts can destroy your rights and overburden you with obligations.

Be careful!

PAYING DOESN'T MEAN BUYING

One of the most important things you can take away from my book is the fact that simply because you paid for something doesn't necessarily mean that you own the intellectual property rights to it. A lot of people don't seem to realize this but often, what you are paying for is a license to use the IP, not actual ownership of the IP.

In case you have forgotten, once you make it big, the sharks will circle and take advantage of everything that you rely on in your business that is not yours. You need to take proper care of IP coming IN your door, and simply paying someone to do something for you just won't cut it.

While intellectual property rights are a very strong weapon, their purpose is to protect the weakest party, the individual creator, by giving him an opportunity to make the best use of the products of his mind without getting ripped off. When some people say that it is only greedy corporations that benefit from IP laws, it's usually because they hate capitalism and corporations, not because they understand how intellectual property works.

The corollary from the two Big Secrets you've just learned, "intellectual property is only as good as your ability to defend it" and "contracts may be stronger than IP", is that when an artist ends up with a really bad deal that allows a big corporation to exploit the artist without giving the artist much in return means,

- the artist did not have a strong bargaining position and would have sold his soul to get the deal;
- the artist did not care or did not even read what he was signing away;
- the corporation, in turn, did care about the language they used to acquire whatever they wanted to get from the artist, so they drafted the contract accordingly; and
- the corporation then used all of its might to enforce the provisions of the contract to a T.

Again, intellectual property gives you the ammunition. It does not give you the balls or the brains to use it. You have to acquire these separately.

What intellectual property gives creators is the right to control how others can use what they had created. If you want to buy this right from the creator, you are supposed to do something very specific about it. You have to put in writing that not only are you buying the tangible, physical stuff, you are also buying the rights to the intellectual property itself. If you don't do this, you only get the tangible stuff. Remember the story when the director owned copyright in the movie and the producer owned the physical film?

When you buy a book in the store, you own the paper on which it is printed, but you don't own the copyright in the book. When you download a program to your computer, you own the file, but you don't own the intellectual property in the program. When you buy a car with intermittent windshield wipers, you buy the car, including its intermittent windshield wipers, but you don't buy the patent that gives you the monopoly to build cars with intermittent windshield wipers. When you buy an iPhone, you buy the iPhone, but you don't buy Apple's logo or the iPhone trademark.

If you want to buy intellectual property, you are supposed to be very specific about it and put everything in writing.

One of my favourite analogies about the tangible-intangible dilemma is buying a refrigerator. You want to make sure that you own both the fridge itself *and* the cold that it generates. One is kind of useless without the other. Granted, we don't run into these issues with refrigerators, but many business owners look at websites, marketing materials, software, and other stuff that they pay for exactly the same way. They assume that when they're buying the fridge, they're buying the cold as well. Not necessarily. When you are buying something that embodies what can be someone else's intellectual property, make sure you buy both the embodiment *and* the IP.

BUT I PAID FOR IT!

Paying somebody is not the same as having a written contract that explicitly says that the author transfers all rights to you. If you don't have that contract, you don't own that IP—plain and simple.

A judge may be sympathetic to your situation, given that you paid a lot of money for something, but if you don't have it in writing, there's really very little the judge can do. You still don't own the IP. At the very best, you will have a limited license to use it.

Here's what this usually means in plain terms:

- it's not your asset, so you can't sell it;

- it's still *their* asset, so they are free to sell it to whoever they want, including your competitors; and

- you can't make any changes to it without their permission.

This can be a big problem because when businesses hire people to create websites, marketing materials, videos, and similar content, they expect that they will own all rights to them and that their competitors will not have the legal right to have an identical website.

WHAT DO YOU MEAN I CAN'T CHANGE MY WEBSITE?!

I recently got a call from a really frustrated business owner. He told me that several years ago, he paid a web designer to build a website for him and a freelance photographer to take pictures of him for the website.

Now, he said, as his business evolved, he wanted to start using the photos in his offline printed marketing materials. He also made a few changes to the website to reflect the growth of his business.

"Can you imagine that?" he said. *"The photographer refused to give me the originals for free, and the web designers sent me a letter stating that I can't make changes on my own, and that I have to hire them, at some ridiculously high price!"*

I asked, *"Do you have a written contract with them?"*

He said, "*I don't have a contract with the photographer, but I do have the contract with the web designer.*"

"*What does your contract with the web designer say?*" I asked.

"*Well, it says that they will create this web design for me, and that I will pay them. So they created the web site, and I paid them. What else do I need?*"

"*Does the contract say somewhere that they assign copyright in the web design and that you own it?*" I asked.

He replied, "*No, but what does it matter if it says here, plain and simple, that they created it FOR ME?!*"

My response went along the lines of, "*This is the classic case of when you buy the tangible stuff without buying the IP behind it. Since you only have a license, not ownership, the company that built the website can contact you and demand that if you want any changes, you have to hire their company to do the changes.*

"*Even if you want to hire a new company, you can't because you only have a license to use the website as is and you do not have the right to modify it. The company that built the website is the only one who has that right.*

"*They could also sell the same design to anyone else, including your competitor.*

"*And as for the photographer, she retained ownership in the photographs that she took of you as well. She can't sell them to others because of your personality rights, but you still don't own the copyright in them, because you never bought it from her.*"

After he shared with me what he would like to do to the photographer, the designer, the lawyers, and those who write IP laws, he asked, "*So what are my options?*"

I said, "*There are three things you can do. One, you can just pay them what they are asking to make the necessary changes and get the necessary files. Two, you can renegotiate the agreement with them and do what you should have done in the first place, that is buy the IP outright, so that you don't have to have this conversation ever again. Three, you can redo the entire thing with someone else, making sure that the new website does not look anything like the old website and that you have a proper contract this time."*

Understandably, he hated all three options. But this is what you will be left with if you neglect to take proper care of the IP coming IN.

PROTECT YOURSELF AT ALL TIMES

Whenever you have someone create content for you, make sure they sign an agreement stating that you own the product. If the person won't sign the contract, then look for someone who will. It's not enough to simply pay for something to be made for you—you need that contract as well.

Although oral contracts are good enough for most purposes, they are not good enough for the purpose of assignment of copyright. Canadian law is very specific in that the contract must be in writing.

Oh yeah, one last thing, it's a lot easier to sign the right contact before your money has left your pocket and landed in the pocket of someone who has promised to do something for you. Most web designers would not have an issue signing a document that says that you own the design they have created for you *before* they get paid to do the work. Getting them to sign something *after* they've already spent your money would be very difficult.

GET THAT CONTRACT SIGNED

When I was starting my business, I didn't have a lot of money. I needed a logo so I used a design contest website to create one. Before I did this, I shopped around and found a design platform that agreed to have the winner sign an addendum to their standard agreement stating that I would own the logo. The platform's standard agreement lacked several very important points that I knew I had to address.

It took a fair amount of back and forth but we finally came to an agreement. The designer signed everything. He sent me a scan of his ID and a signed copy of the agreement, and I was very happy.

I was planning to use the same service to develop my website, but then the site owners said, "*You know what? It's too much hassle. We're not going to do this anymore. We're just going to use our standard agreement, and if you don't like it, don't use our service.*"

I didn't because I didn't want to end up in a situation, although the risk was probably small, where somebody had control over what I wanted to do with my website.

Make sure that when you pay somebody to do something for you, you own it.

I outsource a lot of technical work, and a substantial part of it implies creation of IP by contractors. Even for small projects on oDesk.com, I never give the project to someone who refuses to confirm, through oDesk's messaging system, that I will own the IP rights to what they create. In fact, I don't even look at the bids of those who refuse to assign their IP to me.

I require that those who bid to do the work on my project, message me with the following:

"*I, <your name> of <your address>, in exchange for the opportunity to be selected to provide <description of the services>, hereby undertake never to disclose confidential information that I may receive in connection with my provision of services, and agree to assign and hereby assign to Trademark Factory International Inc. ownership of any intellectual property rights that may subsist in the work product that I may create as a result of providing the services.*"

Granted, this is not a full-blown written contract, but it will be sufficient for most small projects.

I strongly recommend that you read my article "*10 Tips on*

How to Choose a Web Designer—a Copyright Lawyer's Perspective",
where you will learn some specific things you need to look out
for in an agreement with your designer. The article is posted at
**http://mincovlaw.com/blog-post/10_tips_on_how_to_choose_a_
web_designer**

EMPLOYEES AND OWNERSHIP

One important exception to the rule that paying doesn't mean
buying relates to employees.

If you have hired someone as an employee, then the law says
that whatever they create within the scope of their employment
duties belongs to you as the employer.

This only works if:

- there is a true employment relationship between you
  and the worker (i.e. the worker is a salaried employee);

- the IP was created within the scope of employment
  duties of the employee; and

- there is nothing in the employment agreement that
  says otherwise.

But it is really a poor practice to rely on the default provisions
of various laws when you can back your arrangement up with a
written contract that would also deal with important details that
are not addressed in such laws. Remember, contracts are stronger.
They are also much clearer. Or at least they should be.

The main reason for getting employees to sign a contract is that
it just makes your life easier. You don't have to worry about arguing
with an employee over ownership because it's already been settled
before work has even begun. You don't have to argue whether

creating certain types of IP is within the scope of the employee's duties because you would address that in the contract. You don't have to argue over whether the employee is to be paid extra if you use the IP. You don't have to argue over whether you should let the world know that the IP had been created by the employee (this is about the author's moral rights which we'll deal with in Part II of this book). You don't have to argue over anything that you have properly addressed in the written agreement. That's what written agreements are for!

I guarantee that if you have written agreements with your employees where you properly address intellectual property issues, you'll thank me if your employee creates something for your business that generates you a lot of money, and you can point out to the overly eager employee that no, you own it, and no, they can't get a slice of your pie.

ALWAYS KEEP THESE TEN BIG SECRETS IN MIND

These 10 Big Secrets are, in my opinion, crucial to how you approach everything in your business. They are especially important in helping you figure out what to ask a lawyer.

Often when a client comes to me and asks, "*Well, what if we use somebody else's work without their permission, would that be okay?*" My response is always the same.

I tell the client, "*You're asking several questions piled into one. The answer to the question, 'Is this perfectly legal?' can be very different from the question, 'How likely is it that we're going to have any problems if we do it?'*"

The vast majority of business owners are not really interested in finding out whether doing something is 100 percent legal. What they are interested in is the degree of the risk they will face by doing something. Remember the section on risk management.

Make sure you always focus on not only your own IP that you want to protect from others (IP going OUT), but also on the IP coming IN.

Make sure you have a meaningful IP strategy that matches your business strategy. Otherwise you are bound to pay for unnecessary services and neglect to secure what is necessary.

Always think whether your actions contribute to a better story. Remember, judges don't look for better law—they look for the better story.

If you have something worthy of protection, protect it! Don't expect a piece of paper to do all the work for you. The piece of paper may be your most powerful weapon, but only if you use it.

While focusing on IP is very important, make sure you don't lose track of the fact that it is even more important to build a successful business that offers products and services that the public is willing to pay for. Intellectual property owned by successful businesses is worth a lot more.

Don't neglect the power of a contract. Contracts can make you and break you. If you don't pay attention to your contracts, you will be in trouble.

One of the most important types of contract is the one whereby you acquire the intellectual property in what others create for you. Remember, just because you pay them, does not mean that the IP they create is yours. You have to specifically address that in your contracts.

With this in mind, we will now jump into discussing specific areas of intellectual property, but make sure you read the next part through the prism of what you have just learned in Part I. I guarantee that this will allow you to see how to apply this knowledge in your business.

PART II

AREAS OF INTELLECTUAL PROPERTY

You have already learned that intellectual property is just an umbrella term for several areas of law. They all relate to rights designed to protect creations of the human mind. These areas of law protect different kinds of IP in ways that vary from one area of law to another.

Many textbooks have been written on each area of law, and each has so many tiny little details that it is easy to lose focus and get distracted by relatively minor things.

Don't get me wrong, these details are very important if you are a lawyer drafting a contract or preparing a lawsuit. However, if you are not a lawyer and you don't want to become one, the first thing you need to learn is how to easily tell one area of IP from all others.

To put it simply, nobody will take you seriously if, in an attempt to be your own lawyer, you write to someone that you have patented your trademarks or registered your trade secrets. This is more than a matter of knowing the terminology. This is about truly *understanding* the difference between these areas of law.

My purpose with this book is to help you understand intellectual property on a basic level, so that you can immediately identify the different areas of IP as they apply to your business, and if need be, look up the relevant section in this book or go through a more detailed book on the subject.

What you should know about IP right away is that different areas of intellectual property apply to different scopes of objects. Each area has its own tight boundaries and exceptions; each has its own rules for what the protection provides, and how long it lasts.

I found that the best way to address complex concepts, such as the different areas of intellectual property, is by using shortcuts. I call them Magic Words. One Magic Word per area of IP. One Magic Word so powerful that it will immediately focus your mind on a particular area of intellectual property.

At this point, they are probably meaningless to you. But you will understand their meaning as you continue to read this book.

Let me introduce them:

- The magic word for *Copyright* and *Neighbouring Rights* is **HOW**,
- The magic word for *Trademarks* is **WHICH**,
- The magic word for *Patents* is **WHAT**,
- The magic word for *Industrial Designs* is **WOW**,
- The magic word for *Trade Secrets* is **HUSH**,
- The magic word for *Contractual Rights* is **WHATEVER**.

COPYRIGHT AND NEIGHBOURING RIGHTS: *HOW*

Most people have heard the term copyright, but not neighbouring rights. Neighbouring rights relate to an area of law that is very close to copyright, even though it protects a slightly different scope of objects. In fact, in Canada, neighbouring rights are officially called "copyright in other subject matter." They are also known as "related rights."

You will understand why I chose *HOW* as the Magic Word for copyright and neighbouring rights as you keep reading this chapter. We'll start with what can be protected by copyright and neighbouring rights, and then I'll explain the reasoning behind choosing this Magic Word.

Because most of what is covered in this chapter will equally apply to both copyright proper and to neighbouring rights, in order to avoid using the term "copyright and neighbouring rights" throughout this chapter, I will be using the term "copyright" to cover both copyright proper and neighbouring rights. Having said that, when I am comparing copyright proper with neighbouring rights, I will be using the term "copyright" in the sense of "copyright proper."

WHAT DO COPYRIGHT AND NEIGHBOURING RIGHTS PROTECT?

Copyright can protect a vast scope of things. When I say "things," I don't mean physical objects. I mean the results of human creativity that are embodied in those physical objects. This is crucial to understand.

If you read Big Secret #10 carefully, you will remember that when you buy a book in the store, you own the paper on which it is printed, but you don't own the copyright in the book. Just like ownership of the paper does not give you a copyright in the work that is printed on that paper, copyright in the work does not give you ownership of the paper on which it is printed. These are two separate ownerships, even when one cannot be imagined without the other.

So when I say that copyright protects certain things or objects, I am referring to the immaterial, intangible objects—objects that you can't touch any more than you can touch your memories, your imagination, or money on your VISA card. In this last example, you can touch the card itself or you can use it to get cash, which you can also touch, but you can never touch the money that is available to you *while it's still on your card*, because this is your intangible asset. Same thing goes for copyright (and other intellectual property objects).

THINGS THAT CAN BE COPYRIGHTED

Among objects that can be protected by copyright are books, songs, films, videos, photographs, illustrations, paintings, drawings, maps, articles, marketing materials, pamphlets and other writings, user manuals, website contents and look & feel, and computer programs, including HTML, javascript and PHP code.

It is not uncommon for a physical object to have multiple copyrights embodied in it. One of my favourite examples is a music CD (and if you buy music from iTunes, the same still applies, because copyright is not about the physical medium). It will have separate copyrights for music, for lyrics, for the cover art, for any photographs used in the cover art, for any of the fonts used in it, the order in which the songs are arranged on that album, performances, and the sound recordings. All of those

> are separate copyrights that can be and often are owned by different owners. When somebody downloads an album off The Pirate Bay, it's not just one case of copyright infringement; it's usually several at the same time.

Copyright protects original literary, dramatic, musical, and artistic works.

- Literary works are essentially written or recorded words, numbers, or symbols, and include books, articles, blog posts, and software. Software is written as computer code, so it was decided that software should be given exactly the same protection as a literary work.

- Musical works include compositions of music with or without lyrics.

- Dramatic works are works that are written or are created to be performed by one or more characters and include films, plays, scripts, and videos. It's sometimes very difficult to differentiate a dramatic work from a literary work because one often becomes the other.

- Artistic works are two- and three-dimensional works of fine graphic or applied art and include paintings, photographs, sculptures, maps, and architecture.

In most countries, this breakdown of original works into literary, dramatic, musical and artistic is for illustration purposes only, since pretty much any type of human creativity that is covered by the Magic Word *HOW* can be protected by copyright. Canada's approach is slightly stricter, albeit not strict enough to render copyright powerless. Even in Canada, copyright covers a very wide scope of IP objects.

Neighbouring rights are a relatively new addition to the system of copyright, which originally only protected authors. Neighbouring rights cover performances, sound recordings, and broadcasts.

- Performances include:
  - ✓ performances of artistic, musical, or dramatic works;
  - ✓ recitations of literary works; and
  - ✓ improvisations of dramatic, musical or literary works.

- Sound recordings are recordings of any sounds, which may or may not be recordings of performances of works.
- Broadcasts (called *communication signals* in Canada) cover TV and radio broadcasts, whether or not they incorporate works, performances, or sound recordings.

WHAT ARE THE REQUIREMENTS FOR PROTECTION?

Of all types of intellectual property, copyright has the lowest requirements for protection.

To satisfy the requirements for protection, the works, performances, sound recordings and broadcasts must be:

- minimally original; and
- expressed in some objective form capable of being perceived by others.

If these requirements are met, your works, performances, sound recordings, and broadcasts are *automatically* protected by copyright. You don't have to register them anywhere, you don't have to disclose them to anybody—just express something original in some objective form.

The protection of neighbouring rights is also automatic. Once you've performed your performance, it is protected. And if you perform the same thing a thousand times, each of the thousand performances is protected, separately from all the other ones. Once you've made a sound recording, it is protected. Once you've broadcast your communication signal, it is protected.

With neighbouring rights, you will see that copyrights love to breed. A single song can generate thousands of performances, each of which will receive separate protection. And if each of these performances is recorded, each sound recording of each performance will also receive separate protection.

It is often said that copyright arises *upon creation* of the work (or performance, sound recording, or broadcast), and that no formalities are required for copyright protection. This makes copyright a very serious weapon in skilled hands.

We'll discuss this further when we move on to the registration of copyright, but let's first get a handle on what "original" and "expressed in an objective form" mean.

"Original" does *not* mean brilliant, unique, unusual, unlike anything anyone has ever written, or one of a kind. "Original" in copyright terms simply means *"not copied from a pre-existing source"*.

IS THIS SUPPOSED TO BE ORIGINAL?

This book may not be unlike anything anyone has ever written on the subject. And, although, I flatter myself that it is a great book, copyright does not care if it's a great book. From the copyright perspective, this book can be completely devoid of any literary, scientific, or any other value. As long as it was not copied from another source or sources, it is "original".

Did I read many books on the subject before I wrote this book? You bet!

Did I look through competitors' literature? Absolutely!

Does this book cover similar topics as theirs? Of course!

Did I copy this book from something that had existed before? No. Wouldn't that be ironic though?

Is this book "original"? Yes. And this is why it says © *2013–2015 by Andrei Mincov and Trademark Factory International Inc.* on the credits page.

One of my father's favourite sayings was, "*If your music does not sound like anything anybody has ever heard, this means that nobody's gonna give a damn about your music.*"

He didn't suggest that all composers should steal from each other. What he meant was that good composers are well educated to be able to build upon previous generations to create something new and original. One can trace Bach's influence in Mozart's and Beethoven's music. One can trace Mozart's influence in Schubert's and Chopin's music. And so on, and so on.

A similar observation was made in the book *Made to Stick*: "*All creative ads resemble one another, but each loser is uncreative in its own way.*"

Also, if you simply make a copy of an existing sound recording, then your copy or your sound recording will not qualify for its own protection because there is nothing original about your copy. On the other hand, if an artist allows five different sound engineers to record his performance, each of the 5 recordings will be protected, even though these recordings may sound identical.

Copyright does not care about the artistic value of a work. Neither does it generally care about its size. Some countries, Canada among them, tend to specifically exclude from copyright protection single words and really short phrases. European countries do not generally have this "word limit", but still require that whatever is to be protected by copyright be the result of creative work.

"*Expressed in some objective form capable of being perceived by others"* is what many lawyers refer to as the requirement of fixation. This means that the work, performance, sound recording, or broadcast must exist separately from the person who created them.

YOU NEED TO WRITE IT DOWN

I've been planning to write this book for over a year. I kind of knew what it would cover and had some ideas about how it would be structured. For as long as all these great ideas existed nowhere but inside my head, they were not protected by copyright. They were not protected by copyright because they had not been expressed in any form that would allow anybody to read or otherwise enjoy this book.

However, as soon as I started jotting down the drafts for the book, these drafts satisfied the requirement of fixation because they became the *"objective form that is capable of being perceived by others."* Each of these drafts was and is protected by copyright.

Every time I add another word to this manuscript, it adds to the scope of what is protected by copyright.

While the previous sentence was still forming inside my mind, it was not protected. Once typed, it is protected by copyright.

It's that simple!

The performance, the recording, or the broadcast must also be expressed in some form capable of being perceived by others. Just because you're a great performer who has come up with a great idea about how to perform a particular work, if the idea is still in your head, then it doesn't get protected. Your performance is protected the moment you've delivered it in a manner that allowed someone other than yourself to somehow perceive it (by hearing, viewing, or otherwise)—whether or not the performance was recorded or broadcast.

WHAT COPYRIGHT DOES NOT PROTECT

Because the requirements for copyright protection are so low, it is crucial that you understand the boundaries of what can and cannot be protected by copyright. There are, in fact, many things that, although closely related to what is protected by copyright, are outside the scope of copyright protection.

Here they are:

IDEAS

The most important limitation is that copyright does not protect ideas. It protects an *original expression* of these ideas. It protects the form, in which these ideas are expressed. In other words, it protects *HOW* the ideas are expressed.

This is precisely why the Magic Word for copyright is *HOW*. And if there is one thing you need to remember about copyright, it's this.

Let me give you a few examples.

Let's go back to this book. First, I had an idea that it would be nice to write a book. That idea was not protected by copyright. Then I decided that the book will be about intellectual property. This idea was not protected by copyright either. Then I decided that the first part of the book will be about the 10 Big Secrets, and the second part of the book will be about different areas of intellectual property. That idea was not protected by copyright. Then I jotted down the structure of the book in a WinWord document. That document was no longer an idea, it was a literary work protected by copyright. However, at that time, this was all that existed in an objective form. So the actual contents of the book were still an idea that was not protected by copyright. As I am writing these chapters, one by one, they stop being ideas and become works protected by copyright.

Copyright in a book does not protect what the book is about since books can have similar plots and ideas. Copyright in a book protects the actual sequence of the letters and the words in that book. This is how we can have multiple textbooks on math. They all cover the same subject. They all have similar problems and charts. The idea (*this will be a textbook on math*) is not protected by copyright, but the actual textbook, with its particular sequence of lessons, each with its own examples and illustrations, is.

Same with music—copyright doesn't protect the general ideas that are on an album or in a song. Copyright protects the actual sequence of the notes.

Same with software—copyright doesn't protect the idea of what the software accomplishes. It protects the actual code and the actual graphic interface.

Another example can be seen in photographs. If ten photographers go and shoot the sunset over a building without using special lights or other special features, the photographers will each own the copyright in their own photograph even if their photograph is almost indistinguishable from photographs that other photographers have taken. The idea (*it would be a nice location for a sunset picture*) is not subject to copyright but the actual photograph is. On the other hand, it may be difficult in case of a dispute for each particular photographer to prove that it was his, and not somebody else's photograph that was used by the defendant.

FACTS

Copyright doesn't protect facts. When something happens, different newspapers or different TV news anchors will all be able to convey the information; although, they need to do it in different ways. What copyright protects is *HOW* they have expressed those facts, whether it's in words or in videos or some other way, but the facts themselves cannot be protected by copyright.

For example, if I read a newspaper article and then simply copy the article word for word, then I am guilty of copyright infringement; but, if I retell that article in my own words then there is no copyright infringement. There is no one *HOW* anymore. It's their *HOW* and it's my *HOW*; and they are different.

In other words, nobody owns the news. But whoever shapes the news into a consumable news piece, owns that piece. They own the *HOW* of the piece.

FUNCTIONALITY

Copyright does not protect methods, processes, or algorithms. It doesn't protect the functionality of products. As you'll learn later in this book, the only way to protect functionality is through patents.

For example, you came up with a great new type of bicycle. It's so good that you wrote a booklet about it with colourful illustrations. Copyright will protect the text in your booklet and the illustrations, but it will not protect you against anybody who may wish to build the actual bicycle—*that* is not protected by copyright.

MASS-PRODUCED STUFF

In Canada, copyright does not protect aesthetic elements of mass-produced items. That is any items produced in a quantity of more than 50. If you want those protected, you need to register them as industrial designs. We'll discuss industrial designs later in this book. I should note that in most other countries, instead of the "either–or" situation, there is an overlap between copyright and industrial designs.

In Canada, once an item has been produced in a quantity of more than 50, unless you registered its aesthetic elements (i.e. its visual features) as industrial design, you have no protection. In most other countries, even if you don't have a registration as an industrial design, you can still rely on good old copyright to protect the design as an artistic work.

So if you're mass-producing something that has a unique shape and you're not protecting it through industrial designs, then you're not protecting it at all, at least not in Canada.

There are also things that cannot be protected through neighbouring rights:

UNDERLYING WORKS

Neighbouring rights do not protect underlying works. For example, if an actor performs a speech from Shakespeare, the performance will be protected by neighbouring rights (copyright in other subject matter), but it will not revive the protection for the underlying work itself (i.e. Shakespeare's play). Shakespeare will remain in the public domain. Just because a performer performs it and receives protection for his performance does not change anything in terms of protection of the underlying work by Shakespeare.

UNDERLYING IDEAS

If a performer performs something that cannot be protected by copyright, such as a mere retelling of a fact or an idea, the performance will be protected but not the fact or idea. If somebody decides to shoot a video of themselves retelling their next great idea ("*I will write this great book about this and that, and it will cover such and such and all of that sort of thing*"), the video of you saying that will be protected, but it will not allow you to stop other people from creating the same book because at that point in time, it is just an idea, and ideas are not protected by copyright.

STYLE OF PERFORMANCE

Neighbouring rights do not protect the general style of performance. If you are the first musician to use a particular instrument or a particular style of performance then while your individual performances will be protected, your style won't be—because the style of performance is essentially the same thing as an idea in copyright. It's too broad, and copyright is not designed to give you that protection.

PROFESSIONAL SECRETS OF SOUND RECORDING

Neighbouring rights also don't protect professional secrets of sound recording. Let's say you're a professional sound engineer and you figured out a way to have your guitar sound larger than life and your kick drum sound like a basketball (*du-dum, du-dum*), then while your actual sound recordings where you implemented these ideas *will* be protected by neighbouring rights, the secrets or the style themselves will not be protected.

HOW LONG DOES COPYRIGHT LAST?

In Canada, the general term of copyright in a work is the entire life of the last surviving co-author plus fifty years after their death. In most countries, this term is the entire life plus seventy years. If the work has been co-authored by several people, the term of protection will last for the entire term of their lives until the last co-author dies. From that moment on, you'll count either fifty or seventy years. After that period has expired, then the work will fall into the public domain when anybody can use it without asking permission.

Subject to several special cases, performances are protected for 50 years after the end of the calendar year in which the performance took place. Sound recordings are protected for 50 years after the end of the calendar year in which the sound recording was made. Broadcasts are protected for 50 years after the end of the calendar year in which the communication signal was broadcast.

WHERE IS COPYRIGHT PROTECTED?

Not only are your works, performances, sound recordings, and broadcasts protected automatically upon their creation, they are automatically protected *worldwide* (with a few insignificant exceptions) because of the international treaties to which most countries are parties.

If you create the work in Canada, it will be automatically recognized pretty much everywhere else in the world. Also, if you steal material from somebody who lives in Pakistan, they can still sue you wherever you are using it, and they don't need to do anything to acquire that extra-territorial protection.

Likewise, most countries are parties to international treaties that provide protection to performances, sound recordings, and broadcasts originating from other countries. Again, there are a few exceptions, but for all practical purposes, they are mostly irrelevant.

Unlike most other areas of IP, no initial investment is necessary to give you protection worldwide. The combination of automatic and worldwide protection makes copyright a very powerful tool that you can use and that can be used against you. Use it wisely and be careful!

WHO OWNS IT?

The general rule is that copyright is owned by the individual authors who created the work unless there is a true employment relationship between an individual and a company for which the author works.

People need to be very cautious about this because independent contractors and freelancers don't fall into the category of having a true employment relationship. This means they will own the copyright in whatever they create, even if they create it for somebody else. Authors who do something for someone else—even when they're paid to do it—retain their authorship and continue to be the copyright owners. As we discussed in Part I of this book, one of the Big Secrets is that just because you pay somebody to create something for you doesn't make it yours.

The *Copyright Act* provides an extra layer of protection for the weaker party, the creator, by requiring a publisher, a film company, or any other company that wishes to use a specific piece of work or own the copyright in that work to get the creator of the work to sign a written agreement. This written agreement must explicitly state that the author is transferring the copyright. The author needs to basically say, "*Yes, not only do I allow you to use my work, I also assign to you my right to that work.*" Unless you have this in a written agreement, the individual author will continue to own the copyright in a particular work.

PUBLIC LICENSES AND OPEN SOURCE

One of the common misconceptions about open source software and other materials offered on the terms of public licenses such as GPL and Creative Commons is that they are not protected by copyright.

> They are. And they have an owner (or owners).
>
> The reason you can use them without having to enter into individual license agreements with the owners is that the owners have decided to exercise their exclusive rights in the form of granting you a license on particular terms.
>
> If you accept the terms of this license, you can use the work pursuant to them.
>
> But, as you have learned, a license does not deprive the owner of the rights in what had been licensed to you, with the only exception being that the owner cannot prevent a legitimate licensee from using the licensed object, as long as the licensee uses it according to the terms of the license.
>
> Thus, while you usually don't have to pay to use open source software, it is still protected by copyright and has an owner.

As mentioned, where a true employment relationship exists, the copyright will be owned by the employer. There are several tests of what constitutes a true employment relationship, but typically if you have been hired and are receiving a monthly salary to develop something that's relatively well-defined and you create something within that scope, then the employer will own the copyright.

While this makes it slightly easier for employers to deal with their employees in terms of who owns copyright, it also creates a sense of false security because the default provisions of the *Copyright Act* don't address all the issues that should normally be addressed in an employer/employee relationship.

For example, the rights to pre-existing works, something that the employee had created before he became an employee, and also the materials that the employee created while he had been employed by others are not addressed. Neither do the default provisions set out in the *Copyright Act* address moral rights, so it's always a good idea to have a contract reflect all of that and more and be as specific as possible even when the default provisions exist.

I should also mention joint ownership, which is one of the murkiest sides of copyright. As you have learned, intellectual property, and copyright in particular, is not just about the money. It is also about control. So when you have joint ownership of copyright, it's not enough to figure out who gets how much money from the use of the work. Often, the more important question is who can make decisions how to use the work. Essentially, the two possible options here are:

1. any one of the co-owners is fully authorized to grant licenses or make an assignment; or

2. the decision to grant licenses or make an assignment requires consent of all co-owners.

Unfortunately, there is no conclusive answer in Canadian law as to which of these two options applies.

What this means is that every time you may end up in a situation where copyright will be jointly owned by two or more parties, make sure to have a written agreement that clearly states who is authorized to grant licenses and make assignments. Without it, you are setting yourself up for a judicial disaster.

MORAL RIGHTS

Additionally, Canada provides limited protection for moral rights. Moral rights are technically separate from copyright itself, even though these rights arise at the same time as copyright, and pursuant to the same laws. Copyright focuses on protecting economic rights while moral rights focus on protecting the personal rights of the author who created the work.

In Canada, they include the right to the integrity of the work and the right to be associated with the work as its author. The right to the integrity of the work allows the author to prevent any unauthorized modifications of the work that can detrimentally reflect on the reputation of the author.

For example, if somebody takes a novel and turns it into a pornographic movie, the author of the novel can go after the producer of that movie even if they allowed the transformation of the novel into "*a movie*". Of course, if the author knew and agreed that the movie could be pornographic then the author can't claim that his moral rights were infringed.

SOME DIRTY HUMOUR CAN NEVER HURT A BOOK ABOUT LAW

Let this story be your guide when you think about moral rights. A well-known composer who only writes serious classical music gets a phone call. The voice on the phone asks if the composer would be willing to write music for the film they have just launched in production.

The composer says, "*I'm sorry, I don't write music for films. I only write serious music. I write symphonies, operas, ballets, cantatas. I don't waste my talent on such vulgar things as music for movies.*"

The voice on the phone says, "*I understand. We know the scale of your talent. That's why I'm calling. Would you reconsider?*"

The composer says, "*No, I'm not interested.*"

The producer says, "*We were planning to pay you 3 million dollars if you say yes.*"

The composer goes, "*When do I start?*"

And so the composer ventures into new territory. He works day and night and composes all that he's required to compose.

When he's done, he receives a letter from the producer. It has a cheque enclosed, and also an invitation for the world premiere.

The composer puts on his best tuxedo, hires a limo and arrives at the address indicated in the letter. He enters the hall. And, to his horror, it's absolutely empty. Except for him and a couple in the front row, there is nobody there.

He would have thought that he'd come to the wrong place if the lights hadn't gone out and the familiar title of the film that he had been working on hadn't appeared on the screen. After the title, his name appeared in huge letters next to the words: "*Music by*". So he decides to stay.

He sits in the last row and watches.

He realizes that he had been engaged to write music for a *porn* film.

He is presented with all sorts of scenes between different numeric and gender combinations of women and men—all of that in complete silence, not even a hint that any music had ever been written for it. He wonders, "*Why did they need a composer for this, especially since they are not using any music?*"

Finally, two hours into the film, he sees the scene between a man and a dog. He can't stand it anymore and is about to leave, furious, but then the sounds of his majestic music fill the room. This sounds like the best thing he has ever written in his life.

He can't just sit there and so he dashes to the couple in the front row. He sits next to them and whispers, "*Listen, this is MY MUSIC!*" only to hear: "*Shut up and don't bug us! This is OUR DOG!*"

The moral of the story is, if you care *how* your work is to be used (or more importantly, *not* to be used, make sure to specify that in your contract).

But, really, things don't have to go this far. One of the most famous cases on moral rights in Canada dealt with the rights of a sculptor to prevent a mall from tying Christmas ribbons around the necks of geese that the sculptor had created for the mall. The courts agreed with the sculptor that this intrusion constituted infringement of his moral rights.

Additionally, moral rights allow authors to prevent the use of their works in association with a product, service, cause, or institution. For example, it is one thing to license your song to be included in a movie, but quite another if your song is used as the background jingle for a condom commercial. Moral rights allow creators to decide if any particular association between their work and someone else's products or causes is acceptable to them. In certain cases, they allow authors to craft sophisticated licensing policies whereby fees depend on how the works are used.

A separate moral right is the right to be associated with the work as its author. This means that authors have the right to demand that their names be indicated whenever the work is used. Even if you allow somebody to use your work and you have a contract that states that the licensee will have the right to republish your book or sing your song or use your software, that license does not take away your moral right to demand that your name be indicated in one way or another whenever your work is used.

In Canada, this protection is limited by a phrase in the *Copyright Act* which states that this right is only available to authors whenever it's *"reasonable to expect that the name be indicated"*. In most other countries, there is no such limitation, so this moral right can become extremely powerful and it's something that should always be taken care of in contracts.

In Europe, moral rights are significantly more developed and include:

- the right to be known as the author of his work (*droit à la paternité*);
- the right to prevent others from falsely attributing to you the authorship of a work that you have not in fact written;

- the right to prevent others from being named as the author of your work;
- the right to publish a work anonymously or pseudonymously, as well as the right to change your mind at a later date and claim authorship under your own name;
- the right to prevent others from using your work or your name in such a way as to reflect adversely on your professional standing (*droit au respect du nom*);
- the right to prevent others from making deforming changes in your work (*droit au respect de l'œuvre*). This right may sometimes be limited to the right to prevent others from making deforming changes in your work *provided* that such changes might damage your honour and reputation (*droit à s'opposer à toute atteinte préjudiciable à l'honneur et à la réputation*);
- the right to publish a work, or to withhold it from dissemination (*droit de divulgation*);
- the right to withdraw a published work from distribution if it no longer represents the views of the author (*droit de retrait*; also, *droit de repentir*).

Moral rights cannot be sold or assigned. They *always* stay with the author or performer. They stay with the author or performer even if they sell the right to use their works or performances. Moral rights stay with the author or performer even if they created their works or performances within the scope of their employment duties, in which case the employer would be the first owner of copyright. Moral rights are *always* retained by the individual whose mind generated something that is protected by copyright.

While moral rights cannot be assigned, in Canada, it is possible to waive moral rights. What this means is that if the author or performer in a written agreement agrees to waive moral rights, he promises not to assert these rights (that he continues to retain) against the person or the company with whom he has the agreement, thereby giving that person or company a blank cheque to do whatever they want with the work or performance.

In most other countries, you *cannot* waive moral rights. So, if you have an agreement that says that an author waives his moral rights, that agreement may be enforceable in Canada, but it will not be enforceable in France.

THE WHERE IS IMPORTANT

If you think that this is irrelevant as long as you have a contract based on Canadian law, think again.

One of the most famous cases on moral rights was when an American film company colorized a black and white film created by an American director after his death, and wanted to show the colorized version in France. The estate of the late director attempted to prevent it and filed a claim in the French court.

The film company claimed that the director was an American, the company is American, the film was made in the United States, the contract between the company and the director was governed by American law, so there was no reason why the contract's provision whereby the director waived his moral rights would not be enforceable in other countries.

The French court held that while copyright is automatically protected internationally through various treaties, the protection is still provided on a national level, which means that U.S. copyright owners have rights according to French laws in France. While in many aspects the French laws are very similar to the U.S. laws, moral rights is where these laws differ substantially.

Because under French law, moral rights cannot be waived, the court refused to enforce the provision of the contract where the director waived his moral rights, and issued an injunction forbidding the film company from showing the colourized version in France and awarded a significant sum to the estate of the late director.

Therefore, if you are obtaining a license to use somebody else's work, you want to make sure that you address their moral rights as well and not simply rely on the norms of the Canadian *Copyright Act* because moral rights are not handled around the world in the same way.

REGISTERING COPYRIGHTS

Although protection is automatic, you may still want to take it one step further and register your copyrights and neighbouring rights.

Copyright registration doesn't create protection—you already have that by virtue of having created the work, performance, sound recording, or broadcast. What it does is it adds certain presumptions and remedies that you can use if you see that somebody is infringing on your right.

Registration in Canada is very peculiar because, unlike in the States, in Canada, you don't deposit the work that you want to register. All you do is notify the Canadian Intellectual Property Office that you have created a work that has a certain title and that you want that title to be registered in your name in Canada. If you write a song about sunshine, that's what you're going to tell them: *"This is a song that I have created. Its name is 'Sunshine'. Here's your 50 dollars."* You then get a certificate of registration. In my opinion, this is a big flaw in Canada's system of registration because it doesn't really provide any information to anyone about what the work really is.

I CAN'T BELIEVE I GOT THIS REGISTERED

A friend of mine boastingly sent me a copy of his Canadian copyright registration certificate for something that cannot be copyrighted.

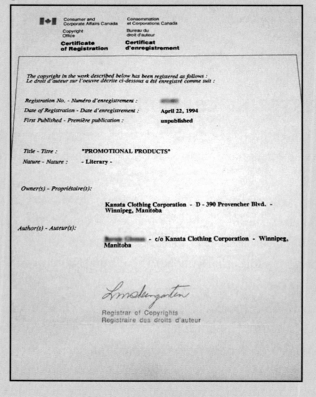

As you can see, the registration is for a literary work called *PROMOTIONAL PRODUCTS*. Thing is, no such work has ever existed. The title is all that my friend came up with and was trying to protect.

Copyright was never designed to protect two isolated words. "Promotional products" is not a literary work, certainly not an original literary work. But the Canadian Intellectual Property Office does not check if you even have the work, let alone if it's original. So they issued the registration certificate.

In this case, the certificate is completely worthless, because it protects nothing. It wouldn't give my friend any additional powers to prevent others from using the phrase "Promotional Products". He would probably be laughed out of court if he decided to use it as evidence of his rights to the "work".

The important thing here is that my friend wasn't trying to trick the Intellectual Property Office, he just didn't know that copyright could not protect the phrase "Promotional Products". He thought that a $50 fee was better than the $450 fee for trademarks, so he filed and it just got registered.

I can only imagine how many similarly worthless copyright registrations have been issued in Canada!

In the United States, when you file for copyright registration, you are required to submit the work itself, and they will look into it and make sure that it's proper subject matter for registration. This allows people to have a reference point to compare their material with any material that has been copyrighted by someone else.

Interestingly, the fees are lower in the U.S. (US$35 compared to CA$50), so I always recommend to my clients who have decided to register copyright that they register both in Canada and the U.S. because Canadian registration will give them certain procedural advantages if they were to have a dispute resolved in a Canadian court, but a U.S. registration will provide the proper evidence to confirm that on a certain date the work existed and that the owner claimed ownership in that work.

WHAT CONSTITUTES COPYRIGHT INFRINGEMENT (WHAT CAN YOU SUE OTHERS FOR)?

Simply put, copyright prohibits others from copying the expression, the *HOW*.

Copyright prohibits others from doing anything with the work, or a substantial part of the work, that only the copyright owner has the right to do unless the copyright owner has given consent.

In respect of works, copyright owners have an exclusive right to do or authorize others to do the following:

- publish an unpublished work (which happens when you post someone's private diary on the web);

- produce or reproduce the work in any material form (which includes making a single copy);

- perform the work in public (which includes playing music in a restaurant);

- create and use any translation of the work (to use an authorized translation, one needs to obtain permission from both the author of the original and the translator);

- convert or adapt a work into a different form (creating derivative works, which means anything that is based on something that had existed before);

- present the work at a public exhibition (which includes hanging pictures on the wall in a hair salon);

- communicate the work to the public by telecommunication (which includes sending it over the internet);

- rent out the work (in case of computer programs or

recorded musical works); and

- sell or otherwise distribute an infringing copy of the work (even if the infringing copy was made by someone else).

In respect of performances, performers have an exclusive right to do or authorize others to do the following:

- record previously unrecorded performances;
- broadcast previously unrecorded performances;
- make copies of unauthorized recordings of the performance; and
- rent out sound recordings of the performance.

With respect to sound recordings, owners have an exclusive right to do or authorize others to do the following:

- publish unpublished sound recordings;
- make copies of the sound recording; and
- rent out the sound recording.

With respect to broadcasts, broadcasters have an exclusive right to do or authorize others to do the following:

- record broadcasts;
- make copies of unauthorized recordings of a broadcast;
- authorize simultaneous retransmissions of the broadcast; and
- demonstrate TV broadcasts in a place open to the public for a fee.

Subject to the defences and exceptions discussed below, if any of these acts are made without proper permission from the rightful owner, it constitutes a copyright infringement.

What you do with those who have infringed upon your rights is up to you. Unless you take action, the infringement will remain unpunished because no one is going to use your ammunition for you. Whether or not to go after infringers (or each particular infringer) should be a part of your IP strategy and risk management. The rule of thumb here is to establish whether the likely costs justify the potential rewards.

Also, remember that whether you can get away with the unauthorized use of others' copyrights will depend on the IP and risk management strategies of those who own the copyright you are infringing. The deeper your pockets, the more likely it is that they will sue you for using their copyrighted works, performances, sound recordings, or broadcasts as part of your successful enterprise.

DEFENDING AGAINST COPYRIGHT INFRINGEMENT LAWSUITS

The general rule for copyright is that nobody can use a work protected by copyright unless they have received permission from the owner of the copyright. There are several exceptions to this rule which you can use to defend yourself in case you are accused of copyright infringement.

I ONLY USED A LITTLE BIT

One defence to copyright infringement is that you used *less than a substantial part of the work*. For example, if somebody writes a book and you use one letter out of that book, you can't be accused of infringing the author's copyright. Likewise, if you just take a word out of it. The more substantial the part of the work that you use, the more likely it is that you will not be able to avoid having a copyright infringement lawsuit on your hands.

HOW MUCH CAN I USE?

Substantiality is a measure of the work *taken from*, not of the work it is *used in*. For example, if you "borrow" someone's painting as an illustration for your 600-page book, this use would be considered substantial, because you used the entire work. It does not matter that it occupies one thousandth of your book. What matters is that you took a substantial part of someone else's work, in this case, all of it.

This issue is not about the *quantity* of what you use but about the *quality*. If what you use represents the core of the work then that will be sufficient to infringe someone's copyright, even if the quantity used is not very large. For example, if a six-minute song has a chorus and in that chorus there is a three-second hook, and you take that three-second hook and use it to advertise your business without permission, then you are probably infringing the copyright in of that song. Just because three seconds is relatively small in relation to a six minute song will not get you off of the hook because everyone will recognize those three seconds as being part of the song. And you don't have any right to use it.

You need to be careful with this defence, but typically, if you can't recognize the original work from the copy, you could argue that you used less than a substantial part of the work.

IT'S IN THE PUBLIC DOMAIN

A second defence is that the work is no longer protected by copyright. We've already mentioned that the work is protected for the life of the author plus fifty or seventy years depending on the country. After that, the work is said to fall in the public domain, which means that anyone can use it without asking anyone's permission.

So if you use a part from one of Shakespeare's plays and somebody accuses you of infringing their rights, you can always say, *"This work is no longer protected by copyright, so I'm not infringing anything."*

> ## TRANSLATIONS AND ADAPTATIONS ARE STILL PROTECTED
>
> An important thing to note here is that while the original work may no longer be protected, you may still be accused of the unauthorized use of translations or adaptations that *are* protected. For example, if you choose to use a modern translation of Shakespeare into another language, you would need to ask permission of the translator, even though you would no longer need to seek permission of Shakespeare's estate.

YOU DON'T OWN IT

The next defence is one that is commonly used by defendants. Basically, you argue that the plaintiff—the person who filed the lawsuit—is not the copyright owner. Essentially, it's a case of a wrong plaintiff. The copyright exists and you've used a substantial part of it, but the person who's claiming that you've done something wrong is not the person who owns the copyright.

This happens more often than you may think. For example, it may occur when the plaintiff is a company who failed to properly obtain the copyright from its independent contractor. In this case, the independent contractor is still the copyright owner even if the company thinks that they are. So, if the company were to sue you for copyright infringement, you could make the case that the company doesn't own the copyright and that the independent contractor still does. Because of this, the claim would be dismissed. Of course, this doesn't mean that the real copyright owner can't or won't sue you.

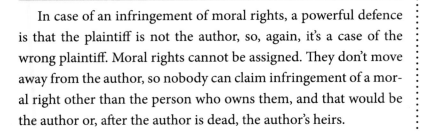

REMEMBER, IT'S NOT YOURS JUST BECAUSE YOU PAID FOR IT

Imagine you hire somebody to shoot a video for your website, and you don't have an agreement in writing with the videographer. You have the video. You pay for the video. You post it on your website. Somebody pulls the video off your website and puts it on their website to advertise their business. You're obviously very unhappy, so you sue them and you say they are infringing your copyright. It actually does constitute a copyright infringement, but it's a copyright infringement of the rights of the videographer, not you or your company. If the videographer is not named as one of the plaintiffs, then the defendant would be able to get away with it simply because the wrong plaintiff filed the lawsuit.

In case of an infringement of moral rights, a powerful defence is that the plaintiff is not the author, so, again, it's a case of the wrong plaintiff. Moral rights cannot be assigned. They don't move away from the author, so nobody can claim infringement of a moral right other than the person who owns them, and that would be the author or, after the author is dead, the author's heirs.

I HAVE A LICENSE

Another defence is that you have a license to use the work. While, of course, it's always better to have a license in writing, there may be cases where the court will imply that you have a license or the circumstances dictate that you do. A license is not necessarily a document but could simply be a permission to do something that you wouldn't normally have the right to do without it.

For example, when you have a guest over in your house and you allow her to stay overnight, essentially what you're doing is you're granting her a license to do something which without the license would have been considered trespassing. You don't have to have an agreement in writing even though staying at your house is something she would not be allowed to do without your permission.

The same thing is true for copyright—without a license or permission to do something, you may be guilty of copyright infringement, but if a relationship exists between you and the author that could be interpreted as permission for you to use something that belongs to the author, then that may be sufficient to act as a valid defence.

MAKE SURE YOU CAN USE IT

Be careful, however. Just because you can find almost anything on the web today does not mean you have a license to use it. For example, images you can find using *Google Images* search engine are not copyright-less. Many of them have owners who diligently monitor their use, and if they catch you using their images in something that makes you money, expect to deal with their lawyers.

TIME'S UP

Another defence is that the time in which you are allowed to file a lawsuit (the limitation period) has expired. In Canada, you can only file a claim in the court if the wrongdoing happened within a certain number of years or months prior to you filing the claim.

In other words, if somebody hit you twenty-five years ago in school, you can't wait for them to become mega-rich and then take them to court claiming how much you've been suffering all these years. This is what's called the limitation period, and it also exists for copyright infringements.

For copyright infringements, the limitation period is three years. If the infringement happened more than three years after you found out about it or after you should have found out about it, then you can no longer file a lawsuit. If you do, then the defendant will always have an opportunity to request that the claim be dismissed simply because the limitation period is over.

IT'S FOR THE PUBLIC GOOD

Finally, in terms of copyright, one of the most common defences is the defence of fair dealing. What the doctrine says is that there may be cases where, in order to provide a benefit to the public, some uses of the work may be permitted without the author's consent. This holds true even if the work is protected by copyright and even if the copyright owner is against such use. Such uses typically relate to the material being used for research, private study, criticism, and news reporting.

The doctrine of fair dealing has been massively expanded in the last couple of years and continues to expand (I think that this trend is wrong and immoral, but the law is the law). Fair dealing has been expanded to include the following reasons to justify unauthorized use of someone else's copyrighted works, performances, sound recordings, and broadcasts:

- use for the purpose of parody or satire;
- use for the purpose of creating non-commercial user-generated content;

- reproduction for private purposes;
- time shifting, which allows you to record an episode of your favourite TV program to watch it later;
- making backup copies;
- use for the purposes of education and, separately, use by educational institutions; and
- copying by libraries, archives and museums.

All of these points can serve as a proper defence against a copyright infringement claim.

What is important to understand is that when using these defences, you really don't know if they will be applied by the judge. This is especially true for fair dealing because it's largely subjective. You don't really know what's fair until the judge tells you.

This ties back to our point that judges don't look for the better law; they look for the better story. It is up to the judge to decide whether your use of the work does or does not constitute fair dealing. If your story is the better one, the judge can use the doctrine of fair dealing to help you avoid liability for unauthorized use of someone else's IP.

TIPS & TRICKS

Below are several tips and tricks that I recommend you consider when it comes to protecting your copyrights.

KEEP DRAFTS

First of all, always keep drafts and backups of everything you create. This is the best way to provide evidence that you created the material because you can demonstrate the developmental process you have gone through to create it.

COPYRIGHT NOTICES

You should use a copyright notice on the copies of your works. A copyright notice is typically a "C" in a circle (©) followed by year of the first publication, followed by the name of the copyright owner.

For example, the copyright notice for this book is, **© 2013–2015 by Andrei Mincov and Trademark Factory International Inc.,** which means that this book was written between 2013 and 2015 and is currently owned by me and my company. And no, you have no way of knowing about the arrangement that I have with my company as to who owns what.

The copyright symbol is not found on standard keyboards. If you are using Windows, hold down the ALT key followed by 0169, or simply hit CTRL + ALT + C in Microsoft Word.

POOR MAN'S COPYRIGHT

A poor man's copyright is when you put your work in an envelope, seal it, and then mail it to yourself. Admittedly, there are many flaws in this from the perspective of evidence because nothing prevents you from doing some switching in the process but, again, the judges are not looking for the perfect story. They're looking for the better story.

You can also email yourself the material but this is even worse than mailing it to yourself because it's fairly easy to tinker with the headers, dates, and times in any email message.

On the other hand, remember the story about outrunning the bear? Your goal is not to have the best evidence in the world. Your goal is to have evidence that is better than the evidence of the other party.

As you've learned in Part I of this book, if you have the better story, the judge will tend to accept your mail and emails as evidence. If the judge doesn't buy your story, then the judge will not believe your poor man's copyright either.

The important thing to do is to always ask yourself two questions: *Do I have a believable story? Am I the more likeable guy between the two parties?* If the answer to both questions is yes, then make sure you help the judge by providing as much quality evidence as you can. If the answer to both questions is no, then you have a problem—regardless of how good your evidence is.

USE CONTRACTS

Enter into proper contracts with anyone who creates original literary, dramatic, musical, or artistic works for you, including your own employees. If you pay somebody to do something for you, make sure that you own it. It's a lot easier to have them sign whatever you want them to sign before you pay them a penny.

While they're still waiting for your money, they'll be much more likely to agree to your version of the contract compared to when they have received their money and don't need anything else from you. At that point in time, they will suddenly be very interested in making sure that they can squeeze more money out of you for doing something that they would have agreed to do for free just a few moments ago.

USE CONTRACT TEMPLATES

Having a lawyer draw up a number of contracts every time you need to sign one in order to protect your copyright can be expensive. I've been drafting copyright agreements for many years. In fact, I've probably drafted hundreds of them. Often, I would get a call from a potential client asking me if I can help them draft a contract. I would give them a quote and often they would realize that my fees were higher than the value of their entire agreement to them. It just didn't make sense given their particular circumstances.

Business owners often face a difficult dilemma: the amount at stake does not justify spending a fortune on having a lawyer draft that perfect agreement that will ideally fit a specific set of facts, yet the free templates available on the internet leave out too many important details or may be governed by laws of a different jurisdiction. In these circumstances, all too often, business owners opt for having no agreements at all.

I really wanted to help businesses bridge the gap between these two extremes, so I decided to offer simplified templates for agreements that address most of the issues that usually arise in generic situations. These templates are the result of almost 20 years of hands-on experience drafting customized contracts for hundreds of clients.

So I made these templates available for you to download from ***http://NiceContracts.com*** at a fraction of the cost that I used to charge for the customized versions. Just to make it clear, these templates cover about 85 percent of what goes into a customized agreement. In fact, I used these templates to draft customized agreements for my clients, they are that good. Yet they cost about ten to twenty times less than the customized ones.

If you can't afford a lawyer to draft a custom agreement for your particular situation, then at least start with a good template. Don't just rely on stuff that you can easily find on the web because most of the time those templates miss out on a lot of important issues and are governed by U.S. law. American copyright law does not generally recognize moral rights and it has the concept of "deemed works-for-hire", which significantly changes how you approach your independent contractors compared to Canada (or pretty much the rest of the world). While some agreement is better than nothing most of the time, it's still likely not good enough.

REGISTER THE COPYRIGHT

The final tip is that if you are in the business of licensing out copyrighted works, consider registering your copyright in Canada and the U.S. While I don't typically recommend that businesses register all their copyrights, if your business model is about licensing your IP, it may be a good idea to register the copyright. You have to be relatively selective about this and only register the copyrights that you ever see yourself trying to defend in court.

ACT NOW!

Time for some homework.

Now that you know what copyright is about, it's time to apply it to your business.

The table on the next page is an extension of the table you filled out when we discussed the IN quadrant for the IP Strategy Review. You did fill it out, right? If not, go back to page 61 and fill it out! I mean it. Seriously.

The purpose of this exercise is to identify everything that you use in your business that can be protected by copyright and to honestly answer whether you have sufficient rights to use them as IP coming IN and if you have taken sufficient steps to protect them as your IP going OUT.

COPYRIGHT & NEIGHBOURING RIGHTS What works, performances, sound recordings and broadcasts am I using in my business?		
Works (books, music, videos, software, manuals, photographs, images), performances, sound recordings, broadcasts	Do I really have a right to USE the IP? If yes, how do I know I have the right to use it?	Do I OWN it? If yes, how am I protecting my rights? (keep drafts and backups? use © symbol? contracts? registration of copyright?)

This table will allow you to instantly see your weak spots. Now you can mend these weak spots in the order of their importance to your business. If your website is crucial to your business and you have nothing to prove that you are allowed to use it, it's a big problem. On the other hand, if you are missing a written assignment for a photograph you once used in your PowerPoint presentation, this can wait until all higher-priority issues have been addressed.

Feel free to download the template for this table (as well as many other goodies) at ***http://ipbook.ca/more*** .

YOUR REFERENCE POINT FOR COPYRIGHT

	COPYRIGHT	**NEIGHBOURING RIGHTS (a.k.a. RELATED RIGHTS)**
What's protected	the *HOW*	the *HOW*

Definition of the protected objects	Original literary, dramatic, musical, and artistic works, that is, an original expression (of an idea) fixed in some (usually, tangible) form
	
	+ Canada also provides limited protection for moral rights:
	  - the right to the integrity of the work;
	  - the right to be associated with the work as its author.
		- fixed or unfixed performances of a work by a performer;
		- sound recordings, including sound recordings of a performance;
		- broadcasts (communication signals).
		+ Canada also has limited protection for moral rights in respect of live aural performances and performances fixed in a sound recording:
		  - the right to the integrity of the performance;
		  - the right to be associated with the performance as its performer.

Classes of protected objects	- books; - songs; - films; - videos; - photographs; - artistic works; - illustrations; - paintings; - drawings; - maps; - articles; - marketing materials, pamphlets and other writings;	- performances; - sound recordings (phonograms); - broadcasts.

	COPYRIGHT	NEIGHBOURING RIGHTS
Classes of protected objects (cont.)	- user manuals; - website contents and look & feel; - computer programs, including HTML; javascript and PHP code; - tables; - lectures; - operas and other musical works; - dramatic or dramatico-musical works; - plays; - choreography; - compilations; - translations; - charts; - plans; - engravings; - sculptures; - architecture; - works of artistic craftsmanship; - sketches; - etc.	
Examples	- Ayn Rand's novel *Atlas Shrugged*; - *Rambo* the movie; - Salvador Dali's paintings; - architectural plans for the CN Tower; - computer code (but not the underlying idea) for Microsoft Windows operating system; - computer code for Facebook; - instructions manual for iPhone;	- any and each live performance of "*I Wanna Be Somebody*" by W.A.S.P.; - sound recording of Michael Jackson's "*Thriller*"; - broadcasts of the Olympics.

	COPYRIGHT	**NEIGHBOURING RIGHTS**
Examples (cont.)	- The Last Command album by W.A.S.P. (separate copyrights in music, lyrics, songs as a whole, compilation of songs as a whole, cover artwork; video for the songs "*Blind In Texas*" and "*Wild Child*", but does not include performances of the songs, sound recording of the songs, which are neighbouring rights, see column to the right); - photograph of Einstein with his tongue out; - etc.	
What is needed to get protection?	The work must be minimally original and must be expressed in some form capable of being perceived by others.	The performance, sound recording, and broadcast must be minimally original and must be expressed in some form capable of being perceived by others.
What it does not protect	- ideas; - plots; - facts; - methods; - most short phrases and slogans; - processes; - algorithms; - features of shape, configuration, patterning or ornamentation as they are applied to useful mass-produced articles (manufactured in 50 or more copies).	- underlying works; - general style of performance; - professional secrets of sound recording.
Enforceable against	Anyone who uses the work without the copyright owner's consent.	Anyone who uses the performance, phonogram, or broadcast without the copyright owner's consent.

	COPYRIGHT	NEIGHBOURING RIGHTS
What constitutes use? / **What are others prohibited from doing?**	Simply put, copyright prohibits others from copying the expression. In greater detail: it prohibits others from doing anything with the work or a substantial part of the work that only the copyright owner has the right to do, unless the copyright owner gives consent. This refers to the exclusive right of the copyright owner to do or authorize others to do the following: - publishing an unpublished work; - producing or reproducing the work in any material form whatever (which includes making a single copy); - performing the work in public; - creating and using any translation of the work; - converting or adapting a work into a different form; - presenting the work at a public exhibition; - communicating the work to the public by telecommunication (which includes sending it over the internet); - renting out the work (in case of computer programs or recorded musical works); - selling or otherwise distributing an infringing copy of the work (even if the infringing copy was made by someone else).	Simply put, neighbouring rights prohibit others from copying the expression. With respect to performances: - recording previously unrecorded performances; - broadcasting previously unrecorded performances; - making copies of unauthorized recordings of the performance; - renting out sound recordings of the performance. With respect to sound recordings: - publishing unpublished sound recordings; - making copies of the sound recording; - renting out of the sound recording. With respect to broadcasts: - recording broadcasts; - making copies of unauthorized recordings of a broadcast; - authorizing simultaneous retransmissions of the broadcast; - demonstrating TV broadcasts in a place open to the public for a fee.

	COPYRIGHT	**NEIGHBOURING RIGHTS**
Where is the owner/ author/ inventor protected?	Each country protects separately, but protection is almost automatically worldwide thanks to international treaties (Berne Convention, WCT, TRIPS).	Each country protects separately, but protection is almost automatically worldwide thanks to international treaties (Rome Convention, WPPT, TRIPS).
Length of protection	In Canada, the general term of protection of the copyright is the life of the author (or the last surviving coauthor in case of co-authorship) of a work plus 50 years after his death. In most other countries, the general term of protection of copyright is the life of the last surviving author or coauthor plus 70 years.	In Canada, 50 years after: - unfixed performance takes place; - fixation of the performance; - fixation of the sound recording; - broadcast takes place.
Can the initial period of protection be extended?	No.	No.
Who owns the right / Who should apply for registration of the right?	The first owner of copyright in a work is usually the individual who created the work (the author). The most notable exception to this rule pertains to works created during the course of employment, in which case the default rule is that it is the author's employer who is automatically the first owner of copyright. Copyright may be transferred to any other person or company. As to moral rights, as in most other countries, they cannot be assigned to third parties in Canada. However, in Canada, it is possible to waive moral rights.	The first owner of the copyright in a performer's performance is the performer. The first owner of copyright in a sound recording is the maker of the sound recording. The first owner of copyright in a communication signal is the broadcaster that broadcasts it. Copyright may be transferred to any other person or company. As to moral rights, as in most other countries, they cannot be assigned to third parties in Canada. However, in Canada, it is possible to waive moral rights.

	COPYRIGHT	**NEIGHBOURING RIGHTS**
Do owners / authors / inventors have some rights if they do not apply for protection?	Yes. Generally, copyright is secured when the work is created. However, there are significant benefits obtained by registration (see below).	Yes. Generally, neighbouring rights are secured when the work is created. However, there are significant benefits obtained by registration (see below).
What are the benefits of applying for protection?	- A registration certificate creates a presumption that the work is protected by copyright; - A registration certificate creates a presumption of ownership of the work; - A registration certificate serves as evidence of ownership of the work; - Registration creates a presumption that the infringer was aware that the work is protected by copyright; - A copyright owner may demand damages from an unaware defendant; - In the U.S., a copyright owner may only claim statutory damages (that is, compensation which is not derived from what the plaintiff lost as the result of the infringement) for infringement of copyright, if the copyright has been registered.	- A registration certificate creates a presumption that the performance, sound recording, or a broadcast is protected as a neighbouring right; - A registration certificate creates a presumption of ownership of the performance, sound recording, or a broadcast; - A registration certificate serves as evidence of ownership of the performance, sound recording, or a broadcast; - Registration creates a presumption that the infringer was aware of the subsistence of copyright in the performance; - Copyright owner may demand damages from an unaware defendant; - In the U.S., copyright owner may only claim statutory damages for infringement of copyright, if the copyright had been registered.
How is the right established?	Copyright emerges merely by virtue of a qualifying work being created.	Neighbouring rights emerge merely by virtue of a qualifying performance, sound recording or broadcast being created.

	COPYRIGHT	**NEIGHBOURING RIGHTS**
How is the right established? (cont.)	Registration of copyright adds certain procedural rights and creates evidentiary presumptions, but is not required to claim that the work is protected by copyright. Copyright exists regardless of whether the work has been registered.	Registration of copyright adds certain procedural rights and affords evidentiary presumptions, but is not a legal requirement for subsistence of the right itself.
Defences & limitations	- less than a substantial part of the work or other subject matter is used; - work / other subject matter is no longer protected by copyright; - plaintiff is not the copyright owner (wrong plaintiff); - in case of infringement of moral rights, plaintiff is not the author or performer (wrong plaintiff); - plaintiff granted the defendant a license; - expiration of limitation period (3 years). Canada also recognizes certain circumstances, in which unauthorized use of another's work does not constitute an infringement. These circumstances form part of the so called fair dealing doctrine, which provides for the following exceptions from the general rule that protected works may only be used with the consent of the copyright owner: - use for the purpose of research or private study; - use for the purpose of criticism or review; - use for the purpose of news reporting; - certain uses by educational institutions; - certain uses by libraries, archives, and museums; - incidental use; - certain uses by broadcasters; - certain uses by persons with perceptual disabilities; - use for the purpose of education; - use for the purposes of parody or satire; - creation of non-commercial, user-generated content; - use by reproducing works for private purposes; - use by recording programs for later listening or viewing; - making backup copies; - use to ensure interoperability of computer programs; - and certain other exceptions.	

	COPYRIGHT	**NEIGHBOURING RIGHTS**
Available remedies	- injunction; - damages (including exemplary and punitive damages); - statutory damages from $500 to $20,000 for each work if infringement is for commercial purposes; - statutory damages from $100 to $5,000 for all works if infringement is for non-commercial purposes; - accounting of profits; - delivery up of infringing materials to the plaintiff.	- injunction; - damages (including exemplary and punitive damages); - statutory damages from $500 to $20,000 for each performance, sound recording or broadcast if infringement is for commercial purposes; - statutory damages from $100 to $5,000 for all performances, sound recordings and broadcasts if infringement is for non-commercial purposes; - accounting of profits; - delivery up of infringing materials to the plaintiff.
When can it be registered?	Because registration is not a prerequisite for existence of copyright, it can be registered at any time. Registration after the infringement will not usually grant the plaintiff the presumptions otherwise made available by the registration.	Because registration is not a prerequisite for existence of neighbouring rights, they can be registered at any time. Registration after the infringement will not usually grant the plaintiff the presumptions otherwise made available by the registration.
How long does the registration take?	2–4 weeks in Canada, unless the Copyright Office staff requests that the application be amended. About 6 months in the U.S., unless the Copyright Office staff requests that the application be amended.	2–4 weeks in Canada, unless the Copyright Office staff requests that the application be amended. About 6 months in the U.S., unless the Copyright Office staff requests that the application be amended.
Are there mandatory maintenance fees?	No.	No.

	COPYRIGHT	NEIGHBOURING RIGHTS
Government fees relating to registration	$50 per work in Canada. $35 per registration in the U.S.	$50 per performance / sound recording / broadcast. $35 per registration in the U.S.
Total ballpark cost if a lawyer / trademark agent / patent agent is involved (including government fees)	$200–$500 per registration.	$200–$500 per registration.

TRADEMARKS:
WHICH

Brands have power over our minds.

Think of the last time you were buying a car. I can guarantee that one of either two things happened. Either you came predetermined to buy a certain make or model of car, or you had a completely open mind and the salesman would rattle off phrases like "this brand is well known for its quality of engineering," and "this brand has the best resell value," and "this brand has been making these cars for the last century," and "this brand is crap, stay away from it." Whichever scenario it was, the brand (or the concepts that are associated with it) influenced your buying decision because there is no way for you to truly *know* each and every aspect of each car on the market to make a 100% objective, unbiased decision. What typically happens is you buy the car within your budget (or usually slightly over your budget) based on your subjective preferences (it just feels better) after you've convinced yourself to believe all the stories that back up the brand.

Think about the food, beer, phones, and clothes that you buy. Think about the services you use: taxis, internet providers, tax return filers, realtors, and restaurants. If you're satisfied with a particular brand's product, chances are when you are looking to buy the same thing again in the future, you will specifically look for the same brand or at least it will quickly find its way to your shortlist.

If brands have so much power over the minds of your customers and prospects, wouldn't you want to make sure that you can *protect* this competitive advantage? Wouldn't you want to make sure that this power stays with you rather than benefit someone else?

That is precisely what trademarks are for.

Here is my definition of a trademark. A trademark is a feature unrelated to the characteristics of your products or services which allows your business to help customers and consumers distinguish your products and services from the identical or similar products and services of everyone else.

This is precisely why the Magic Word for trademarks is *WHICH*—trademarks help consumers pick *WHICH* box they are going to pick from the shelf when they see 10 different brands of essentially the same product.

The scope of what can be trademarked is limited by the function that trademarks are supposed to perform. To simply say that names, logos, and slogans can be protected *if they function as a trademark* would be of no use to you—unless you know what the proper function of trademarks is, so we'll start with that.

I need to mention one more thing just before we get there. Canada uses a hyphen in between "trade" and "mark" to spell trademarks. While "trade-mark" is the official term in Canada, this book uses the more conventional spelling, "trademark", except when the reference is made to the actual name of the Canadian statute, the *Trade-Marks Act*.

WHAT IS THE FUNCTION OF A TRADEMARK?

The function of a trademark is to allow the end consumer to distinguish your products and services from the identical or similar products and services of your competitors. In legal speak this is called "distinctiveness".

If what you chose as your brand cannot perform this function, then it's not a trademark, and it certainly is not a trademark that can be registered.

Here are a few examples to help you understand when the function of a trademark is properly fulfilled.

You go to a food court in a shopping mall and see several chains offering burgers, fries, and drinks. It's not that their recipes are so fundamentally different. Even if they taste differently, the burgers, fries, and drinks themselves look very much the same. What makes them look different is the packaging, the big signs at the back, the uniforms, the bags, and the plastic cups—they are all there to help you choose the burgers, fries, and drinks offered by one company over the burgers, fries, and drinks offered by all the other companies. This is the proper function of a trademark.

However, simply displaying a photograph of a mouth watering burger in a food court to seduce passersby to choose a burger over a pizza or a "healthy", raw, vegan, organic, gluten-free, sugar-free, salt-free, GMO-free celery-stick salad is *not* a proper function of a trademark because that photograph does nothing to distinguish this particular burger place from all other burger places. So there is nothing that functions as a trademark about it.

You need a cab. You know that all the operators in your city are required by law to charge the same rates. You remember that last year when you called company A, the driver was rude, and when you called company B, the driver didn't even show up. So you are not going to give them any more of your business. Instead you look for some other cab companies on the Internet and read reviews on Yelp. Now you know you should use company C, so you call them. Indeed, they are very good, and you add *Company C's* number to your phone in order to use them the next time around. This is the proper function of a trademark.

However, advertising your taxi company as "Vancouver Cabs", "Toronto Taxis", "Airport Cabs", or simply "Taxis", would do nothing to set you apart from your competitors who do the same thing. So, none of these names can be trademarks.

You go to a grocery store to buy some ketchup. You finally find the shelf with ketchup, and, to your surprise, you see that there are 8 different brands of ketchup there. How do you pick one? Subconsciously, you remember a jingle you heard on TV a couple of years ago, praising a particular brand of condiments. Imagine that! It's there on the shelf along with 7 others. So you buy it, even though it's 15% more expensive than the rest. This is the proper function of a trademark.

A label wrapped around the bottle that says, "Buy our ketchup, it's the best ketchup out there" will not be something that acts as a trademark.

WHAT IS A TRADEMARK?

Pretty much *anything* can act as a trademark. It can be invented words—for example, *Xerox* or *iPad*. It can be dictionary words—like *Apple* or *Windows*. It can be a slogan—like *I'm Loving It*. It can be a logo. It can be a character from a book or a cartoon. It can be the shape of a product (called "distinguishing guise" in Canada)—like the *Coca-Cola* bottle. It can be a color, such as the magenta color of T-Mobile or the red soles of Louboutin shoes. It can be a tune, such as the famous Nokia tune. It can also be just a sound or a noise. The first registered sound trademark in Canada was MGM's roaring lion, and, indeed, every time you hear a roaring lion in the beginning of a movie, you don't even have to look at the screen; you'll know exactly who made it. This is the function of a trademark.

One important thing is that simply because you have a trademark doesn't mean you have the monopoly over the word, slogan, or image you chose as your trademark. You only have a monopoly over the association between that word, slogan, or image and the specific goods or services that you offer.

This is how the same trademark BLUE SHIELD can be owned by two completely different entities: one provides medical insurance, the other sells welding equipment.

Another example: T-Mobile doesn't own the color magenta. They cannot forbid an artist to use this color in his paintings. They can't stop other people from using this color in furniture, but they can stop others from using that color in the field of telecommunications.

The function of a trademark is to give you a monopoly over the use of a specific name, logo, or slogan with respect to your specific products and services. Your trademark allows people—your past, current, potential, and future customers—to distinguish your business from everybody else who offers the same or similar stuff.

USING THE TRADEMARK

The word "using" in trademark law differs substantially from the word "using" in the common sense of the word.

"Use," in relation to physical products (goods, or "wares" as they are called in Canada) requires that the trademark be placed on the product itself or its packaging, or that the trademark is otherwise associated with the goods in the mind of the purchaser when he makes the purchase.

The rules are more relaxed with respect to services, and a trademark is considered to be used if it is displayed in the performance or advertising of those services.

A simple website that features the trademark to advertise your *services* is sufficient for the purpose of establishing that the trademark is "used". On the other hand, advertising a *product* is not sufficient for it to be recognized as the use of the trademark. What this means is that simply having a website that talks about your product will not satisfy the requirement of trademark use. However, if you provide an online store where visitors can order your products, that would be sufficient because you are not simply advertising your products, but are actually selling them through your website.

I've mentioned many trademarks in this book. However, this does not constitute "use" in the trademark sense because I'm not offering any products or services under these names. I don't need Apple's permission to mention the *IPAD* trademark in this book, because I'm not selling any electronics. Even if *IPAD* was registered for legal services or books, a simple mention in this book would not be sufficient to constitute use because I'm not using this name to distinguish my book from all other books. I'm not going to sell any more books or legal services just because I use iPad as an example. Nobody would think I am using this name to create an impression that the products or services that I sell are named *iPad*, and nobody would ever think that my services are somehow authorized by, associated with, or licensed from Apple. The moral of the story is that not every mention of a trademark constitutes its "use".

Another thing to consider is the doctrine of exhaustion of rights. If you want to resell your used iPad, you can safely create an ad on Craigslist and openly say that you are selling an iPad. This is because you own the physical device and have the right to dispose of it any way you please. And calling it by its name is the only proper way to refer to it. As long as you don't create an impression that you are an authorized Apple dealer when you're not, it is safe to use the name of the product to sell the antiquated device you purchased 5 months ago. Do not use the logos though.

TRADEMARKS VS. TRADE NAMES

It's important to recognize that trade names are not the same thing as a trademark.

Simply incorporating the business or registering a DBA (*doing business as...*) name is not enough. All it does is prevents your competitors from registering an identical or similar name as their *corporate name*. However, such registration does nothing outside the province where your business is registered. It also does very little to protect you against competitors who might use your brand without using it as part of their corporate name or their DBA name.

While prior use of a trade name *can* help you ultimately succeed in a dispute over your brand, a registered trademark will save you a lot of time and tens of thousands of dollars in legal fees.

For example, if you start a company, ABC Media Inc., in British Columbia, it doesn't mean that you now have a trademark for *ABC* or *ABC Media*. It doesn't become your trademark until you start using it as a trademark. Make sure you have fully grasped the meaning of the term "use" in the trademark law sense.

You only use the trade name as a trademark if you "use" that name as the name or as part of the name of your products or services. For example, Microsoft can protect its trade name because they use the word "*Microsoft*" as part of their product names — Microsoft Word, Microsoft Windows, Microsoft Office and so on.

WHAT TRADEMARKS DO NOT PROTECT

Because the function of a trademark is to distinguish your products and services from similar or identical products and services of others and is not meant to give you a monopoly over those products and services themselves, there are a number of things that cannot function as trademarks or that cannot be registered as trademarks.

Here they are:

GENERIC NAMES

You are not allowed to claim the generic name of a product or a service itself as your trademark. For example, you can't trademark *ACCOUNTING* for accounting services. This means you can't stop other people from using the word *accounting* to describe their accounting services. Similarly, you can't trademark *BADMINTON* for badminton, and you can't trademark *APPLE* for apples. Remember, the function of a trademark is to distinguish the apples of different producers, not to give someone the right to say, *"I am the only one who can sell apples in Canada."*

Some legitimate trademarks have become generic through their wide use. The first well-known trademark to have ever become generic was Linoleum in 1878. But it certainly wasn't the only one. Other famous examples include App Store, Aspirin, Cellophane, Dry Ice, Escalator, Heroin, Kerosene, Kleenex, Laundromat, Videotape, and Zipper. Google is rapidly approaching this status as well, since everyone seems to be "googling it".

If your business relies on its monopoly to use a certain name for a certain product, make sure that you control its use by your own marketing team and by others. This will help you avoid this "genericide" where what used to be a perfectly protectable trademark becomes a generic word that refers to an entire class of products or services. Sometimes you become so happy that your product is adopted by the masses that you can miss the moment when your product is no longer one of a kind, it is *the* kind.

Trademarks that become generic names can no longer function as trademarks and therefore nobody can claim a monopoly over them anymore, whether through registration or otherwise.

DESCRIPTIVE NAMES

Next to generic names are "clearly descriptive or deceptively misdescriptive" marks.

In human terms, *clearly descriptive* means that your trademark is made up of dictionary words (or their phonetic equivalents) which describe some important characteristics of your product or service. For example, you can't trademark *COLOR* for printers, or *SAFE* for cars, or *DEL1SHEWZ* for apples.

Deceptively misdescriptive means that your trademark is made up of dictionary words (or their phonetic equivalents) that would mislead consumers into believing that your products or services have characteristics that they do not possess. For example, you can't trademark *LEATHUR SHOOZ* for shoes that are not made of leather. Likewise, you can't trademark *CALGARY OCEANFRONT PROPERTIES* for real estate services.

You cannot register clearly descriptive or deceptively misdescriptive marks unless you have used them to such an extent that everyone has come to associate your business with that particular name. Until that happens, you can still use such marks in the hope that you will acquire the reputation required to render them registrable. For example, if you have been using *CALGARY OCEANFRONT PROPERTIES* for so long that a substantial number of people across Canada understand that they will be buying *your* services rather than simply think that they would be buying a Calgary house with an ocean view, then your deceptively misdescriptive trademark may become registrable. This is not an easy task though.

Unlike clearly descriptive marks, suggestive marks only give some vague idea about the products and services covered by the trademark, and are registrable. Sometimes the boundary between unregistrable clearly descriptive marks and registrable suggestive marks isn't very clear. This can result in long disputes between applicants and the Trademark Office. Ultimately, it is up to the Trademark Office or the courts to decide one way or the other.

PERSONAL NAMES

In Canada, while you can *use* your personal name as a trademark, as a general rule, you can't *register* a trademark that consists only of your full name or your last name. For example, JOHN SMITH or SMITH would not be registrable.

There are a few exceptions from the rule, however.

If your trademark consists of more than just your name, it will become registrable. For example, JOHN SMITH'S ACCOUNTING no longer violates the rule.

Also, just as in the case of descriptive marks, if you have such a reputation that everyone associates your name with your services, then the name can be registered as a trademark. However, you need to be *really* well known for this to work. Think *Celine Dion* or *Gillette* kind of fame.

Simply using the first name (but not the last name) as a trademark does not violate the rule. So JOHN, JOHN'S, AT JOHN'S and JOHN'S ACCOUNTING would all be registrable trademarks.

Combining several names into one trademark is another way out, for example, SMITH &WESSON would be registrable.

FUNCTIONALITY

In Canada, you cannot trademark something that goes to the functionality of the product itself. Anything that is required in order for the product to function cannot be protected as a trademark. If anything, it should be protected through a patent (which we will discuss in the next chapter).

For example, while it is generally possible to register the shape of a product as a trademark, if that shape is dictated solely by the function of the product, it cannot be registered as a trademark.

IT'S A FUNCTION, NOT A DESIGN!

A good example of function over design can be seen in a 1995 case involving Philips's three-head shaver.

Philips came up with their famous three head electric shaver and registered a trademark on its design. When a competitor started selling similar electric shavers, Philips sued. Philips claimed that the competitor was violating their trademark because the competitor's shaver looked exactly the same as Philips's three head shaver.

The competitor claimed that Philips was not allowed to trademark the design because it related to the function of the product and the trademark was never supposed to grant Philips a monopoly on three head shavers.

The court agreed with Philips's competitor and cancelled the trademark registration, thus allowing the competitor and pretty much everybody else to make three-headed shavers without the fear of attracting Philips's wrath.

UNREGISTERED (COMMON-LAW) TRADEMARKS

In most countries, unregistered trademarks are not protected. In other words, no registration—no protection.

Unlike most of the rest of the world, Canada and the United States afford some limited protection to unregistered trademarks. This protection exists through the availability of the tort of passing off, whereby the plaintiff can recover damages it incurred as a result of the defendant selling products or services while passing them off to be the products or services of the plaintiff.

However, such protection depends on how actively you "use" your trademarks in association with your products and services. This means that in order to stop competitors from using your unregistered trademark, not only should you be able to prove that your mark is distinctive, you should also be able to prove, through surveys, that your trademark is well known to the public in a specific area where it is being used by your competitors. This is different from a registered trademark where your certificate of registration is sufficient to protect you all across the country where the trademark is registered, and you don't have to prove how well people know your trademark.

In most cases, once (or even before) you realize that your trademark has value, it is probably a good idea to register it. While recognition by others (demonstrated by them imitating your brand) may seem flattering, the last thing you want is to spend tens of thousands of dollars and years of your life fighting over something that could have been relatively easy to protect when you were just starting out.

DON'T END UP LIKE A WOODPECKER

You just can't make some things up. Sometimes, I had to think very hard to find a decent example to illustrate a point in this book. But some examples just seem to have been created especially for this occasion.

In September of 2013, an important trademark battle began.

Woodpecker Hardwood Floors (2000) Inc. had been in operation for over a decade but, for some reason, didn't register their trademark, WOODPECKER.

Another flooring company, Wiston International, opened up within a mile of Woodpecker Hardwood Floors (2000) Inc. and the new company registered "WOODPECKER" as their trademark for flooring and related services. The Trademark Office doesn't cite unregistered trademarks against the applications they receive, so they proceeded to register WOODPECKER as the trademark for the second company.

When the old company realized that its competitor succeeded in registering and was actively using its very own trademark, it sued the new company. The old company was eventually able to get an injunction preventing the new company from using the trademark and opening the door to cancel the new company's trademark—because the old company was able to prove that it was in existence long before the new company and that people recognized its name.

The new company appealed, but the old company won again.

So, you may ask, if they won anyway, what difference would it make if the old company had registered its trademark first?

Well, it would have helped them big time—for two reasons.

First of all, if the old company had registered its trademark in the first place, the new company would have never been able to register the same trademark, so this would never have become an issue.

But even aside from that, I can guarantee you that it cost the old company at least $75,000 to win in court, and I wouldn't be surprised if it was closer to $150,000.

If you ever see yourself fighting to keep your own brand, register it as a trademark. It may save you a ton of money!

REGISTERING TRADEMARKS

While registering a trademark can be—and often is—a rather complicated process, for business owners it typically boils down to three stages: *Can* I do it? *Should* I do it? *How* do I do it?

We'll get there in a second, but first, let me tell you about the benefits of trademark registration.

BENEFITS OF REGISTERING TRADEMARKS

While unregistered trademarks are afforded some limited protection in Canada, there are significant benefits that come with registration.

It Covers a Lot of Territory: Registration grants you the exclusive right to use your trademark all across Canada, whereas unregistered trademarks can only protect you in geographical areas where you can prove that your brand is known to enough customers. You don't have to worry about being limited to areas where your reputation or goodwill has been established. A registered trademark protects you in the most remote locations in Canada where nobody has ever heard about your brand.

You Get a Head Start: In Canada and the U.S., your unregistered trademarks are only protected if they are well known to consumers, and your trademark applications will not proceed to registration unless you have commenced "using" your trademark. However, you can still apply to register a trademark before you start offering products or services under that brand to the public. This is called registration on the "proposed use" basis in Canada and registration on the "intent to use" basis in the States. Once you have filed the application, the Trademark Office will not allow anyone else to register a subsequent identical or a confusingly similar trademark. If you know that your new brand will generate some buzz, apply to register it as a trademark before you share it with the world.

You Own It: A registered trademark is presumed valid. Certificate of registration is evidence of your ownership of the mark. Often, showing the certificate to the judge is sufficient to establish rights to the trademark. Now it's up to the other side to prove that you don't own it. In case of unregistered trademarks, you have the burden of proving that your name, logo, or tagline are actually trademarks, and that you own them.

Avoid Confusion: No one can register a trademark that is the same or confusingly similar to your registered trademark. You don't need to do anything because the Trademark Office will filter out all similar trademark applications that are filed after your trademark has been registered. In addition to refusing all trademark applications that are confusingly similar with a registered trademark, in certain situations when the Trademark Office is not sure if the mark is confusing, the Trademark Office will notify the owner of a registered trademark of the other application so that the owner has a chance to oppose the application.

Now People Know It: Registration serves as public notice that its owner has a claim to exclusivity of that mark.

Secure Your .CA Domain: A registered trademark allows non-Canadian owners to register corresponding .CA domain names because it fulfills the "Canadian Presence requirements" of the Canadian Internet Registration Authority (CIRA).

Do It Once, Enjoy It for 15 Years: The term of registration is 15 years, renewable for an unlimited number of times.

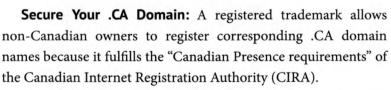

It's Incontestable after Five Years: After 5 years of being registered, a trademark becomes incontestable unless it was registered with knowledge of the prior rights of third parties. This means that even if there are other companies who have been using the mark before the owner of the registered mark, the registered trademark will take priority if it has been on the books for five years. This only works if the owner didn't know about those other companies using the mark.

You Can Sue: Registration provides additional statutory remedies against trademark infringement and depreciation of the value of goodwill. This means that you can demand compensation from somebody who is diluting your brand by doing something that makes it less valuable in the mind of the public. This option is not available for unregistered trademarks. This provides additional ammunition in court if you see your competitor using your trademark without your permission.

Official—Shmofficial: Registration protects you from becoming disentitled of the trademark due to the adoption of a confusing official mark by a third party. Official marks are unique to Canada, and they can trump previously adopted unregistered trademarks. While registration of your trademark will not prevent the issuance of an official mark, the issuance of an official mark will not become a hurdle for your continued use of your trademark. You'd be out of luck in case of an unregistered trademark.

Let's Get Down to Business: A registered trademark is a valuable asset and can be more readily sold or licensed. It also increases the value of a company.

CAN I REGISTER MY TRADEMARK?

This is really the first thing to figure out. If you don't have anything trademarkable, the remaining questions are no longer relevant.

I like to say that *if it's remarkable, it's trademarkable*®. But things are slightly more complicated than that.

There are two big traps that you need to avoid before you can confirm that you *CAN* register your trademark. In European countries, they are called the absolute and the relative grounds for refusal. If your trademark is not refused on either of these grounds, it *CAN* be registered.

Absolute Grounds: At this stage, it is important to confirm that your trademark fulfills its proper purpose of distinguishing your products and services from identical or similar products or services of others and that it does not fall under any of the categories we discussed under *What Trademarks Do Not Protect*. When the trademark has passed this hurdle, you can move on to the next step.

Relative Grounds: The next step is to ensure that your trademark is not identical or confusingly similar with another previously registered or applied for trademark. In Canada and the United States, the registers of registered trademarks are public information, and anyone can conduct trademark searches. Below, in the *Tips and Tricks* section, I provide a few tips how to do it.

If your trademark is not unregistrable under the absolute grounds for refusal and is not confusingly similar with other previously registered or applied for trademarks, then it *CAN* be registered.

The next thing to decide is whether you *SHOULD* register your trademark.

SHOULD I REGISTER MY TRADEMARK?

Once you have established that you have something that meets the requirements for a trademark, you have to take it one step further and figure out if you *SHOULD* register it. Just because you *CAN* register your trademarks doesn't mean that you always *SHOULD*.

A simple answer to this question can be found in Trademark Factory®'s tagline: *"If It's Worth Promoting, It's Worth Protecting!™"*. Indeed, if you spend time, energy and money building your brand, it only make sense that you protect it.

Here's a three-question test I developed to help my clients figure out if it is a good idea for them to register their trademarks.

1) Will my brand be worth fighting for if my business receives a cease-and-desist letter from somebody else demanding that I stop using my own trademark?

Here is a not uncommon scenario. You have been building your business, and then one day, several years down the road, you receive a cease-and-desist letter in the mail from a lawyer representing some other business that demands that you immediately stop using THEIR trademark—that is, in fact, the brand that YOU have been building all along.

The letter typically goes like this, *"I am a lawyer with Bully & Intimidator LLP. I act for Shmooper Systems Inc. It has come to my client's attention that you have been using my client's trademark SUPER SHMOOPER to sell or offer for sale this kind of products and to render, advertise, or offer that kind of services.*

As you are likely aware, my client has been providing these products and services since 1986, and they own a trademark registration (Reg. No. 123,456, a copy of the Registration Certificate is enclosed herewith).

Lest my client not sue you for damages, which we estimate in the neighbourhood of $200,000, we hereby demand that you immediately stop using the name SUPER SHMOOPER to sell or offer for sale any products, or to render, advertise, or offer any services. You are to remove my client's trademark SUPER SHMOOPER from all of your products and their packaging as soon as possible but in any event no later than 3 days after your receipt of this letter. You must remove all references to SUPER SHMOOPER from your website, including its metatags. You must also transfer to my client the domain name SUPERSHMOOPER.COM that you are holding in violation of my client's trademark rights. Close your account with Twitter and rename your Facebook page to remove any references to SUPER SHMOOPER because my client is the rightful owner of the trademark registration."

Now, the important thing to recognize is that it doesn't matter whether you're right or wrong. It doesn't matter whether you were there first or they were there first. What matters is that the other guy has registered the trademark. Trademark registration makes it a lot easier for them to bully you into changing your brand, while at the same time making it a lot harder for you to defend your right to use that trademark even if you were there first.

Essentially, you have two options at this stage. You can comply with the demands and stop using the brand you developed but neglected to protect, or you can start a fight.

If you foresee a possibility that you might end up fighting in court to retain the right to keep using your brand, you should realize that the fight will be very expensive, even if you win because your lawyer will spend countless hours attempting to prove that you have a prior right to the trademark and to cancel the issued registration certificate in someone else's name. While you may get *some* of your legal costs back if you win, in most cases this will not be enough to make you whole. So if you see yourself fighting over your trademarks, you should definitely register them.

Even if you think that you would rather give up, estimate how much it would cost you to change all your signage, marketing materials, company cars, packaging, domain names, website, etc. If the number is more than $15,000, you should certainly register your trademarks.

Your answer to this first question would be *NO*, only if you believe that you would give up your brand without a fight and it would not cost you an arm and a leg to rebrand.

Essentially, this is a risk management question. If you think you may end up in a situation where you would lose a lot of money, whether you fight to keep the brand or just give it up, then it's a good idea to get your trademark registered right away.

2) Would my brand be worth fighting for if you saw your competitor use YOUR trademark to advertise THEIR products and services?

Here is another scenario. You start noticing that you are losing customers to your competitor who is using YOUR trademarks to sell THEIR products and services.

Some of your customers think that you may have a joint venture with the competitor and will often even complain to you about problems they have encountered when buying from your competitor.

Some customers simply don't care. They are just attracted by the power of the brand you created.

If that happened to you, would you consider taking the competitor to court for trademark infringement? If the answer is yes, you must definitely register your trademarks—simply because it would cost you a lot less to win a case against your competitor having ammunition in the form of a trademark registration certificate. Without it, you are guaranteed to spend a bucketload of money.

This is precisely why you don't want to be in the position of somebody who receives that cease-and-desist letter. If you have to fight with somebody who has a registered trademark, you are fighting an uphill battle. Conversely, if you have that certificate of registration, your chances of successfully telling someone to cease-and-desist using your trademark increase exponentially.

3) *If you were to sell, franchise, license out, or expand your business throughout Canada, would potential buyers be willing to pay you more money for your brand?*

A trademark registered in Canada gives you protection all across Canada, including locations where nobody has even heard of your business. Likewise, a trademark registered in the United States gives you protection all across the U.S. This is a great advantage over unregistered trademarks that provide some limited protection to business owners, but only in the area where the public is actually aware of the unregistered trademark.

Trademarks can become an extremely valuable asset for your business if you decide to franchise, expand, or sell it in the future.

So ask yourself, does your brand have any value if you were no longer a part of the business. So JOE'S CAR WASH may be an important brand for Joe, but if Joe sold the business to Harry from another province, would Harry keep using the name JOE'S CAR WASH? More importantly, would Harry pay you an extra dime for the right to use the name JOE'S CAR WASH?

If your brand transcends you personally, then it's a good idea to register the trademark. Think about McDonald's. It doesn't really matter who owns it anymore. It doesn't matter whether there is a person with the last name McDonald working in or on the business. It has value in and of itself.

HELLO KITTY

A good example of why you should register your trademark can be seen in the HELLO KITTY trademark.

This example is based on my personal experience as the father of two sweet daughters. You can't imagine how many times I have been asked, begged, and harassed to buy them various stuff bearing the image of the famous feline. Some of it has even made its way to our home—pens, skirts, stickers, t-shirts, toys, and other stuff.

Do you think the company that owns the brand actually manufactures and distributes all of this stuff? Nope, all they do is simply get paid for licensing out their trademark to whoever wants to use it on their products.

The owners of the HELLO KITTY trademark can charge substantial licensing fees because their brand is so popular. To give you an idea just how popular—think about it: in 2010 it made over $5,000,000,000.00 (yes, 5 billion bucks).

On the other hand, if the value of your business is limited to your charming personality or the location of your business, or both, then maybe you don't need to register. If people find you and buy from you because they like you or because you have a nice location on a busy intersection and your name does not go beyond your circle of acquaintances—then maybe registration is not for you.

If you notice that because of your marketing efforts or because of word-of-mouth or for any other reason, a lot of people are coming to your store on purpose and even travelling a fair distance to specifically come to your store, then you might recognize that there is value to that brand that you want to protect. To protect your brand, you need to register your trademarks.

Another way to look into this is by checking your online statistics. Use services such as Google Analytics or Statcounter to find out how online users find your website. If most of the new visits come from those who used generic keywords, for example "Vancouver trademark lawyer", or "register trademark in Canada", it means that you have done a great job optimizing your website for search engines. It also means that people are not looking for your brand. They are looking for the generic name of the products or services that you happen to offer.

If, on the other hand, most of the new visits come from people who search for your brand, for example "Trademark Factory", then you know you have something that is precious and needs to be protected.

Now, the important thing here is to understand that you don't need to answer *YES* to all three questions. If you answer *YES* to at least one of them, it's a good enough reason to invest immediately in registering your trademarks. A trademark registration can save you tens and even hundreds of thousands of dollars in the long run, and it can also be an asset of massive value in the future if your business becomes successful.

ALL YOU NEED IS ONE

Just to make sure you understand, you don't need to answer yes to all three questions. If your answer is **yes to at least one** of these questions, you should register your trademarks as early as possible.

Ideally, if you realize that you may end up with a brand that will have some value, you should apply to register your trademarks before you start using them. You would do it by filing your trademark applications on the basis of proposed use (intent to use).

TRADEMARK FACTORY®—THIS IS HOW YOU REGISTER YOUR TRADEMARK!

Once you know that you CAN and that you SHOULD register your trademarks, the final step is to figure out HOW to do it.

I created *Trademark Factory*® to make this the easiest question for you to answer.

There used to be only three options for business owners when it came to trademarking.

You could ***file your trademarks yourself***, so you'd only pay the government fees, but, as statistics show, chances are, you will receive a letter from the Trademark Office called an office action (or an "examiner's report"), telling you that your trademark application does not meet their standards. Many unrepresented applicants have no idea how to respond to these, and abandon their trademark applications.

I've seen cases where self-represented applicants drafted their applications so poorly that there was nothing we could do to fix them after they were refused by the trademark examiner. In Canada, after a trademark application has been filed, one cannot broaden the scope of goods and services that the application is supposed to cover. Therefore, if your trademark is deemed too descriptive because of the way you described your products and services, there may be very little you (or your lawyers) can do at this point. In order for the trademark to not be descriptive, you would need to use a broader language for your goods and services, but you can't do this after you have already filed your application. Catch 22!

The net result is that unrepresented applicants will often have spent a lot of time, end up without a registered trademark, and lose all the fees they paid to the government.

On the next page you will find the simplified chart of what happens with the trademark application after it is filed:

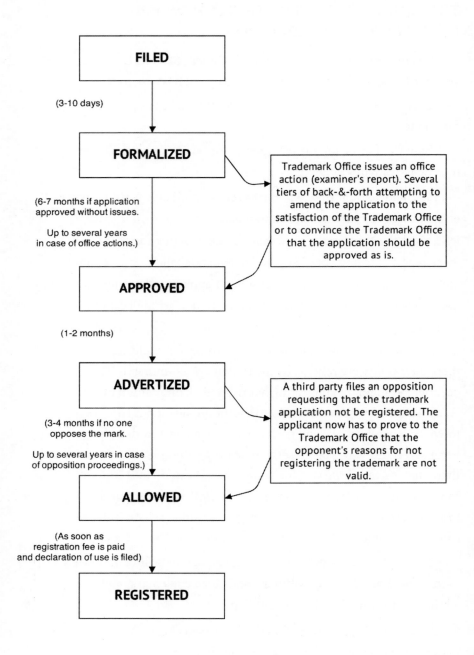

Another option was to ***use online trademark filing websites***. They have automated the filing process to make it easier for business owners to figure out what should go where. They will file your applications for $199, $299, or $399 based on what YOU are going to tell them. But guess what? If something goes wrong, and it happens in more than half of the cases, they are going to send you to one of the law firms that they are affiliated with, and those lawyers are going to charge you an arm and a leg to fix your application. No wonder they are happy to take your money to apply for MICRO-SOFT SOFTWARE!

The third option was to ***use a typical law firm***. In most cases, they will do everything right. But you won't know your budget until the whole process is over, and it usually takes fourteen to eighteen months. They'll send you their two-page schedule of fees, detailing that if *this* happens then they will be charging you *this* amount, and if *that* happens then they will be charging you *that* amount.

Thing is, few business owners know how the trademark registration process really works, so they naively assume that the amount they see next to "drafting and filing trademark application" covers the entire cost of registration as if the rest of the schedule of fees does not apply to them.

Based on this assumption, they start comparing apples to oranges (filing fees with total fees) and end up buying a lemon. I've met dozens of business owners who were lured in by low filing fees, but ended up paying five, six and even seven thousand dollars for a single trademark. The problem is not that it's expensive. The problem is that it's UNPREDICTABLY expensive.

Most law firms use flat rate fees for *some* elements of the trademark registration process, but charge you an hourly fee in the middle when the *real* work of a trademark lawyer happens. Often, law firms will only state their fee for *filing* a trademark application, typically around $700 to $1,000. What you may not realize is that you will be receiving more and more invoices every time the lawyer has to do as little as sneeze at your file. And if an examiner at the Trademark Office finds something problematic about the application, it usually means several hours of billable time, which most clients grudgingly pay because they are already invested in the process. That's how a $700 file sometimes becomes $4,000, $5,000, or even $7,000 file. And you won't know which it will be until the very end.

I know how much time, money, effort, emotion, and love goes into the creation of a successful brand, and it pains me to see business owners who squander their brands by failing to take proper steps to protect them.

This is why I released the report 5 Trademarking Rip-Offs You Should Avoid. Download it at ***http://TrademarkRipoffs.com*** .

There HAD to be a better way. So I came up with the better way. It's called the ***Trademark Factory®***.

We surveyed hundreds of entrepreneurs throughout Canada about the challenges they faced when dealing with traditional lawyers and trademark agents. We identified three big reasons why businesses are hesitant to use trademark professionals:

- There is no way to know how much it will end up costing you until you get the final of the many invoices for services;

- If something goes wrong, you don't get your money back because you are paying for a lawyer's time, not the results; and

- The application is filed by a clerk, and the lawyer does

not see it until there is something wrong with it, at which point you start getting billed by the hour.

We built the **Trademark Factory®** to address all of these concerns and make it as easy as possible for business owners to protect their valuable brands.

We are the first and the only firm on the planet that will offer you an ALL-INCLUSIVE package that will cover the cost of the entire process, from filing to registration for a single, all-inclusive flat fee. If it takes us three hours or three hundred hours to deal with the examiners at the Trademarks Office, your price stays the same. The only thing it does not include is opposition proceedings that third parties may initiate against your application *after* it has been approved by the Trademarks Office. But don't worry, opposition proceedings only happen in just a fraction of one percent of cases. And if you want even more protection that would also cover unexpected oppositions, you can choose our ULTIMATE package.

To get started, you would order your free trademark search from us by filling out the form at **http://freeTMsearch.com**. When we do a free trademark search for you, we will tell you about the registrability of your brand. In most cases, we will be able to offer you our unique 100% money-back guarantee. What this means is, if your trademark does not get approved, you get all of your money back. For many trademarks, we even offer a 100+% money-back guarantee, where you get back not only our fees, but also the government fees. So we refund more than we received from you.

Here's my philosophy: if we tell you that we think your trademark is registrable and take your money, and the government rejects it at the examination stage, it is *immoral* and *unethical* for us to keep your money, no matter how much time we spent on your file. It amazes me that we are the only law firm on the planet with this attitude!

We also guarantee that each and every file is reviewed by a registered trademark agent or a licensed trademark attorney. So it's not a clerk who does the work to be fixed by real professionals later. We do everything right the first time. Because we are not charging hourly rates with our ALL-INCLUSIVE package, our interests are naturally aligned with yours.

We call it the Triple-Peace-of-Mind Guarantee™.

MORE WORK—NO EXTRA PAY

We filed two trademarks for one of our clients: one in the U.S. and one in Canada. The Canadian trademark application went smoothly without any problem.

The United States Patent and Trademark Office (USPTO) found a trademark that they thought was confusing. The USPTO refused to approve the trademark because of that existing trademark. Even though I didn't think that my client's mark was confusing, in this particular situation, it would have been almost impossible to convince the USPTO that they were wrong.

I had to spend several dozen hours trying to convince the owner of that other trademark to permit my client to register theirs and to sign a trademark co-existence agreement, and then to convince the Trademark Office that the co-existence agreement addressed their concerns about any possible confusion. Ultimately, our application was approved.

Honestly, I could almost see that client sitting on her couch laughing every time I sent her updates because she had paid us a fixed fee and I ended up doing all of this unexpected stuff.

That's what's our *Triple Peace-of-Mind Guarantee*™ is about.

We have developed a system of processes that allow us to offer the highest quality of services at a predictable cost. The work is done by a lawyer or a registered trademark agent, not a filing clerk at some online trademarking service.

We can help you register trademarks in Canada, the United States, and European Union, and are working on adding other countries to our menu.

We did our best to make choosing us as your service provider as easy as possible. If you decide that you will benefit from registering your trademarks, **Trademark Factory®** is *an obvious choice!*

But *don't take our word for it.* We dare you to find another firm that offers some, let alone all, of these guarantees.

No, seriously. If you see the value of registering your trademarks but are not sure that we have the best offer on the market, feel free to shop around, but make sure you ask these questions:

- Can you quote a fixed fee for the entire process from start to finish?
- Will you charge me for the initial search of registered trademarks to confirm my trademark is registrable?
- Will you charge me an hourly rate to respond to office actions?
- Will you charge me extra every time you receive something from the Trademark Office and notify me about it?
- If the Trademark Office refuses to register my trademark, will I get my money back?

Many of our customers became our customers because they have done just that. They called other law firms, listened to their evasive answers, and then gave us their business.

HOW LONG DOES TRADEMARK PROTECTION LAST?

Unregistered trademarks are protected for as long as the business carries on and continues to "use" them.

For registered trademarks, you will need to renew the registration. In Canada, you have to renew your trademark registration every 15 years. The renewal term is 10 years in most other countries.

Of course, you need to keep providing the same service or selling the same kind of products under the same trademark. If you begin selling a product that falls into a completely different category, then you need to file a new trademark application because trademarks do not give you a monopoly over the word or image, only over the association between such words or images and specific goods and services. So to protect the new association, you need to register a new trademark.

Like most countries, in Canada, if you don't use your trademark for three consecutive years, anybody can apply to the Canadian Trademark Office and request that your trademark be cancelled for non-use. If you can't prove that you have been actively using your trademark for the three years immediately preceding the request to cancel your registration, then the Canadian Intellectual Property Office will strike your registration off the register.

You would then have to go through the same process again to re-register your trademark but the chances are that you won't be able to get your trademark back. Most of these cancellation proceedings are started with the sole purpose of filing a new trademark application for somebody else. So you would need to kill an existing trademark application to occupy the same spot, which isn't always easy.

WHERE ARE TRADEMARKS PROTECTED?

In the countries that recognize unregistered trademarks, they are protected only in the geographical areas where your products or services are widely known.

Registered trademarks are protected in the countries where they were registered. If you register in Canada, then your registration will only cover Canada and not the rest of the world.

If you are only interested in conducting business in Canada, then this is not a problem because your Canadian trademark registration is federal and protects you throughout all of Canada.

But what if you target many markets at once?

Unlike most other countries, Canada is currently not a party to the Madrid Agreement or the Madrid Protocol, which allow you to file a single trademark application, in one language, and just put check marks next to the countries where you want it protected.

Just as I was about to send this book to the printers, the Government of Canada "tabled" five intellectual property law treaties in Parliament to harmonize Canada's patent, trademark, and industrial design laws with those of other countries. Among these treaties is the Madrid Protocol.

"Tabling" of a treaty in Parliament by the Minister of Foreign Affairs is the first procedural step after the signing or adoption of an international treaty towards its ratification and subsequent implementation. What this means is that various specific issues around ratifying and implementing the treaties in the national laws of Canada will soon be voted on.

I hope that by the next edition of this book, Canada will be a party to the Madrid Protocol so that Canadian businesses can finally protect their brands internationally without having to spend a fortune.

But for now, if you are looking to develop international markets, you have the following options for protecting your trademark outside Canada:

1. File individual trademark applications in every country where you want trademark protection. This means lawyers, a lot of lawyers, and a lot of bills to pay.

2. If your company has "a real and effective commercial establishment" in a country that is a member to the Madrid Agreement or Madrid Protocol, then you could apply for an international trademark in that country. A real and effective commercial establishment is typically when you have a branch, an office, or a daughter company in that other country. Simply having sales in that other country is not sufficient for the purposes of using the Madrid Agreement or Madrid Protocol to file for international trademark protection.

3. Set up a new company outside of Canada. For example, you could set up a new company in the U.S. and then file for an international trademark on its behalf.

The option you should choose will depend on your specific circumstances. The Madrid system only makes sense if you want to file your trademark application in a large number of countries (at least five). Then it will allow you to save a substantial amount on the fees. Another reason to use it is if you are planning to file in countries that have varying official languages, since a Madrid application allows you to file your application in a single language that you are familiar with.

If you only want to add a country or two, don't bother with setting up a corporate presence outside of Canada. If you are seeking worldwide domination on a limited budget, set up a company outside Canada and file an international trademark application on its behalf.

DON'T FORGET GRACE

Another thing you should consider is that you have a 6-month grace period after filing your very first trademark application. During this grace period, you can decide to file in other countries with an option to rely on the priority date of your first application.

Let me give you an example. Let's say, you came up with a unique brand, MNBVCXZ and filed to register it as a trademark in Canada on January 1, 2013. You haven't filed any other trademarks just yet. But the brand quickly became so popular that somebody decided to take a free ride on its popularity and filed a trademark application for the same mark in the U.S. on April 15, 2013—before you had a chance to do it.

Are you out of luck in the States now?

Yes, unless you file your own application there no later than July 1, 2013 and specify that you are relying on your Canadian application dated January 1, 2013. If you do file before July 1, 2013, then the U.S. filing of the third party will be thrown out, because you would have an earlier date (January 1, 2013). If, however, you only file on July 5, 2013, then you will have missed the 6-month grace period and the April 15, 2013 priority date will trump yours.

At this point you will be out of luck.

WHO OWNS THE TRADEMARK?

The trademark owner is the person or the business entity which uses or controls the use of a trademark. Trademarks can be assigned to other people or companies, but the new owner must use the trademark and the use must not confuse the public as to who the owner of the trademark is.

For example, if there is a manufacturer and a distributer of a product and the manufacturer decides that the distributor will own the trademark, then you have to be very careful with marking the packaging of your products. You must make sure the public is not misled into believing that the manufacturer owns the trademark when it's the distributor because this can lead to the cancellation of the trademark for both the manufacturer and the distributor.

Likewise, if the trademark is used by a licensee of the trademark owner, it is crucial that no confusion arises as to who owns the trademark and on what grounds the licensee is using it.

One other thing to consider when licensing out your trademark is that the licensor has an obligation to exercise control over the quality of products and services offered by the licensee under the trademark. The purpose of this quality control is not to prohibit licensees from selling poor quality stuff. The purpose of the quality control is to eliminate confusion whereby the quality of products and services offered by the licensor is substantially different from the quality of products and services offered by the licensee under the same brand. The quality must be substantially the same even if that quality is awful. It's about consistency and lack of confusion.

WHAT CONSTITUTES A TRADEMARK INFRINGEMENT (WHAT CAN YOU SUE OTHERS FOR)?

Trademarks are enforceable against anyone who "uses" (in the trademark sense of the word) your trademark in association with goods or services for which the trademark is registered. You can also sue anyone who uses your trademark in a way that causes or is likely to cause confusion with the registered trademark.

What this means is that you can take action against anybody within the same or similar field of business who uses your trademark in such a way that is likely to cause confusion among customers.

The protection that trademarks grant is two-fold. First, trademarks protect the owner against the owner's property being stolen by somebody else. Trademarks also protect the public from being misled into buying something different from what they thought they were getting. In other words, a customer who plans to buy a specific product from a specific company should be able to easily tell which product is which.

There are many remedies available to you if someone infringes on your trademark. If you prove your case, you can:

- Get an *injunction* ordering the infringer to stop using the trademark;

- Get *damages* requiring the infringer to compensate for your losses;

- Get an *accounting of profits* which means that the infringer will be required to pay you everything that the infringer made using your trademark; and

- Demand the *destruction, exportation, or other disposition* of the offending goods.

DEFENDING AGAINST TRADEMARK INFRINGEMENT LAWSUITS

If you are accused of trademark infringement, there are a number of defences that you can rely on to defend yourself. Likewise, when you are accusing somebody of trademark infringement, these are the defences that you may encounter.

I DIDN'T "USE" IT

If your use of the trademark does not constitute "use" in the trademark sense, then you are not infringing anyone's rights. In other words, unless you are using someone else's brand to sell or offer for sale specific products or services, you are not using it in a way for which you can be sued.

THE TRADEMARK OWNER AIN'T USING THIS TRADEMARK

If the trademark owner has not "used" its own registered trademark for over 3 consecutive years, you may just have gotten a *Get Out of Jail Free* card.

You may ask, *"How often does it happen that you get sued over a trademark that has been abandoned by the trademark owner?"*

More often than you'd think. Because the important thing is *what* had been registered and *what* is being used.

Often, in order to save a little bit, a business may register a combined mark that consists of both the name and a logo. Then, as the business develops and the marketing people keep playing with the design, the logo morphs into something else, it moves to a new location, changes in size and color. At the end of the day, the current version of the brand may look substantially different from what was registered.

If the trademark owner is no longer using the original trademark as it was registered, and the current branding is substantially different from it, then the registered trademark may be cancelled for non-use. If it is the only registered trademark that the plaintiff has, then the plaintiff has just lost the ability to sue you for trademark infringement, because the trademark is no longer there.

Oops.

DON'T GET FAT, GET EVEN

Often, trademarks evolve together with the business. Logos change, fonts change, layouts change.

If you registered one trademark but are using a modified version of that trademark, you are running a serious risk of losing your registration.

There was a company that registered an image of a skinny penguin as its trademark. As its business evolved, the penguin got fatter and fatter.

After a while, another company came to the market under a logo that looked suspiciously similar to the thin penguin.

The first company sued. The second company attempted to kill the skinny penguin mark on the ground of non-use.

The judge in that case (probably driven by the better story of the plaintiff) decided that the trademark should not have been cancelled but noted that the plaintiff came dangerously close to losing its mark.

The moral of this story: you are better off registering separate elements of your combined brand as separate trademarks—the name, the logo, the tagline. Don't dump them all up into a single trademark, because if you change the overall look over time, you run the risk of losing everything.

And if you changed your name, logo or tagline substantially— register the new versions as separate trademarks as well.

THE TRADEMARK WAS NOT REGISTRABLE AT THE DATE OF REGISTRATION

If a trademark did not meet the criteria to be registered but it slipped through the Trademark Office and got registered anyway, then the trademark can be attacked because it did not meet these criteria.

THE TRADEMARK IS NOT DISTINCTIVE

If the trademark does not perform the function of distinguishing a company's products and services from products and services that are similar or identical, then you can argue that it's not really a trademark, and so you didn't infringe anything.

THE WRONG PERSON SECURED THE REGISTRATION

If a person had rights to use a trademark, and someone else simply ran to the Trademark Office to register it first, then a claim can be made that the person secured the registration improperly. Since the trademark was secured improperly, the trademark holder has no right to stop you from using it.

I WAS FIRST

If you started using a brand in good faith before the plaintiff registered their trademark, you would have the prior right. Remember the *WOODPECKER* story? However, to rely on this argument you would need to prove that you had been using this brand *as a trademark*, and that a substantial number of people knew your business under that trademark. Simply coming up with a name is not enough.

BUT THIS IS MY NAME!

If you are using your own name as a trade name (for example, JOHN SMITH ACCOUNTING if you are an accountant whose real name is John Smith), then someone else's trademark registration should not really concern you.

Be careful, however, because this must really be your own name, you must use it as a trade name, and you must use it in good faith.

You cannot change your first name to "Donald" and your last name to "Trump" and expect to get away with calling your Bed & Breakfast "TRUMP INTERNATIONAL HOTEL & TOWER".

I LIVE HERE

If you are making a good faith use of the geographical name of your place of business, then you can defend yourself against allegations of infringing upon a descriptive trademark that contains that geographical location. For example, if you are a lawyer in Vancouver, you can continue calling yourself a Vancouver lawyer even if somebody somehow manages to register *VANCOUVER LAWYER* as a trademark. Likewise, if someone registers a trademark *YALETOWN BBQ*, you would not be prohibited from continuing to use the same name if you are selling BBQs and are located in the Vancouver district called Yaletown.

THE TRADEMARK OWNER ACQUIESCED TO THE USE

In plain English, this means that if the trademark owner did something that lead you to believe that the owner was not interested in defending the trademark, then the trademark owner can no longer rely on that registration to go after the defendant.

This is sometimes referred to as the obligation of the plaintiff to defend their trademark. It's not as rigid in Canada as it is in the

U.S., but it still exists. If somebody openly uses a registered trademark owned by somebody else and that owner does nothing for a long period of time, then they can't just wake up and decide to sue you for trademark infringement.

TIPS AND TRICKS

There are a number of things you can do without seeing a lawyer to ensure that your trademark can be registered and protected.

CONDUCT A SEARCH

When (or even better, *before*) you adopt a brand in Canada, make sure you conduct a free search of registered trademarks. The last thing you want is to dump money into building a brand that you can't own.

You can start with your own search using the links below, but make sure you also order your free, no obligation, trademark search and registrability opinion from Trademark Factory® by filling out the form at ***http://freeTMsearch.com***. A lot more goes into a proper trademark search than simply checking whether someone had previously registered the exact same brand that you came up with.

Here's what you should do on your own:

> **Canadian Intellectual Property Office (CIPO):** Use ***http://bit.ly/cipo_tmsearch1*** to search the database of all trademarks registered and applied for in Canada.

> **United States Patent and Trademark Office (USPTO):** Even if you're only interetested in protecting your brand in Canada, it's usually a good idea to check out your trademark in the States as well because you

may want to expand your business at some time. Use ***http://bit.ly/uspto_tmsearch1*** to get there.

Google: Search for your brand using Google. This will tell you how many pages there are that have references to your potential trademark.

If you see a ton of people using your brand for similar products and services, then maybe your trademark is not as distinctive as you would like it to be, and you may be building a castle in the sand.

If there aren't too many, or there are some but they're in a completely different industry, then you should be relatively safe. It's very rare that you'd come up with a term that nobody in the world has ever used before, unless it's a made-up word. This is why made-up words are the easiest to protect as trademarks because they are so unique.

There are a few tips for searching.

Let's say you came up with the name AMAZING SHMOOPER DUPER PLUM, EH? and you are planning to provide plumbing services in Calgary.

This is what I'd search for (if you don't understand the syntax search, check out ***https://support.google.com/websearch/answer/134479***):

amazing shmooper duper plum eh

"amazing shmooper duper plum, eh"

+amazing +shmooper +duper +plum +eh

shmooper

duper

amazing shmooper duper plum eh +Calgary

"amazing shmooper duper plum, eh" +Calgary

+amazing +shmooper +duper +plum +eh +Calgary

+shmooper +Calgary

+duper +Calgary

amazing shmooper duper plum eh +plumbing

"amazing shmooper duper plum, eh" +plumbing

+amazing +shmooper +duper +plum +eh +plumbing

+shmooper +plumbing

+duper +plumbing

+plum +plumbing

Domainsbot.Com: You can check to see if your domain name is available by using DomainsBot.Com. Here you can search through multiple domain name databases to see how many domain names similar to your brand name have been already taken. It will also show you different combinations of domain names that are available.

If all of your domain names are taken by somebody, then you will have a problem with your online presence.

NameChk.Com: NameChk.Com is an internet site which allows you to check over a hundred social media platforms to see if your name is available. Obviously, you won't need to register on all of these platforms, but there are several that can be very important for your business, such as Facebook, YouTube, Twitter, LinkedIn, Yelp, and possibly others, depending on your business.

If they're all taken, then it's an indication that you may run into problems with other people. If they are not taken, then you may want to go ahead and register them in your name so that when your brand becomes well known, you won't have to buy the names from somebody who was quicker to figure out the value of your brand.

Even if you find that people have been using a similar trademark or you find some links, or even a couple of hundred links, this may not indicate a huge problem. What you want to make sure is that you know the marketplace, you know the competition, and you know who might be upset if you decide to use that trademark for your business or register it as a trademark.

USE A TRADEMARK SYMBOL

Once you have decided to use a particular brand for your business, start putting a trademark symbol (™) next to it.

What the ™ symbol says to the public is that you are using this logo, name, or tagline *as your trademark*. In fact, this means that you *yourself* think that it is your trademark. However, it has an added advantage because a lot of people don't know trademark laws and think that there is something more required from a business owner before they can place the ™ sign next to their trademark. Customers may take you more seriously, even though all you had to do was insert an extra character in all of your branding and marketing materials.

Sometimes you'll see an "R" encircled (®). This means that the trademark is registered. While the ™ sign means that you yourself think that it is your trademark, the ® sign means that you yourself think that it is your trademark, and the government agrees. Be careful, because you can get into a lot of trouble for using the ® symbol if your trademark is not actually registered, so don't use it if you only have an unregistered trademark. The U.S. laws carry some heavy penalties for unauthorized use of the ® symbol.

Don't try to find the ™ sign on the keyboard. It's not there. But, if you are using Windows, you may hold down the ALT key followed by 0153 and you will see a nice TM sign (™) right there.

In Microsoft Word, you can also hit CTRL + ALT + T to achieve the same result.

To get the registered trademark symbol, hold down the ALT key followed by 0174, or simply hit CTRL + ALT + R in Microsoft Word.

DOCUMENT YOUR USE OF YOUR BRAND

Keep logs of your use of the mark on your website. Make printouts. Save receipts from the printer shop where you printed your business cards. Save invoices of you selling your products bearing your trademarks. Try to save as much evidence of prior use as possible.

If there is a dispute about the priority to the trademark, the path to success would be to demonstrate prior use. Just because you told the Trademark Office that you had been using the mark since 1890 is not enough. You must be able to back it up with evidence.

Make sure you have it.

REGISTER YOUR DOMAIN NAME

Again, you want to register your domain names before your brand becomes known because there will be a lot of people who will want to profit off your inability to foresee the value of your own brand. It's a lot easier (and cheaper) to buy a domain name from **TMFDomains.Com** at $8.99, compared to having to beg somebody to sell it to you for a few thousand dollars.

You may end up owning dozens of useless domain names at some point in time, but the investment is miniscule compared to what you may be saving if your brand becomes known and popular.

DON'T FORGET TO RENEW YOUR DOMAIN NAME

While I was a lawyer in Russia, a huge multinational company that was a client of the law firm I worked for decided to save 20 bucks and not renew their Russian domain names.

There were three domain names they decided not to renew. They had a long internal correspondence in the office debating whether to renew and they finally decided to not renew.

This company is making billions, but they still wanted to save 20 bucks. They let the domain names expire, only to find that the next day, one of their distributors in Siberia grabbed and registered them in his own name.

The company tried to reason with him, without success. At the end of the day, the dispute grew into a full-blown litigation.

After several court hearings, we were able to secure the transfer of the domain names to our client, but trust me when I tell you that their legal fees were s-u-b-s-t-a-n-t-i-a-l-l-y higher than the $20 they had saved by not renewing the domain name. Did I mention, they spent a ton of money on their lawyers?

REGISTER YOUR TRADEMARKS

We've already discussed the benefits of registering your trademarks on page 178. If you have answered *yes* to at least one of the *"Should I Register My Trademark"* questions, do it as soon as you can.

If you are serious about your brand, you owe it to your business to protect it.

To put it another way, if you are not protecting a valuable asset, be honest with yourself and answer a simple question—are you running a business or is it just a time-consuming hobby?

ACT NOW!

Homework time again.

Here, you need to identify everything that can serve as a trademark in your business. Then you need to honestly answer whether you have sufficient rights to use each of the marks as IP coming IN and if you have taken sufficient steps to protect them as your IP going OUT.

This table will allow you to instantly see your weak spots. Now you can mend these weak spots in the order of their importance of these trademarks to your business. If your logo is crucial to your business and you have nothing to prove that you are allowed to use it, it's a big problem. If you chose not to register one of your taglines as a trademark, this can wait until all higher-priority issues have been addressed.

Feel free to download the template for this table (as well as many other goodies) at ***http://ipbook.ca/more*** .

TRADEMARKS		
What distinguishing features am I using in my business?		
Mark (name, logo, image, sound, color)	**Do I really have a right to USE the IP? If yes, how do I know I have the right to use it? (trademark search? company name search? Google? namechk. com? license from logo designer?)**	**Do I OWN it? If yes, how am I protecting my rights? (use ™ symbol? registered trademark? use ® for registered trademarks? contracts?)**

YOUR REFERENCE POINT FOR TRADEMARKS

	TRADEMARKS
What's protected	the *WHICH*
Definition of the protected objects	A mark (words, names, symbols, devices, sounds, smells, trade dress) used to distinguish the goods and services of one business from similar goods and services of all other businesses. + In Canada, it is possible to register the non-functional shape of a product or its packaging (called distinguishing guise, or "trade dress"). + In Canada, it is also possible to register certification marks (i.e. marks used to demonstrate that goods and services of different companies meet certain criteria set out by the owner of the certification mark)
Classes of protected objects	- word; - symbol; - logo; - design; - slogan; - trade dress; - non-functional shape of the product or its packaging.
Examples	- iPad name; - - "I'm Lovin' It" slogan; - Mickey Mouse character; - Coca-Cola bottle; - MGM Roaring Lion sound; - Nokia tune; - magenta color registered by T-Mobile.
What is needed to get protection?	The mark must be distinctive (i.e. it must be used to distinguish the goods and services of one business from similar goods and services of another business), and not confusingly similar to another trademark.

What it does not protect	- company names, unless they are used to distinguish goods or services; - the generic name of goods or services for which the trademark is used (i.e. can't use "apple" as a trademark for apples); - marks that are clearly descriptive or deceptively misdescriptive of the goods or services, unless the mark has become distinctive; - personal names unless they have become distinctive as trademarks; - functional elements of the product's shape.
Enforceable against	Anyone who uses the trademark in association with goods or services for which the trademark is registered or otherwise in a way that causes or is likely to cause confusion with the registered trademark.
What constitutes use? / **What are others prohibited from doing?**	With respect to goods (wares), a trademark is deemed to be used if: - the trademark is marked on the goods; - the trademark is otherwise associated with the goods in the mind of the purchaser; - the trademark is marked on the goods' package; - the trademark is marked on the goods or the goods' packaging, if the goods are exported from Canada. With respect to services, a trademark is deemed to be used if the trademark is used or displayed in the performance or advertising of those services. Third parties are prohibited from causing confusion in the minds of consumers between their goods or services and those of a trademark owner. In case of registered trademarks, the confusion is implied if someone uses another's trademark in association with goods or services for which the trademark is registered.
Where is the owner/ author/inventor protected?	Only in those countries where the trademark protection is sought. Unlike Canada and the U.S., most countries do not recognize unregistered trademarks, so the protection only extends to countries where the trademark has been registered, and a small number of countries where the trademark has not been registered but has been used by the trademark owner to distinguish its goods or services.

Length of protection	As long as business continuously uses the trademark in connection with the goods or services with which the trademark is associated.
	For registered trademarks, a renewal is required in Canada every 15 years. The renewal term is 10 years in most other countries.
Can the initial period of protection be extended?	Trademark protection is indefinite (see above). However, maintenance is required (periodic filings and fees).
Who owns the right? / Who should apply for registration of the right?	Trademark owner: the person or the business entity (e.g., corporation) which uses or controls the use of the trademark.
	Trademarks can be assigned to another person or company, but the new owner must use the trademark, and the use must not confuse the public as to who is the owner of the trademark.
	Trademarks can also be licensed to another person or company. However the licensor is required to exercise control over the quality of goods and services offered by its licensees under the licensed trademark.
Do owners / authors / inventors have some rights if they do not apply for protection?	Yes. So long as you are not infringing on another trademark, some rights in a trademark can be acquired by simply using it in commerce. However, a registered trademark provides additional significant benefits (see below).
What are the benefits of applying for protection?	- Registration protects your trademark all across Canada, whereas unregistered trademarks can only protect you in geographical areas where you can prove that your brand is known to enough customers;
	- You can apply to register a trademark before you start offering products or services under that brand to the public. Unregistered trademarks are only protected if they are well known to the public;
	- A registered trademark is presumed valid. A certificate of registration proves ownership of the mark. Often, showing the certificate to the judge is sufficient to establish rights to the trademark. In case of unregistered trademarks, you must prove that your name, logo, and tagline are actually trademarks, and that you own them;
	- Registration serves as public notice that its owner has a claim to exclusivity of that mark;

What are the benefits of applying for protection? (cont.)	- The term of registration is 15 years, renewable an unlimited number of times; - After 5 years of being registered, a trademark becomes incontestable, unless it was registered with knowledge of the prior rights of third parties; - Registration provides additional statutory remedies against trademark infringement, depreciation of the value of goodwill, and losing the rights to the trademark as a result of the adoption of a confusing official mark by a third party; - A registered trademark is a valuable asset and can be more readily sold or licensed. It also increases the value of a company.
How is the right established?	Common law trademarks: through use in trade. Registered trademarks: through registration with trademark offices in the countries where trademark protection is sought.
Defences & limitations	- the trademark is not "used"; - the plaintiff's trademark is invalid; - the plaintiff's trademark was not registrable at the date of registration; - the plaintiff's trademark is not distinctive; - the plaintiff abandoned the trademark; - the plaintiff was not the person entitled to secure the registration; - plaintiff's fraud; - prior concurrent use of the trademark by the defendant in good faith; - good faith use of the defendant's personal name as a trade name; - good faith right to use, other than as a trademark, of the geographical name of the defendant's place of business; - good faith right to use, other than as a trademark, of any accurate description of the character or quality of the defendant's goods or services; - acquiescence + delay (plaintiff's conduct that leads the defendant to believe that the plaintiff will not enforce its legal right against the defendant).

Available remedies	- injunction; - damages; - accounting of profits; - destruction, exportation, or other disposition of offending goods.
When can it be registered?	In Canada, a trademark application can be filed on the basis of actual use or an intent to use, but no registration will be issued until the use of the trademark has commenced. Unlike Canada and the U.S., most countries allow registration of trademarks that have not yet been used.
How long does the registration take?	18–24 months in Canada. 9–15 months in the U.S.
Are there mandatory maintenance fees?	Regular renewals every 15 years. In Canada, the renewal fee is $350. The trademark must continue to be in use by the trademark owner to avoid the risk of it being cancelled at the request of a competitor.
Government fees relating to registration	In Canada, for the filing of a trademark application, the government fee is $250. If the trademark is allowed, the registration fee is another $200.
Total ballpark cost if a lawyer / trademark agent / patent agent is involved (including government fees)	$1,700–$7,000 per registration

PATENTS:
WHAT

Patents are as close as you're going to get to protecting the substance of your brilliant idea. This is why the Magic Word for patents is *WHAT*. While most textbooks will say that patents don't protect ideas—and in fact they don't—it is as close as you can get.

> ### UTILITY
>
> Patents discussed in this chapter are called *utility patents* in the States, to distinguish them from *design patents,* which will be discussed in the chapter dedicated to *industrial designs.*
>
> The reasoning behind the name is that patents, or utility patents, deal with the functional and utilitarian elements of inventions, not their looks.

It all starts with an idea. You come up with a brilliant new zadget or a brilliant new way to make existing zadgets. Now what?

Let's assume that you have an entrepreneurial mind (otherwise, it probably would have been too painful for you to read this deep into the book—in fact, you probably wouldn't have even made it through the first chapter). So your entrepreneurial mind tells you, "*I gotta figure out a way to make a bucketload of money on this!*"

You think back of all the episodes of *Dragons' Den* and *Shark Tank* that you've watched religiously, and you remember what Kevin O'Leary, Mr. Wonderful, always asks, "*Anyone can make your zadgets, and if they're any good then a big company with a really big foot will pick up your idea and crush you like the cockroach that you are. What have you done to protect your idea?*"

Indeed, what?

If your idea can easily be understood and replicated by looking at your zadget, then you can't protect it through a trade secret (we'll get to them soon). If there is nothing unique about how your zadget looks, then you can't protect it through an industrial design (we'll get to them in the next chapter). If it's not about the name of your zadget, then trademarks are also out of question (by now you're supposed to know that). And it doesn't look like copyright would be the proper way to protect it either, unless you are going to protect the actual code of the software used to run your zadget.

If the uniqueness of your zadget is about *WHAT* your zadgets do or about a particular way they do *WHAT* they do, then a patent is really the only way for you to have the legal right to forbid everyone else from making your magnificent zadgets.

A patent cements your first-to-market advantage by giving you the legal right, for a relatively short period, to stop everyone else from competing with you by making or selling your zadgets.

What you do with this first-to-market advantage is up to you. Importantly, you should not look at your patent as the government's permission to use your own invention. You don't have to patent your invention in order to use it. The purpose of the patent is to give you the ammunition to *stop others* from using your invention.

Let's start with the definition. A patent is a form of recognition by the government of the patent owner's time-limited monopoly to use an invention. We'll dissect it in just a moment.

WHAT IS AN INVENTION?

The Canadian *Patent Act* defines an invention as "any new and useful art, process, machine, manufacture or composition of matter, or any new and useful improvement in any art, process, machine, manufacture or composition of matter."

Let's simplify this definition and replace the serious legalese with its down-to-earth substitutes. What we get is that an invention is "any cool stuff or any cool improvement to existing stuff."

Now, that makes sense!

The term "cool" replaced the words "new and useful". We'll discuss what this means in the *Requirements for Protection* section.

The term "stuff" replaced the words "art, process, machine, manufacture or composition of matter". I know it's easy to get intimidated by a futile attempt to actually understand what this means, but for the sake of simplification, "art" and "process" refer to a *method* of performing some meaningful function or accomplishing some meaningful result, while "machine", "manufacture" and "composition of matter" refer to something *tangible* that is capable of performing some meaningful function.

So, an invention is basically a cool method, something tangible that's cool, a cool improvement to an existing method, or a cool improvement to something tangible.

Here are some famous examples of cool methods:

- improved method of transmitting vocal and other sounds telegraphically (Bell's telephone);
- Nicola Tesla's method of electrical power transmission;
- Priceline.com's method of reverse auctions to buy airline tickets over the internet;
- streaming of audiovisual content over the internet; and
- Amazon's 1-click process.

And here are some famous examples of cool tangible stuff:

- Edison's light bulb;
- intermittent windshield wipers featured in the movie

Flash of Genius;

- King Gillette's razor;

- Viagra;

- Michael Jackson's system for creating an anti-gravity illusion (that he used for his *Smooth Criminal* performances); and

- Henry Ford's carburetor.

If you are visual like me, I know that you will find the chart below helpful:

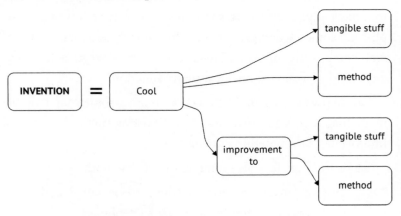

TWO TYPES OF PATENTS

There are two types of patents based on the kind of invention that they protect. However, there's more to it than simply *what* they protect. The important difference is *how* they protect your invention.

These two types are: *product patents* that protect cool tangible stuff and cool improvements to existing tangible stuff, and *method patents* that protect cool methods and cool improvements to existing methods.

Either type of patent contains a list of so called *claims*, which is a fancy way of describing the features that make your invention new and useful. Patent claims define the extent of the protection conferred by a patent.

YOU'VE BEEN HIT BY A SMOOTH SYSTEM FOR ENGAGING SHOES WITH A HITCH MEANS

So, if you're wondering what exactly Michael Jackson patented, you would need to look at the list of the claims in his patent. There are 13 claims in total, of which there are 3 independent claims and 10 claims that rely on one of these three independent claims.

I will only cite the first two claims from the patent. The first one is independent and the second one depends on the first. This should give you a good idea about the insanity that goes into the drafting (and also reading) patent documents.

So here they are:

"1.　　A system for engaging shoes with a hitch means to permit a person standing on a stage surface to lean forwardly beyond his or her center of gravity, comprising:

at least one shoe having a heel with a first engagement means, said first engagement means comprising a recess formed in a heel of said shoe covered with a heel slot plane located at a bottom region of said heel, said heel slot plate having a slot formed therein with a relatively wide opening at a leading edge of said heel and a narrower terminal end rearward of said leading edge, said recess being larger in size above said terminal end of said slot than is said terminal end of said slot; and

a second engagement means, detachably engageable with said first engagement means, comprising a hitch

> *member having an enlarged head portion connected by a narrower shank portion to a means for raising and lowering said head of said hitch member above and substantially level with or below said stage surface, said head portion being larger in size than said terminal end of said slot and said shank portion being narrower than said terminal end of said slot, wherein said hitch member can be moved through apertures in said stage surface between a projecting position raised above said stage surface and a retracted position at or below the stage surface, and when said head portion of said hitch member is raised above said stage surface, said first engagement means can be detachably engaged with said projecting hitch member, thereby allowing a person wearing the shoes to lean forwardly with his or her normal center of gravity beyond a front region of said shoes, and maintain said forward lean.*
>
> *2.   The system of claim 1, wherein said slot in said heel slot plate is V-shaped, with the mouth of the V at the leading edge of said heel."*
>
> So there you have it. The patent prevents anyone from making the system described in any one of the claims listed in the patent. And yes, it is your responsibility to figure out if your product would be caught by the claims in any of the patents out there.

Product Patents: A product patent allows you to stop others from making and selling (or enabling others to make or sell) the product described in the patent. For example, if you have a patent on zadgets, then nobody can make or sell zadgets or anything else that has *all* of the characteristics of at least one claim listed in your patent.

Method Patents: A method patent allows you to stop others from using or enabling others to use the method described in the patent. For example, if you have a patent on a new way to make zadgets, then nobody can make zadgets using the method that has *all* of the characteristics of at least one claim listed in your patent. Importantly, a method patent will not stop others from making zadgets using other methods. Depending on how your patent is drafted, it may also be able to let you stop others from making wadgets and xadgets if their manufacturing would require using your patented method.

Often, you would have claims relating to both the product and the method in the same patent. So you can have claims that will stop others from making and selling zadgets *and* also claims that will stop others from using a particular method to make them or a particular method of using them to achieve a certain result.

It is important to clearly understand what it is that you are trying to prevent others from replicating. For example, let's say your name is Henry Reardan, and you have invented a new kind of alloy, Reardan Metal. This alloy is going to bury the competition. Now you need to decide what is it that you are going to patent. Is it the composition of the alloy itself? This will allow you to prevent anyone from making and selling an alloy with that same composition. Or are you going to patent a new way of pouring metal that yields superior results as evidenced by your Reardan Metal? This will allow you to prevent anyone from making and selling *any* alloy, regardless of its composition, as long as it's made using your method. Or maybe you should patent both the alloy and the method?

Patents of these two types can cover a wide range of human knowledge and include:

- mechanical patents;
- electrical patents;
- biotech patents;
- software patents; and
- business method patents.

In the U.S., more than anywhere else, we've seen a lot of software and business method patents. For example, Google has just received a patent on their method of providing free driver-less taxis to an advertiser's business location. Imagine seeing an ad that asks you, *"Like our stuff? Would you like us to pick you up and take you to our store for free?"* Now you can't implement this idea in your business, unless you get Google's permission.

However, not every country welcomes software and business method patents as much. Some countries expressly disallow this type of patents. Canada is somewhere in the middle, because software and business method inventions are not expressly unpatentable, but there is a significant hurdle to overcome to get them patented.

REQUIREMENTS FOR PROTECTION

It's important to remember that there is no such thing as an unregistered patent. If you don't register the patent then your invention will remain unprotected.

So what do you need to get your invention patented? In other words, what are the patentability requirements?

There are four main requirements for getting a patent to protect your invention. The first three refer to the actual invention and the fourth requirement refers to what you need to include in your patent application. You need to meet all four requirements in order to get a patent.

THE INVENTION MUST BE NEW

In order for an invention to be classified as new, the invention must have never been made public by anyone, anywhere. Even if it's your own invention, you are still not allowed to disclose it to the public until you have filed for the patent.

Disclosing doesn't just mean publishing in a scientific magazine. It means providing enough information for those sophisticated in the area of knowledge to which your invention pertains to understand the substance of your invention.

This may include selling your product or even writing an article on your blog about your product or your revolutionary new process.

If you share your invention with an investor under a non-disclosure agreement, and the investor keeps it to himself, it does not count as a public disclosure and would not hurt your chances of getting your invention patented.

But once the information is out there, even if the inventor is the source of disclosure, the invention is no longer new.

When I say, "out there", I mean "out there anywhere". Even if you only make your product available in a single store in a small village in Moldova, this may be enough to destroy your chances of getting a patent—not just in Moldova but anywhere in the world.

You're probably thinking to yourself, *"How on earth would the patent examiner in the U.S. find out about our test sale in Moldova?"*

Chances are he won't, unless your competitor somehow finds

out and provides the information to the examiner, or to the judge who may invalidate your patent even after it was registered.

The moral of the story is not that you should never sell your products in a single store in a small village in Moldova. The moral of the story is that you should always know how selling your products in a single store in a small village in Moldova will fit with your overall IP strategy. If you have no plans of filing for a patent, feel free to sell your products in Moldova, Zanzibar, Winnipeg, or New York. The more the merrier. But if your IP strategy presumes that you will be attempting to patent your invention, then you must not sell your products in Moldova until you file your patent application because the risk, however remote, is just not worth it.

Having said that, you should know that in Canada and the U.S., there is a grace period of twelve months for you to get a patent after you've disclosed your own invention to the public. This grace period is unique, so don't rely on it anywhere else.

DON'T FORGET ABOUT GRACE #2

You invent a zadget. You don't tell anybody anything about it. You just build a small number of them. You decide to sell 50 zadgets in Moldova on February 15, 2015, and they go on sale there on March 1, 2015. Let's assume that your competitor somehow finds out about your Moldova adventure and will not hesitate to inform the Patent Office or the judge if he needs to. What this means is that your invention is unpatentable in most of the world, even if you choose to file for a patent in Germany on March 2, 2015.

You can still file your patent application in Canada and the U.S. with at least some hope for success, if you do it by February 28 of 2016. However, if you do it on March 2, 2016, then your invention becomes unpatentable in Canada and the U.S. as well.

Just to be clear, let's say someone else invents a zadget and sells it in Moldova on February 15, 2015. You just happen to be on your honeymoon there and you just happen to visit the store with zadgets on the shelf. With thoughts, *oh, that's a great idea*, you return to Canada and file for a patent in your own name. Then, the grace period does not apply because you are not the person who had disclosed the invention.

The bottom line is, you need to be careful about what you disclose about your invention so that you don't lose your opportunity to get a patent and be rewarded for your hard work.

THE INVENTION MUST BE USEFUL

In addition to being new, the invention must also be useful. This doesn't really mean that your invention has to be of some particular use to anybody. It just means that your invention has to provide at least some identifiable benefit and that it can be made and used.

In the U.S., this requirement is referred to as "utility", hence the term "utility patent" being used in the States. The invention must *do* something.

In Europe, this requirement has the form of an "industrial applicability" test, which is slightly different but still reflects a similar idea—there must be something about the invention that would make it capable of being reproduced over and over again with the purpose of performing a certain function or achieving a certain result.

Either way, this requirement is the easiest to meet because as long as your invention can be made and as long as it can produce some meaningful result, you meet the requirement.

TELL ME, DOCTOR, WHERE ARE WE GOING THIS TIME?

Coming up with an idea that it would be great to have a time machine is not enough to make your idea patentable, even if you are the first person who's ever thought about it.

Unless you know (and share with the Patent Office) how to actually build one and how it will work, you haven't demonstrated that your invention is useful.

"*Wouldn't it be nice*" is not good enough. Hypothetical devices are not patentable.

One of the underlying ideas behind the patent system is that the public should be able to use inventions after the patent expires. If the patent does not provide enough information for the public to do that, then there is very little value that the public receives in exchange for granting the monopoly to the patent owner. This is the reason why usefulness is a requirement for patent protection.

THE INVENTION MUST NOT BE OBVIOUS

This requirement is typically the hardest to meet, and this is where a lot of tension arises between the Patent Office and the inventor.

You may have to deal with the patent examiner's objections regarding obviousness if your invention is not described in a single existing source (in which case it would not have been new) but results from combining a number of already known components.

Let me take you back for a second. I hope you still remember that a patent is made of *claims* that define the features of your invention. Remember the first requirement—that the invention be new? The claims in your invention are not "new" if somebody already disclosed or made available to the public something that fully describes what you are trying to cover with your claims. For example, if you invented "a system that allows a person to lean forward beyond his center of gravity by fastening his shoe to the stage by means of a system that comprises a special shoe heel and a hitch that attaches the shoe to the stage", you didn't invent anything new because your invention is described in Michael Jackson's patent. So your invention would not be patentable.

But what if you have invented "a system that allows a person to lean backwards beyond his center of gravity by fastening his pants to the wall by means of a system that comprises a special belt and a hitch that attaches the belt to the wall?" This was not described in Michael Jackson's patent. So the analysis would move on to whether your invention is obvious or not.

The determination of whether or not an invention is obvious relies on a mythical person who knows everything that currently exists. This person knows every single patent out there, every single journal, every single magazine article, and every single blog post. The person knows everything but is totally incapable of inventing anything new even if his life depended on it. So the question the patent examiner asks is, *"Would this person be able to come up with what you're trying to patent?"* If the answer is yes, even a person with zero creativity could still put two and two together and come up with the same solution, then your invention is obvious, and you cannot get a patent. If our mythical person would look at what you've come up with and think, *"Wow, I'll be damned. I knew about this part and I certainly knew about that part. But I wouldn't for the life of me think that you could combine them to get such an amazing result,"* then your invention is non-obvious and you have managed to go over the steepest hurdle of patentability.

Here's another example. Let's say, someone has a patent for a hammer, and there is someone else who has a patent for a nail remover. Let's say you're the inventor who comes up with an idea that you could place the nail remover on the opposite side of the hammer. Again, your invention is new (because neither patent described what you invented), but is it obvious?

While this is supposed to be objective (that's why they came up with the standard of the mythical all-knowing uncreative person), like any other legal fiction, it is applied by humans, and humans are inherently subjective. In these situations, be prepared for some back-and-forth with the Patent Office when they claim that your invention is obvious. You'll say, "*Well, if this is so obvious, how come nobody has come up with this yet?*" And they'll say, "*Maybe they have, they just didn't do anything public with it?*" And you'd say, "*This is such a great idea, I'm sure that if somebody came up with it, we'd hear about it.*" And so on, and so on.

Your ability to win this argument is your No. 1 reason why a professional should deal with your patent application. Again, I'm not one, so I'm not tooting my own horn here. It is just a fact of life that it is very difficult to overcome these objections unless you really know what you're doing.

THE PATENT MUST TEACH THE PUBLIC

Let's say you've cleared all three hurdles for patentability—you've invented something that is new, useful, and non-obvious. There is one more thing you should *do* to ensure that your invention is patented.

The philosophy behind the patent system is that you are granted a time-limited monopoly in exchange for teaching the world about your invention. When your patent expires, anyone will be able to use it as they please. It's like the government telling you, "*We'll give you this magic sword if you tell us and everyone where your treasure is. And you can use that sword for a while to keep peo-*

ple off. But then we're going to take that sword away. And anyone can come and take your treasure."

DON'T MESS WITH THE GOVERNMENT

This reminds me of when a Mafia gang took on a deaf-mute man to run their deliveries, feeling it would be safer having someone who can't overhear their conversations and who can't tell on them. One day when he was to deliver a large sum of money, he never showed up with it. The mobsters tracked him down but he had no money on him. As none of them were able to use sign language, they brought in an interpreter.

Mobster: *"Where is the money?"* (Interpreter repeats the question using sign language.)

The bag man replies with the sign language. The interpreter says, *"He says he had to ditch it in the river because the cops were onto him."*

Mobster: *"I'm not fooling around! You better tell me where that money is!"* (Interpreter again uses sign language to repeat the question.)

The interpreter relays the bag man's answer, *"He swears he is telling the truth. He had to get rid of it."*

The mobster pulls out a big gun and points it between the deaf man's eyes. *"Tell me where that money is, or I'll kill you right now!"*

The bag man, sweating profusely, says in sign language, *"It's inside a shoebox under a loose floorboard in my bedroom closet."*

The interpreter says, *"He says he doesn't know where it is and he doesn't think you have the guts to pull the trigger."*

BOOM!

The moral of this story is that when you are telling the Patent Office about how your invention is supposed to work, you can't tell them that you had to ditch the money in the river. If you don't teach the public about your invention, you have not fulfilled your end of the bargain, and your patent will not be valid, even if you somehow manage to get it registered.

> In fact, this is precisely what recently happened to the Viagra patent in Canada. The Supreme Court of Canada found that Pfizer patented Viagra without specifying which of the various chemicals used in it was the active ingredient.
>
> The Court found that "Pfizer benefited from the law, obtaining exclusive monopoly rights by not disclosing [the active ingredient] in spite of their obligations under the law" and cancelled Pfizer's patent.
>
> The cancellation of Pfizer's patent opened the door for generics that perform the same function and the same formula. The only thing that now makes Viagra different from generics is the trademarked name. The manufacturers of generics are allowed to make the pill using the same chemical formula that used to be patented, but they are not allowed to call it Viagra.

You have to write the patent so that people reading it will know how to produce or use it. You can't have a patent and write it in such a way that people who have read the patent would not be able to make or use your product or method after your patent expires.

In this sense, patents are the opposite of trade secrets. In order to get a patent, you must disclose the details of your invention so everyone can make it once your patent has expired. As you will learn in the chapter about trade secrets, the only way to protect your trade secrets is by keeping your information to yourself.

If you can sell your product without fear of your secret being compromised, and you know that the lifespan of your invention is more than 20 years (think of the *Coca-Cola* recipe), you might be better off not filing for a patent. However, if anyone who buys your product would be able to take it apart and figure out the great idea behind it, then you would not be able to protect your invention through a trade secret, and would need to get a patent in order to stop others from using it.

WHAT CAN'T I PATENT?

There are a few things that you are not allowed to patent.

DISCOVERIES OF EXISTING NATURAL ORDER

You cannot get a patent unless you have an invention. If you've discovered how something in nature works, you can't patent this. This is a discovery, not an invention. You have discovered how nature works but you are not *changing* anything about how nature works, and you are not providing any solution to an existing problem. Likewise, you cannot patent mere scientific principles or abstract theorems.

You may, however, patent specific inventions that are *based* on such discoveries, principles, and theorems.

NON-FUNCTIONAL ELEMENTS OF AN INVENTION

You can't protect the way the product looks with a (utility) patent, unless there is a specific useful function that depends on the appearance.

Let's take Michael Jackson's example again.

It would not be proper subject matter for a patent if you came up with the idea that the shoe must be black, or shiny, or with a diamond buckle because this has nothing to do with creating the anti-gravity effect.

However, if you realized that the heel of the shoe must be made of rubber matching the color of the shoe in order to allow you to hide the lock, this could be patentable, because there is a direct link between the appearance and the function of the invention.

You might be able to protect the looks through other areas of IP, usually through industrial design protection, but you can't get a utility patent on it. Utility patents only deal with functional parts of an invention.

SOMETHING THAT REQUIRES PROFESSIONAL SKILLS

You cannot patent an invention that requires application of professional skills for it to function, unless such skills are perfectly controllable and reproducible as part of the benefit of your invention.

For example, it is not possible to patent a method of winning a patent infringement lawsuit if nobody but brilliant litigators can take advantage of the information disclosed in the patent. If a mediocre lawyer who reads your patent can't win patent infringement lawsuits, then the invention, however clever it might be if used by brilliant minds, cannot be patented.

The reason behind this is that patents are not designed to protect inventions that can only be used by brilliant minds.

IT'S IMPOSSIBLE TO MAKE

You can't patent an idea unless you can actually make something out of it. We already discussed this in the section looking at the usefulness of patents. You can't patent a time machine if you have no idea how to actually make one.

IT'S NOT NEW OR IT'S OBVIOUS

Again, we discussed this under the requirements for getting a patent. You cannot get a patent on inventions that are not new or that are obvious based on the level of knowledge at the time the patent is applied for.

If your invention doesn't add anything or doesn't add substantially to what is known to specialists knowledgeable in the area of your invention, you cannot get a patent on that. If your invention is about nuclear reactors, you cannot claim that your invention is new because your neighbourhood butcher knows nothing about it. The important thing is whether those who know everything about existing nuclear reactors would find that you have invented something that had not been known before.

TELL THE WORLD, MAKE IT A BETTER PLACE

Sometimes, inventors who do not have the budget to patent their inventions make a deliberate public disclosure of their inventions in order to make sure that they can safely *use* them without someone else running to the Patent Office to patent them.

What this does is it makes the invention unpatentable—by them or by anyone else. This is called *poisoning the well.*

Just because the invention is not patentable does not mean that it cannot be *used*. In other words, "unpatentable" means that nobody can successfully get a patent monopoly on the invention to prevent you from using that invention.

You have to be very careful with this though. It's not uncommon for an invention to be based on other pre-existing inventions, some of which may be patented.

Let's go back to the example of the hammer and the nail remover. Let's say the patent on the hammer and the patent on the nail remover are still in force, and you come up with the invention of the nail remover being placed on the opposite side of the hammer. You decide that you don't want to deal with patenting your invention so you publish your idea on your blog for everyone to see. Once you've published the idea, nobody can get a patent on it anymore.

This does not mean you can start making hammers with nail removers. You would *still* need the permission from both the owner of the hammer patent and the owner of the nail remover patent to do that. Likewise, the hammer patent owner would not be able to make the combined tool without the license from the nail remover patent owner, and vice versa.

WHERE ARE PATENTS PROTECTED?

Patents are only valid in the country where you have requested protection. If you don't have a patent in a particular country, then your invention isn't protected there. This means if you have a patent for the U.S., but not Canada, then anyone can make or sell your product in Canada.

Once you've applied for a patent in one country, you only have twelve months to apply for patent protection in other countries. After the twelve months are up, anyone can make and sell products in any country not covered by your patent.

This is a different 12-month grace period than the one afforded to inventors who disclose their inventions in Canada and the U.S. before filing a patent application because:

- it applies to all countries, and not only to Canada and the States; and

- it only applies to disclosures made to a patent office in a patent application.

For example, you can't get a patent in the United States, wait for five years to see how well your product sells, and then apply for patents in Canada, Australia, and New Zealand. Your twelve month grace period is long gone, so you are not allowed to apply for any more patents for the same invention.

DON'T FORGET ABOUT GRACE #3

Once you have filed your patent application in the first country, it becomes what is called prior art for everyone else who may come up with the same or similar ideas in the future, making all future patent applications no longer new, and thus not patentable. Prior art is the aggregate knowledge and information that has been made available to the public that might be relevant to a particular invention.

This is precisely why the 12-month period is called the grace period.

If not for the 12-month grace period, you would need to file your patent applications at the same time in all countries where you would like to file. Otherwise, your disclosure to the first patent office would act as prior art against your own patent applications elsewhere.

The fact that you need a patent in every country where you want protection means that getting a patent can be very expensive, especially if your market is the entire world. Most businesses need to find a compromise and pick and choose which markets are the most important to get patent protection in.

Most business owners start with the United States as the primary market for patents because the United States is the biggest market out there, while the costs of getting a patent there are comparable to the costs of getting a patent in other countries. So, if you want to get a patent, you normally start with the United States and then you have 12 months to add other countries depending on your target market.

HOW LONG DOES PATENT PROTECTION LAST?

A patent lasts for twenty years after the date of application. This is important because the clock doesn't start running once the patent is granted—it starts running as soon as you apply.

The normal amount of time it takes to get a patent is about four to six years and all of this time is counted as part of the duration of the patent. This means that you actually only have a patent for fifteen years or so.

You can't sue others for patent infringement while your patent application is being examined, but it does not mean that someone can get away with stealing your invention as long as they stop a day before your patent is registered. After your patent application is published, you can send a cease-and-desist letter to whoever may be using your invention. This will put them on notice that this is *your* invention and demand that they immediately stop using it. If your patent is successfully registered and the bad guys ignored your warnings, you can go after them not only for what they did *after* the patent was registered but all the way back to when the invention was published. This is why you put "*patent pending*" on products for which there is a filed patent application.

SHOULD I GET A PATENT?

Because getting and maintaining a patent is very expensive, the lifespan of the patent is one of the most important considerations in deciding whether or not to get a patent.

You also need to decide if there will still be value in your invention by the time the patent is issued. Since it takes four to six years to get a patent, if your invention is going to be obsolete before you are even granted a patent, you may decide to not bother.

You also need to decide if your invention will remain valuable after the patent expires. Remember, in order to get a patent, you need to disclose all the details of how to use or make your invention. If your invention is still relevant and valuable after twenty years, people will be lining up to use it and there is nothing you can do to stop them. This is precisely how the generics market works in the pharmaceutical industry. One company develops a new drug, enjoys a brief monopoly, and then it's fair game for anyone else to copy it.

There may be situations where you would be better off keeping the whole thing to yourself as a trade secret in an attempt to continue making a profit from your invention. In other words, can you make money through your invention while keeping it a secret?

Essentially the thought process should go like this:

1. Is it valuable?

2. If it is valuable, can I protect it by any means other than a patent?

3. If I can't protect it other than through a patent, is it patentable?

4. If it's patentable, is it *really-really-really* valuable?

If it's patentable and really-really-really valuable, find the money and file for the patent. Otherwise, don't bother.

WHAT CONSTITUTES A PATENT INFRINGEMENT (WHAT CAN YOU SUE OTHERS FOR)?

Patent infringement occurs whenever anyone, without your permission, uses something described in at least one claim of your patent in the country where you have a valid patent. The patent claims define the extent of what the public is not allowed to do.

If the use is not covered by the claims in your patent, then it is not a patent infringement. This is why it is so important to draft your claims broadly enough to make sure that potential infringers cannot easily get away with modifying some unimportant characteristic of your invention.

For example, if you only have a single claim in your patent that states that you are claiming a "tool for the purpose of driving nails into walls and consisting of a metal head of a certain shape and a wooden handle", then it would not be an infringement of your patent for anyone to make and sell hammers with plastic or metal handles.

Compare this with a patent for a "tool for the purpose of delivering an impact to an object, which tool may consist of a heavy head and a handle". This wording would catch hammers made of any materials.

This is what patent lawyers mean when they say that the patent is broad or narrow. The narrower the patent, the easier it is to get (because the narrowness increases the chances that the invention so narrowly worded would be new and non-obvious), but also the easier it is for someone to find a way to not infringe on it.

On the other hand, the broader the patent, the stronger your weapon will be because significantly more things are going to be caught by it. But this also means that it may be very difficult to get one.

The usual strategy is to first file for as broad a protection as humanly possible, and then carve out pieces of the patent as the patent examiner cites objections, thus navigating towards a narrower, yet still enforceable patent.

As with most other areas of intellectual property, there are two main remedies available to you if someone is infringing on your patent.

You can ask for an **injunction**. This is when the judge orders the defendant to stop using your invention as covered by your patent. This usually means that the defendant must stop making or selling a particular product, or using a particular method.

The other remedy is **damages**. This is when the judge orders the defendant to pay money to you to compensate for your losses from the patent infringement. On top of compensatory damages, the court may in some circumstances award punitive damages to punish the defendant for blatant infringements.

DEFENDING AGAINST PATENT INFRINGEMENT LAWSUITS

If someone accuses you of patent infringement, there are a number of steps that you can take to defend yourself. Some of these steps are similar to the steps discussed in the section on defending yourself from claims of copyright and trademark infringement. Again, if you sue someone for infringing your patent, expect some of these defences to be used against you.

I DIDN'T USE IT

As you've just learned, if you did something that is not covered by at least one claim of the plaintiff's patent, then it is not a patent infringement.

If you can figure out a way to prove that you are making or selling something that does not have all of the features described in the patent, you will be off the hook.

In our example about the hammer with a wooden handle, if you are *not* using the wooden handle, you have a good argument that you did not use the patent.

Please note that *adding* features to someone else's patentable invention would not relieve you of liability for infringement. For example, if you started selling hammers with nail removers, just because the hammer patent did not contain anything about nail removers would not be a valid defence because your unit still has a metal head and a wooden handle.

THE PATENT IS INVALID

You can claim that the patent is invalid, and therefore, you couldn't have infringed on someone's claim. There are a few things you could address. You should look into:

- whether at the time of the patent application there existed prior art that made the invention not new;
- whether at the time of the patent application the invention was obvious;
- whether the patent covers subject matter that is improper (for example, some countries prohibit patents relating to cloning of human forms);
- whether the patent has been obtained by fraud; and
- whether the claims are drafted properly.

THE PATENT HAS EXPIRED

If more than 20 years have passed since the patent filing date, the patent has expired and can no longer be used against you.

I WAS USING IT FIRST

If you can prove that you have been using material covered by someone's patent before they filed their patent application, then you might not be guilty of patent infringement.

YOU DON'T OWN IT

You might want to try and prove that the person who is suing you does not actually own the patent. This might be the case where an inventor filed the patent but then assigned that patent to a company. If the inventor sues you, you can claim that the inventor no longer holds the patent.

ACQUIESCENCE AND DELAY

If you can show that the patent owner knew about the patent infringement for some time but decided not to pursue it, then you may not be guilty of patent infringement. This occurs when you are openly making and selling your product, and the patent owners knows about it but waits for a number of years until you have started to make money before bringing a claim.

The patent owner does not have to sue right away but the owner does need to let you know that he is not happy with what you are doing. This puts you on notice that the patent owner is *not* acquiescing to your use and removes this defence from your arsenal.

This goes for your own patents as well. Even if you are not planning on suing, you should send a cease and desist letter to someone who is infringing on your patent so you leave yourself the right to sue at a later date.

YOU GAVE ME A LICENSE

For this to work, you would need to prove that the patent owner agreed to let you use the patented invention. While nothing beats a written contract that plainly states that the licensor is granting a license to the licensee, there are situations when you can provide sufficient evidence for the court to agree with you that the patent owner indeed has granted you permission to use the invention—even if you don't have a proper written agreement.

TIME'S UP

There is a time limit to how long a person can wait before claiming patent infringement. If the plaintiff has known that somebody has been infringing on their patent but has not done anything about it for six years, the plaintiff is prohibited by law from suing the defendant for an infringement.

TIPS AND TRICKS

There are a number of tips and tricks that you can use when it comes to patents. Not every tip will fit your situation but most will be helpful.

CONDUCT A PATENT SEARCH

If you think you've come up with a new product, a new service, or a new way of doing something, then the first thing to do is to check whether you're really the first to do it. Just because nobody's doing it doesn't mean that you're the first who came up with this idea. More often than not, you'll be surprised how many people think the same way and have come up with similar ideas. There are a number of steps you can take to do a patent search.

Check Google: Sounds obvious, but really check the web to see if someone has done or disclosed something similar. Often, we are so in love with our ideas that we are blind to the possibility that we might not be the first ones to give birth to them.

Do a Google Patent Search: Google has its own U.S. patent database search engine (google.com/patents). Because the U.S. is the biggest market, it's very unlikely that somebody would have a patent in Canada but not in the States. Always start the patent search with what's registered in the States.

Check Free Patents Online: Another database that you can check is Free Patents Online (freepatentsonline.com).

You need to be careful when doing your own patent search because it is very likely that you will miss important information. It's not about the quality of the database; it's about how you frame the search. Unless you know what you're doing, you could end up missing many critical details. While you can do the search yourself, I always recommend that my clients use a professional patent searcher. It could end up saving you a lot of money in the long run. You don't want to start spending money developing a product only to find out later that you can't get a patent on your idea.

WHAT DO YOU MEAN I'M NOT FIRST?

Several years ago, I thought I had invented an amazing way to sell books to lawyers. I was beyond excited because I knew that nobody was doing this.

I did my own search and found absolutely nothing. I was ecstatic. I thought I had discovered a source of passive income that was going to last me a lifetime. I was about to go and spend about $20,000 to get a patent on my invention in Canada and the U.S.

Just before I was about to shell out the money, I thought

maybe I should do a patent search with somebody who has more experience doing patent searches. I hired a patent attorney in the States who did a search for me, and he came back with a ninety-page report, essentially burying any chances of my invention ever being patented anywhere.

That pretty much killed the whole idea right there because I knew that the only way for me to protect the idea was to get a patent, and that turned out to be something that could not be done.

In fact, there were several patents that my method of delivering books would infringe on even if I decided to use it without getting a patent. So the problem was not just that I could not protect the IP going OUT, but also that that I had problems with IP coming IN.

I'm still disappointed that I couldn't make any profit on that idea, but what I'm really happy about is that I saved myself a lot of money and a lot of time by not trying to develop an idea that I couldn't use myself, let alone patent.

The purpose of the patent search is not to tell you that the road is clear. The purpose of the search is to show you all the roadblocks. If you see too many roadblocks, then you might realize that it is useless to file for a patent because it will either not be registered, or it will eventually be worded so narrowly that, in effect, it won't cover anything. If there are some roadblocks, then it is precisely the function of a good patent attorney to draft your patent application in a way that navigates around all these roadblocks.

Contrary to what you might think, having no roadblocks to your patent might also be a concern. It may mean that you haven't framed your search correctly—it's very seldom that somebody comes up with something today that's absolutely new. It's always going to have to borrow something from somebody. The question is, *"Have you invented something that's sufficiently innovative to merit protection on its own?"*

FILE A PROVISIONAL PATENT APPLICATION

In the U.S., you can apply for a provisional patent application. A provisional patent application basically lets the Patent Office know that you are planning on filing a regular patent application at some point soon but you don't want to make the information public just yet. You have one year to decide to file a regular patent application, re-file the provisional application, or abandon the provisional application all together.

The advantage of a provisional patent application is that you don't have to disclose the details of your invention to the public although you do need to disclose some details to the Patent Office. This will give you a priority date. A priority date means that anybody who files their patent application within one year after you file your provisional patent application will be denied protection because you were there first.

You need to be careful with this for two reasons. If you decide to file for a regular patent, it has to follow what you wrote in the provisional patent application. You can't just change all the details when applying for a regular patent. The details need to match your provisional patent application. This means that you should still have a professional do it for you, and most of them will recommend drafting your provisional patent application almost with the same carefulness (and almost for the same budget) as a non-provisional patent application.

Also, if at the end of the one year that the provisional patent protection lasts, instead of converting your provisional patent into a non-provisional patent, you decide to simply file another provisional patent application, you will get a new priority date. If someone filed a patent in the U.S. Patent Office before you file your second provisional patent application, you're toast because there will be somebody with an earlier priority date. It doesn't matter that you had an initial provisional patent application with a prior date because your first application will be deemed to have been abandoned and not converted into a non-provisional patent.

The main reason for a provisional patent application is if you were looking for investors. You could show them the provisional patent application to help boost confidence in your invention.

One last thing to remember is that provisional patents are only good for the United States. Do not assume that they are also available in other countries. Most probably, they are not.

ACT NOW!

Ready for some more homework?

Here, you need to identify all novel products and methods you use in your business. If you think you're using something that you might patent or that might have been patented by someone else, you should reflect this in the table (regardless of whether or not it is indeed new, useful, and non-obvious). Then you need to honestly answer whether you have sufficient rights to use it as IP coming IN and if you have taken sufficient steps to protect it as your IP going OUT.

This table will allow you to instantly see your weak spots. Now you can mend these weak spots in the order of their importance to your business. If your ability to make zadgets is crucial to your business and you have nothing to prove that you are allowed to make and sell them, it's a big problem. On the other hand, if you chose not to apply for a patent on a novel method of attaching stamps to your outgoing mail, this can wait until all higher-priority issues have been addressed.

Feel free to download the template for this table (as well as many other goodies) at ***http://ipbook.ca/more*** .

INVENTIONS		
What inventions am I using in my business?		
Invention (novel product or process)	Do I really have a right to USE the IP? If yes, how do I know I have the right to use it? (patent search—freedom to operate? Google search? license?)	Do I OWN it? If yes, how am I protecting my rights? (did not disclose more than 12 months ago? provisional patent in the U.S., patent application in U.S. and Canada and elsewhere? contracts?)

YOUR REFERENCE POINT FOR PATENTS

	PATENTS
What's protected	the *WHAT*
Definition of the protected objects	Any new, non-obvious, and useful art, process, machine, manufacture, or composition of matter, or any new, non-obvious, and useful improvement in any art, process, machine, manufacture, or composition of matter.
Classes of protected objects	Functional features of: - tools; - devices; - machines; - processes; - methods; - ingredients.
Examples	- Intermittent windshield wiper; - Streaming of audiovisual content over the Internet; - Amazon's 1-click process.
What is needed to get protection?	The invention must be new, useful, and not obvious, and the inventor must "teach" the public how to make and use the invention in the patent application.
What it does not protect	- discoveries of the existing natural order; - non-functional elements of an invention; - inventions that are impossible to make (for example, the time machine); - inventions that are obvious based on the level of knowledge at the time the patent is applied for.
Enforceable against	- For product patents: anyone making or selling a product that has all the main features covered by the patent; - For process patents: anyone using the process to achieve a result that has all the main features covered by the patent.
What constitutes use? / What are others prohibited from doing?	- making, constructing, using, or selling a product patent; - using a method described in the patent.

Where is the owner/ author/inventor protected?	The countries where the patent is granted.
Length of protection	20 years from the date of filing for the patent application.
Can the initial period of protection be extended?	No.
Who owns the right / Who should apply for registration of the right?	Inventor. Patents can be transferred to another person or company.
Do owners / authors / inventors have some rights if they do not apply for protection?	No.
What are the benefits of applying for protection?	It is the registration of a patent that creates protection. Without registration, the invention is not protected for what it stands.
How is the right established?	Through issuance of the patent by patent offices in the countries where patent protection is sought.
Defences & limitations	- the plaintiff's patent is invalid (prior art, obviousness, improper scope of claims, fraud, non-statutory subject matter); - plaintiff's patent has expired; - defendant's prior commercial use; - plaintiff does not own patent (wrong plaintiff); - antitrust violation; - acquiescence + delay (plaintiff's conduct leads the defendant to believe that the plaintiff will not enforce its legal right against the defendant); - plaintiff granted the defendant a license; - limitation period has expired (6 years).
Available remedies	- injunction; - damages (including exemplary and punitive damages).

When can it be registered?	In Canada, an application must be filed no later than 1 year after the first public disclosure of the invention anywhere in the world.
	Provisional patent applications in the U.S. normally are not considered public disclosure, but every non-provisional patent application or any other public disclosure of the invention anywhere in the world will trigger the commencement of the 12-month period during which patent applications must be filed in all countries where the patent protection will eventually be sought.
How long does the registration take?	4–6 years.
Are there mandatory maintenance fees?	Yes. Annual maintenance fees are required to keep an application / patent alive. The fees range from $100 to $450.
Government fees relating to registration	Filing of an application $400. Request for examination fee is $800. Final fee for registration is $300. * Only half of the fees are payable by universities and companies with 50 employees or less.
Total ballpark cost if a lawyer / trademark agent / patent agent is involved (including government fees)	$5,000–$15,000 per registration

INDUSTRIAL DESIGNS: *WOW*

The magic word for industrial designs is *WOW*. This is because industrial designs protect the look (the thing that makes you go wow) of products.

Industrial designs are called *design patents* in the United States. In fact, industrial designs have many similarities with patents, or *utility patents* as they are called in the U.S.

Similarly to regular (or utility) patents, industrial designs are a form of recognition by the government of the design owner's time-limited monopoly to use the design.

How often is it that we go to a store and we see two almost identical products by different companies on the shelf? One of them looks slightly better than the other, so we buy the one that pleases our eyes more.

The function of industrial design is to stop anybody else from copying that distinctive look of your product. So what you acquire through registration of your *WOW* as an industrial design is the right to prevent others from making or selling products to which your industrial design has been applied.

Industrial designs can be found in many industries. Jewellery, fabric design, cutlery, tools and hardware, electronics, packaging and containers, furniture, cars, musical instruments, office supplies, toys, lighting, cosmetics, washing machines, watches—pretty much anything which depends on the look of the product as one of the main selling features can, and often should, be protected through industrial designs.

POWERFUL DESIGNS

The most famous litigation around design patents must be the battle between Apple and Samsung in the U.S., where Apple accused Samsung of infringing on a number of Apple's design patents, including the notorious design patent on rectangular devices with rounded corners.

A lot of people still think that industrial designs are the weaker link compared to regular patents.

But the verdict of over *one billion dollars* that the jury awarded Apple against Samsung for design infringement should be sufficient to convince you otherwise.

As a business owner, I'm sure you understand that anything that can generate a billion dollars is a good thing to have on your side.

Granted, the chances of your industrial design being worth a billion bucks are not very high. But in a situation when you see your competitor copy the looks of your products, you'll be glad to have extra ammunition to protect your competitive advantage. And your industrial design registrations may be just what the doctor ordered.

WHAT DO INDUSTRIAL DESIGNS PROTECT?

Industrial designs protect the uniqueness of how a product looks. Not what it does, not what it's for, nor what it's about. It protects what your customers find pleasing to the eye. To put it more formally, industrial designs protect aesthetic, cosmetic, or visual qualities of products.

These qualities can refer to shapes (the famous "rectangular devices with rounded corners" on which Apple got the design patent for its iPhones and iPads), arrangements (Google's graphical user interface), patterns (Louis Vuitton's patterns applied to bags, purses, fabrics, etc.), or ornaments (Christmas decorations).

As you will learn in the next section, you cannot protect functional elements of products through industrial designs. If the looks of your product are simply the result of your product's function, then you can't protect them through industrial designs.

This is the crucial difference between patents (utility patents) and industrial designs (design patents). One protects the functionality and the other protects the looks. These two can never overlap, even if they are supposed to protect the same product. For example, there are a great many functional inventions inside the iPhone. They can and are protected through utility patents. But they do not protect the shape of the phone. On the other hand, the design patent on the shape does not protect any of the functions that the phone is capable of performing.

While the utility/design patent dichotomy is relatively straightforward, by now you should see that industrial designs could overlap with two other areas of intellectual property—copyright and trademarks.

Most countries allow an overlap between copyright and industrial designs, but in Canada, there is a special rule that removes designs of mass-produced products from copyright protection. "Mass-produced" according to Canada's *Copyright Act* means a product is made in a quantity of more than 50. The logic behind this rule is that the design of whatever is mass-produced can and should be protected as an industrial design, and if the owner of the design does not wish to protect it as such, then the owner does not deserve to have it protected at all. Another possible reason is that unlike copyrights, which are protected automatically, without the government making any money on registrations, industrial designs *must* be registered in order to be protected—for a fee.

Whatever the reasons, in Canada, if you haven't registered the designs of your mass-produced products as industrial designs, you have no protection. This means that anyone can use your design and there is nothing that you can do about it.

The other possible area of overlap is trademarks. The perfect example is the shape of the *Coca-Cola* bottle. As you will learn, the lifespan of an industrial design is very short, while trademarks can last forever. If you're asking, *"Why would anyone want to register industrial designs if the same thing can be protected as a trademark?"*—go back to the chapter on trademarks and read what it means to use something *as a trademark*. Unless you are using the design to allow customers to tell your products and services from the identical or similar products and services of everyone else, you are not using it as a trademark, so you cannot claim trademark protection over the design.

Coca-Cola used the shape of the bottle religiously to make sure that consumers recognized it among all other manufacturers of carbonated soft drinks. But not all designs are used like that. For example, Christmas decorations or shapes of car parts are rarely used as trademarks. This is when you want to protect the design as such, not just the mental association between the design of the product and the product's manufacturer.

WHAT INDUSTRIAL DESIGNS DO NOT PROTECT

There are a number of important things that cannot be protected as industrial designs. Some of the things that cannot be protected through industrial design can be covered by other methods of protection though.

FUNCTIONAL ELEMENTS

As you've already learned, industrial designs don't protect the functional elements of a product's appearance. If the design is dictated by the function of the product, then it does not meet the requirements for industrial design protection.

For example, if the handle of a cup was designed so that it doesn't get hot or so that it causes less strain on your fingers, then you can't protect the shape of the handle with an industrial design because your design goes to the functionality. The only way to protect functionality is through getting a traditional utility patent. And yes, utility patents are much harder to obtain.

On the other hand, if you design the handle of your cup to look like an armadillo, which has nothing to do with functionality but everything to do with the looks, then the design could be protected as an industrial design.

WHY CAN'T I USE INDUSTRIAL DESIGN?

The reasoning behind this is simple – the laws are set up this way to make sure that you don't try to get what should properly be protected by a patent (which is the most hard-to-get type of IP protection, both in terms of how much it costs and what is required to get it), through other forms of IP protection.

Judges often call this *making sure that you don't claim patent protection under the guise of the trademark or industrial design.*

INVISIBLE ELEMENTS

Industrial designs don't protect features that are invisible at the time of purchase or during normal use. This is why you can't get industrial design protection on the inside of an engine because the inside of the engine is not something you typically see when you buy a car.

Again, industrial designs are supposed to protect the looks that make the customers go *WOW!* Nobody can be impressed with the looks of what they can't see. And even if you are really impressed with the engineering of a particular part of a mechanism, it doesn't count because you only see it after you take the product apart, and in order to take something apart, you should have already bought it, at which point the industrial design protection becomes irrelevant.

METHODS, PROCESSES AND PRINCIPLES OF CONSTRUCTION

You can't get industrial design protection on processes or ways of doing things. If you come up with a new way of rounding up corners on rectangular devices, this method needs to be protected through a regular patent.

Likewise, you can't get industrial design protection on principles of constructing a product or on materials used to construct that product.

However, you can claim an industrial design over the actual designs generated using your method. Remember, just the looks, just the good looks.

ART

Even though industrial designs are just about the looks, you can't use industrial design to protect art which has a value independent of the product. For example, you can't take a photo, place it on a T-shirt and then apply for protection on the art through industrial design. The photo has a value separate from the T-shirt so the photo needs to be protected through copyright.

REQUIREMENTS FOR INDUSTRIAL DESIGN PROTECTION

The requirements for industrial design protection are lower than for regular (utility) patents, but for the most part are still higher than the requirements for trademarks and copyright.

The main requirement for industrial design protection is that the design cannot be identical or confusingly similar to a design previously published anywhere in the world or registered in Canada as an industrial design by somebody else.

For example, you can't go to Egypt, find a nice fabric design and claim it as your own in Canada. Likewise, if somebody has registered an industrial design without making it public in Canada, you still can't register it by yourself or use it.

Essentially, compared to a utility patent, design patents in Canada only have the requirement that they be new, but no usefulness or non-obviousness requirements apply.

One other thing to consider is that registration of an industrial design does not give you the monopoly over the design itself, only a monopoly over the design as it is applied to particular products that you specify in your application. For example, if you came up with a shape of a diamond ring and protect is as an industrial design, that registration will not prevent others from using the same shape for office supplies.

D IN A CIRCLE

There is another way in which Canada is different from all other countries when it comes to intellectual property laws. Here we have a special symbol that owners of industrial designs should place next to their registered designs. The symbol is a capital letter "D" in a circle with the name of the owner of the

> industrial design next to it. Because Canada is unique in using this symbol, it not only does not exist on keyboards, but also does not exist as part of any fonts that I am aware of. So don't bother looking for it. Ask your designers to hand draw one for you.
>
> All jokes aside, if you do get your industrial design registered in Canada, make sure you mark it with the D in a circle because without it, you may have limited options for defending your design.

HOW LONG DOES INDUSTRIAL DESIGN PROTECTION LAST?

In Canada, industrial design protection lasts for ten years after the registration and it takes about six to twelve months for the designs to be registered. The owner must also pay a maintenance fee after five years to keep it alive.

In the U.S., design patents last for 14 years from the date of registration with no maintenance fees.

Whatever the term of protection, it cannot be renewed or extended.

The term of protection is very short compared to pretty much all other areas of intellectual property, especially copyright. This creates a big disadvantage for Canadian businesses that develop industrial designs because according to Canadian law, the companies can't protect them through both copyright and industrial design.

In Canada, an application for industrial design protection must be filed no later than one year after the first public use of the design. However, not all countries have this grace period, so you have to be very careful about making your designs public.

WHERE ARE INDUSTRIAL DESIGNS PROTECTED?

Industrial design only protects your design in the countries where the industrial design is registered.

You may ask—how come you just said that "*I can't go to Egypt, find a nice fabric design and claim it as my own*" and a few pages later say that "*the design is only protected in the countries where it is registered*"?

There is really no contradiction there.

The former deals with whether you can *register* your design if an identical design has been used elsewhere by someone else. And the answer to that question is, *no, you can't.*

The latter deals with whether you can get away with *using* someone else's design in a country where it is not registered. And the answer to this question is, *yes, you can, unless it's protected as copyright or a trademark.*

WHAT CONSTITUTES AN INFRINGEMENT OF AN INDUSTRIAL DESIGN (WHAT CAN YOU SUE OTHERS FOR)?

During the term while your industrial design is valid, nobody can make, import, sell, rent, offer or expose for sale, or rent any products to which an identical or a very similar design has been applied. Of course, because registration of an industrial design presupposes that the protection is granted in connection with a specific type of products, it is only an infringement if your design is applied without your consent to a similar type of products.

Just like with most other areas of intellectual property, if someone is infringing on your industrial design, there are two main remedies available to you.

You can ask for an ***injunction***. This means a judge will order the defendant to stop using your design. This usually means that the defendant must stop making or selling a particular product, unless the design is changed.

The other remedy is ***damages***. The judge will order the defendant to pay money to you to compensate you for your losses from the infringement. On top of compensatory damages, the court may in some circumstances award punitive damages to punish the defendant for blatant infringements.

Please remember that damages would be unavailable to you in Canada if you didn't mark your design with the D in a circle and the defendant can prove that he didn't know and had no reasonable grounds to suspect that your design was registered.

DEFENDING AGAINST INDUSTRIAL DESIGN LAWSUITS

If someone is claiming that you are using their industrial design, there are a number of defences that you can use. Again, if you are suing someone who you think is infringing upon your industrial design rights, be prepared for the defendant attempting to use these defences against you.

I DIDN'T DO IT

If you're accused of infringing somebody else's design, the first defence is to simply deny it. You could claim that your design is sufficiently different from the one registered by the plaintiff.

Alternatively, you can claim that the products to which you apply the design are sufficiently different from the products for which the industrial design was registered.

YOU CAN'T REGISTER THAT

The next defence is that the plaintiff's design does not meet the requirements for registration. For example, you can claim the design was published by someone else before the plaintiff applied to register it. You can also claim that the design actually deals with the functionality of the product, or that it's not visible to the customers when they buy the product.

YOU'RE TOO LATE

You could claim that the design was published more than one year prior to the application for registration. There is only a one-year grace period during which you can apply to register the industrial design after you have published it. If this period has passed, then the design can't be registered.

YOU LIED

Another defence is to claim that the declaration accompanying the application for registration was false. You could claim that the design was not original.

I DIDN'T KNOW

You could also claim that you didn't know about the registration because of plaintiff failed to mark products with a D in a circle. If you go this route, you will still have to stop using the design but you wouldn't have to pay any damages.

Please remember that this symbol is only relevant to Canada. So you cannot use the argument that because there was no special sign on someone else's product, you should not have to pay damages in another country. It's not going to work.

YOU DON'T OWN IT

Another defence is that the plaintiff is not the registered proprietor or an exclusive licensee of the design. If the designer passed the industrial design to a company, the designer can't be the one to sue you for using the design. Of course, you could still get sued by the company that does own the design.

I HAVE A LICENSE

You can also argue that you had permission from the owner to use the design through a license. As with all other types of IP, it's best if you have a written agreement that clearly spells out your right to use the design, but you may use other evidence to prove that the industrial design owner agreed to let you use the design.

IT'S EXPIRED

There are actually two parts to this defence. Since the owner of the industrial design has to pay a maintenance fee five years after the initial registration, you can argue that this fee was not paid and the registration lapsed.

You can also claim that the registration has expired because more than ten years have passed.

TIME'S UP

You can also claim that the limitation period has expired. The time limit for a person to bring a lawsuit against you for industrial design infringement is three years. If you can show that the plaintiff knew or should have known about your infringement for more than three years, then the plaintiff is no longer allowed to sue you.

I THOUGHT I COULD USE IT

You can also claim that the plaintiff did something that led you to believe that the plaintiff would not object to your use of the industrial designs. You would have to show that you used the industrial design openly and that the plaintiff knew about it but didn't do anything to stop you.

ACT NOW!

I know you've been waiting for some more homework.

Here, you need to identify everything about your products that looks awesome. Then you need to honestly answer whether you have sufficient rights to use it as IP coming IN and if you have taken sufficient steps to protect it as your IP going OUT.

This table will allow you to instantly see your weak spots. Now you can mend these weak spots in the order of importance of such designs to your business. If your ability to apply a particular design is crucial to your business and you have nothing to prove that you are allowed to do it, it's a big problem. If you don't make or sell physical products, or if there is nothing special about your designs, feel free to skip this step.

Feel free to download the template for this table (as well as many other goodies) at *http://ipbook.ca/more* .

INDUSTRIAL DESIGNS		
What novel designs am I using for my business's products?		
Design	**Do I really have a right to USE the IP? If yes, how do I know I have the right to use it? (Google search? license?)**	**Do I OWN it? If yes, how am I protecting my rights? (registered as industrial design in Canada? registered as design patent in the U.S.? using D in a circle symbol? contracts?)**

YOUR REFERENCE POINT FOR INDUSTRIAL DESIGNS

	INDUSTRIAL DESIGNS (a.k.a. DESIGN PATENTS)
What's protected	the *WOW*
Definition of the protected objects	Non-functional features relating to the shape, configuration, pattern, or ornament and any combination of those features that, in a finished article, appeal to and are judged solely by the eye.
Classes of protected objects	Ornamental designs for any tangible products (not pure art and not relating to the function).
Examples	- design of a chair; - design of jewellery; - watch face plate; - pattern of a fabric.
What is needed to get protection?	The design must not be identical or confusingly similar to a design previously used anywhere in the world or registered in Canada by someone else.
What it does not protect	- functional elements of the product's appearance (can't protect a cup's handle for the function that it performs, but can protect the aesthetics of it); - features that are invisible at the time of purchase or during normal use; - processes; - principles of construction; - construction materials; - art that is of value independent of the products to which it may be applied.
Enforceable against	Anyone making or selling products to which a registered design has been applied.
What constitutes use?	Making or selling any product to which an industrial design has been applied.
What are others prohibited from doing?	

Where is the owner/ author/inventor protected?	The countries where the industrial design is registered.
Length of protection	In Canada, 10 years after the registration of the industrial design. In the U.S., 14 years after the registration of the design patent.
Can the initial period of protection be extended?	No.
Who owns the right / Who should apply for registration of the right?	Proprietor of a design. Industrial designs can be transferred to another person or company.
Do owners / authors / inventors have some rights if they do not apply for protection?	No.
What are the benefits of applying for protection?	It is the registration of an industrial design that creates protection. Without registration, unless other forms of intellectual property (notably, copyright or a trademark) cover the design, anyone can apply the design to their products.
How is the right established?	Through registration of the industrial design (issuance of a design patent) by intellectual property offices of the countries where the protection is sought.
Defences & limitations	- denial of infringement; - the plaintiff's design is not proper subject-matter for registration; - design was published more than 1 year prior to the application for registration; - the declaration accompanying the application for registration was false; - the design is not original; - defendant's lack of knowledge about registration because of plaintiff's failure to mark the products with D in a circle → injunction only remedy; - plaintiff is not the registered proprietor of the design (wrong plaintiff); - defendant had a license;

Defences & limitations (cont.)	- lapse of registration through failure to pay maintenance fees; - registration expired; and - limitation period expired (3 years).
Available remedies	- injunction; - damages (including exemplary and punitive damages); - accounting of profits; - disposal of any infringing product.
When can it be registered?	In Canada, an application must be filed no later than 1 year after the first public use of the design.
How long does the registration take?	6–12 months.
Are there mandatory maintenance fees?	Yes. To keep a Canadian registration in force for the full 10-year term, a maintenance fee of $350 must be paid before the 5th anniversary of the registration date. No maintenance fees are payable in the U.S.
Government fees relating to registration	$400 per design.
Total ballpark cost if a lawyer / trademark agent / patent agent is involved (including government fees)	$1,500–$3,000 per registration.

TRADE SECRETS:
HUSH

The magic word for trade secrets is *HUSH*. It should be pretty obvious why I'm using *HUSH* as a magic word. Trade secrets, also known as *know-how* or *confidential information,* refer to your right to prevent others from using or disseminating your confidential information without your permission.

Trade secret protection results from a combination of what you *do* and what *contracts* you enter into. You may have noticed that the next chapter of this book is dedicated to contracts. But there is something special about the contracts relating to trade secrets. You will find out what this is in just a second.

WHAT CAN BE A TRADE SECRET

Trade secrets protect know-how, confidential information, and any other information that has actual or potential commercial value as a result of it being unknown to others. Pretty much anything can be a trade secret—customer lists, recipes, business processes and systems, business plans, data related to sales performance of key sales personnel, phone sales scripts, checklists, internal policies, even new inventions for which you haven't filed a patent application.

ALWAYS COCA-COLA

Probably the most famous example of a trade secret is the recipe for *Coca-Cola.*

The original *Coca-Cola* recipe was patented in 1893 making the original formula public knowledge. When the recipe was changed, the company decided not to patent the formula again, choosing instead to keep it a secret. This way, the formula is not disclosed to the public, including Coca-Cola's competitors, and the protection does not expire with the expiration of the patent. Today, the formula is stored in a fancy vault. In fact, Coca-Cola has made its trade secrets one of its strongest marketing weapons.

People are conditioned to value something that is secret more than what is readily available to them. When they are told that the carbonated soft drink that they buy is actually made using a secret recipe that the company spent millions and millions of dollars protecting, they automatically attribute extra value to what they drink.

Ironically, I don't drink *Coca-Cola*, but I cannot help admiring the company's smart use of intellectual property to build and protect their brand.

Anything you keep confidential that gives you some sort of a competitive advantage *because* you keep it confidential can be a trade secret.

REQUIREMENTS FOR TRADE SECRET PROTECTION

As long as your secret can stay within your own head, you don't need to do much more to protect it than simply keeping it nicely tucked in there. If someone else comes up with the same idea, tough luck, but a trade secret would not have protected you against this scenario anyway.

Generally, you can't use the legal system to protect your secret until you either document it (when you write down your secret formula) or share it with someone (when you either tell your secret to someone or when you use the secret so that others can figure out what it is). Trade secret protection does not defend the actual secret. It only defends you against acts of others who might disclose or use the secret in breach of their implied or expressed obligations of confidentiality. If no one came in contact with your secrets, which by definition is only possible if you express these secrets in some form that others can perceive, then nobody owes you any obligation to keep your secrets confidential, because nobody knows what your secrets are.

So the rest of this chapter will only deal with trade secrets that you act on by using them in your business, by disclosing them to others, or by somehow documenting them.

There are four basic requirements for something to be defined as a trade secret.

YOUR SECRET HAS ACTUAL OR POTENTIAL COMMERCIAL VALUE

Not all secrets are trade secrets.

If you eat chocolate ice cream before going to bed and keep this away from your wife or your fitness trainer, most likely this secret is of no commercial value—either to yourself or to anyone who might somehow find out about it. The only exception would be if you somehow discovered that eating chocolate ice cream before going to bed does something uniquely positive to your business.

Just to be clear, secrets about bad things you may have done, even if they are capable of destroying you and your business if revealed, are still not trade secrets because your knowledge of the secret does not add anything to your bottom line.

Coca-Cola makes money selling carbonated soft drinks using their particular formula, and a huge chunk of that money comes from it being able to claim that no one else has the same recipe. This secret has actual commercial value.

You have developed a brilliant marketing strategy for your business which, if implemented, will give you a tremendous competitive advantage. But if your wealthier competitor figures it out and starts using it as well, you will lose a ton of money. This secret has potential commercial value.

Google has developed an algorithm by which it ranks websites in its search. There are thousands of people who'll tell you that they will do their best to get your website on page 1 of Google, but they don't *really* know the entire algorithm, because it's Google's trade secret. But if Bob SEOmeister tortured the algorithm out of a Google employee, then Bob would dominate the industry. This secret has both actual and potential commercial value.

WELL DEFINED

In order for something to be protected as a trade secret, it needs to be well defined. If you accuse someone of stealing your trade secret, you need to be able to properly tell what it is and also pinpoint to the judge that whoever stole your secret *knew* that it was *your secret*.

If you are entering into agreements with third parties, the information about what needs to be kept confidential has to be specific and detailed.

The trade secret can be difficult to define in a non-disclosure agreement without disclosing the secret itself, but unless you can do that in some measure, your non-disclosure agreement will be very weak.

For example, you can't simply state that, *"Whatever I'm going to tell you, you promise to keep confidential."* It won't work because if the recipient really discloses something and then you try to enforce the agreement, no court in the world is going to agree with you that the recipient really understood what they were supposed to keep secret. At the very least, you have to define the area of knowledge that pertains to the trade secret.

You must describe the subject matter of your trade secret with sufficient detail to separate it from matters of general knowledge, and to permit the recipients of your confidential information to ascertain at least the boundaries within which the secret lies.

NOT PUBLICLY KNOWN

This one should be fairly obvious. If something is already publicly known, then it can't be a trade secret. It also means that if someone does figure out your secret (through legal means) then you can no longer claim it as your trade secret.

For example, if you were somehow able to figure out the recipe for *Coca-Cola* and you did this without breaking into their vault or breaching a contract, then nothing stops you from sharing this information with the public. Once the information becomes publicly known, the recipe is no longer a trade secret.

Essentially, there are three ways how your secret can become publicly known without anybody violating your rights: you may deliberately choose to disclose the secret to the public, you may fail to take proper steps to keep your secret confidential, or someone may simply independently figure it out.

Either way, just like you can't put toothpaste back in the tube, once your secret is out, it's no longer a secret. You have no one else to blame but yourself.

Of course, the toughest pill to swallow is when somebody figures out your secret on their own. It's not unusual for us to over-value our ability to create something unique. Whenever you are choosing to protect something through a trade secret as part of your IP strategy, ask yourself—and be brutally honest—*"How difficult would it be for my competitors to figure out what my secret is if they were to analyze my products and services with a fine-tooth comb?"* Don't rely on trade secret protection unless you are sure that your secret is not easily breakable.

MUST BE KEPT SECRET BY THE OWNER

This doesn't simply mean that the owner of the trade secret should refuse to share the secret with anyone. The owner has to take clear, specific steps to ensure that the secret is kept secret. This means you need to keep things locked up, you need to have employees sign confidentiality agreements and whatever else you can do to show that you are actively trying to keep your secret safe.

For example, if you have all your secret documents lying around in your office and a cleaning lady comes by and sees those documents, takes a photograph, and publishes them on Facebook, that's it. It's no longer a secret because you didn't have a confidentiality agreement with employees, and you didn't take proper steps to keep those documents secret.

If the defendant can prove that you didn't really care to keep your secret confidential, the judge will have very little sympathy for you. Trade secrets is one of the areas where creating the better story is essential. A story about your competitor breaking into your office in a ninja suit through a window on the 28th floor is very different from a story about your competitor readily spotting your secret in a pile of documents carelessly scattered around your desk while in a business meeting with you.

WHAT CAN'T BE A TRADE SECRET?

From what you have learned in this chapter, you should be able to find the answer to this question.

Essentially, there are three large categories of what does not constitute a trade secret.

The first one is information that has no actual or potential commercial value. If it can't create a competitive advantage, it's usually not a trade secret.

The second is information that has already been disclosed or is generally known to others as long as that information didn't come through a breach of a contract. This is pretty obvious. If other people already know about it, then how could it be a trade secret?

Finally, what could qualify as a trade secret would no longer be treated as such if you squander it by failing to take reasonable steps to protect it. If your secret is as valuable as you claim it to be, you need to demonstrate to the judge that you took adequate measures to keep it to yourself. You also need to show the judge that you let anyone who might come into contact with your secret know that it is your secret and cannot be used outside some very strict boundaries.

REGISTERING TRADE SECRETS

Gotcha! Trade secrets cannot be registered.

The protection exists by virtue of the information being secret. In other words, unlike patents where the protection is granted to you in exchange for disclosing the information to the public, with trade secrets, it's the opposite. They're only protected as long as

you fully control who has access to that knowledge.

In fact, it's not technically correct to say *"the owner of a trade secret"* because trade secrets are not owned. A trade secret is controlled. You are attempting to gain or retain a competitive advantage by taking steps to limit access to your confidential information.

If you have invented something truly amazing, one of the decisions you must make as soon as possible is whether you want to disclose the invention to the public to get stronger, but shorter and more expensive, protection through the patent system or whether you will be able to capitalize on your invention while keeping it confidential. If you invented something that will retain commercial value after 20 years (the duration of patent protection) and you know that no one will decode your invention even if they come in contact with the actual products and service that your invention is embodied in, then it might be better to simply stick with trade secrets and not bother with patenting. The obvious benefits of trade secrets is that they are relatively cheap (unless you are building an insanely expensive vault), and they can last forever, or at least as long as the secret remains uncracked.

On the other hand, if your secret can be easily decoded, deciphered, cracked, or reverse engineered, then you would lose trade secret protection the moment your product hits the shelves because you have just demonstrated your failure to take reasonable steps to protect your secret.

Importantly, as you have learned in Part I of this book, you should not try to fit your overall business strategy to whichever type of IP you like better. You must always start with assessing your business strategy, and then figure out what kind of IP better suits your situation.

In other words, don't lament over the difficulties of patenting something that cannot be patented or of protecting as a trade secret that which cannot be protected as a trade secret. Your thought process should go like this: this is what I have, this is what I would like to achieve with it, what is the best way for me to get there?

WHERE ARE TRADE SECRETS PROTECTED?

The territory covered by trade secrets is essentially any country which recognizes your right to protect your confidential information. Most countries protect confidential information in some shape or form, but some of them have specific requirements that you must follow.

For example, a country might require you to mark every page of your confidential materials with a stamp saying, *Confidential Information*. If you don't do this, then it might no longer be considered to be a trade secret.

So you should look into the confidentiality requirements for each country where you are interested in protecting your information.

HOW LONG DOES TRADE SECRET PROTECTION LAST?

In theory, trade secrets can be protected for as long as the information remains unknown to the public while still being of actual or potential commercial value.

In practice, of course, very few secrets can truly stand the test of time. With time, either the secret is leaked, or the protected information simply becomes irrelevant.

What's important is that the secret serves you and your business for as long as it continues to provide you with a competitive advantage.

WHAT CONSTITUTES AN INFRINGEMENT OF A TRADE SECRET (WHAT CAN YOU SUE OTHERS FOR)?

No one who receives access to your trade secrets through an agreement with you is allowed to violate the terms of that agreement. The agreement usually includes an obligation not to use or further disclose your trade secrets other than as specified in the contract.

If you shared your trade secret with an investor and had him sign a non-disclosure agreement (NDA), and the investor blabs about it on his blog, then you can take action against that investor for disclosing your trade secrets. You can only take action against someone who received your trade secrets and only if you can show that this person knew or should have known that disclosing the information was in violation of the recipient's confidentiality obligations.

For example, if Company A discloses some information to Company B under an NDA, then Company A can enforce the terms of the non-disclosure agreement against Company B if Company B discloses that information to Company C.

However, it would be very difficult for Company A to go after Company C because Company C did not promise anything to Company A. In legal terms, this is called *privity of contract*. This concept limits your ability to enforce contracts to only those who entered into a contractual relationship with you. With trade secrets, you can take it one step further and enforce the confidentiality regime against Company C, but only if you can prove that Company C knew or must have known that the disclosure by Company B would be in breach of its obligations to Company A.

This is usually a difficult thing to prove since Company C could simply claim that they thought it was okay for Company B to give them the information. In this scenario, you are back to square one and your only remedy would be to go after Company B. If Company B has no money to pay you for your losses, you're out of luck.

A properly drafted non-disclosure agreement should cover more than just non-disclosure. A very important part of these agreements is non-use.

Let's say, you came up with an amazing new recipe and you would really like to have your favourite restaurant serve this new dish. You would also like to get something out of this deal. So you meet with the executive chef and have him sign an NDA according to which you will disclose your secret recipe. Not only do you want to make sure that the chef does not disseminate your secret further, you also want to make sure that the chef does not actually use the recipe unless you get paid.

A good NDA would cover the following aspects:

- define the secret;
- confirm that the secret is being disclosed to the recipient;
- state the purposes for the disclosure;
- explain the expectations of the disclosing party in disclosing the secret;
- set limits to how the recipient is allowed to use the secret;
- explicitly list what the recipient is not allowed to do with the secret (usually, non-use, non-disclosure, and non-competition); and
- clearly state the negative consequences that will strike the recipient if the recipient chooses to breach the contract.

> You can download a template of a one-way Non-Disclosure Agreement at *http://NiceContracts.com* .
>
> This template covers situations when you are about to disclose some confidential information to someone else for a particular purpose, and need to make sure that this information will remain confidential. You are not assuming any obligations of confidentiality, just the recipient of your confidential information.

Let's recap for a second.

Remember, at the beginning of this chapter, I said that trade secrets are a combination of what you *do* and what *contracts* you enter into?

As you can see, the *"what you do"* part is about you taking steps to protect your secrets. If you don't do certain things, you don't have anything to protect.

The contracts you enter into is *how* you are protecting your secret. The protection will really only be as good as your contract. If your contract only says that the recipient can't disclose the secret but leaves out the issue of whether the recipient can implement your secret, it is unlikely that you would be able to prevent the recipient from using your secret if the recipient diligently prevents your secret from further disclosure.

Now, let's assume you've taken all the right steps to establish that you have a trade secret, and you've entered into all the right contracts to define how your secrets are to be treated by others. What if the contract is breached?

Your remedies would be an ***injunction*** (when the judge orders the recipient to stop using or disclosing the trade secret) and ***damages*** (when the judge orders that the recipient—or a third party, if you're lucky—pay you money).

It is prudent to identify the measure of your potential losses in the non-disclosure agreement in case of breach. For example, if you specify sanctions in the contract, and the recipient *still* chooses to violate the contract, you will have a much easier argument in court as to why your secret is worth a billion dollars. But be careful. In Canada, you can't implement penalties for breach of contract into your agreement. The idea is that you are not supposed to benefit from someone violating the terms of the contract. In other words, you cannot end up better off if someone chooses to breach the contract compared to if he chose to follow it to a T.

DEFENDING AGAINST TRADE SECRET INFRINGEMENT LAWSUITS

Let's assume you are being accused of unlawful use or disclosure of somebody else's confidential information. There are a couple of defences that you can use.

THAT AIN'T A SECRET

There are a few things you can do based on what you've just learned about what it takes to have trade secret protection.

Can you prove that the secret has no actual or potential commercial value, and so is not a trade secret?

Can you prove that the information had already been publicly known?

Can you prove that the plaintiff failed to take reasonable steps to keep the information secret? For example, maybe the plaintiff disclosed this information to so many people that there was no reasonable expectation that it should remain secret.

I GOT IT FROM SOMEWHERE ELSE

The second defence is to claim that you legally obtained the information independent of the plaintiff. You could claim that you figured the secret out for yourself or someone gave you the information, but you didn't know that this was violating any confidentiality agreements.

For example, if you bought a can of *Coca-Cola*, did a chemical analysis (I wonder how many have tried and failed), and finally figured out the recipe on your own, then the company can't claim you are violating their trade secrets. You cracked their secret, but you never had an obligation not to, so it's fair game. They took the risk that they would be able to control the secret while selling the product based on it, and now the risk materialized. Oops.

YOU WEREN'T CLEAR

The third defence is to claim that the information was not defined clearly so the defendant didn't know the boundaries of what was secret and what wasn't.

If Company A tells Company B that, *"anything we might ever tell you is confidential,"* then this would not stand up in court because it's not clear enough. The agreement would be placing an unreasonable burden on Company B to figure out what information is and what information isn't confidential.

Just so you understand, most NDAs are overbroad, but it is essential for a good NDA to also contain at least *some* specifics that would catch most valuable secrets you are trying to protect. For example, instead of stating that *"anything we might ever tell you is confidential"*, it is much better to state *"the list of ingredients and the recipe of this carbonated soft drink, as well as anything else we might ever tell you, are confidential"*. You may think that the list of ingredients and the recipe would fall under the umbrella of "*anything we might ever tell you*", but you shouldn't rely on the judge being so fascinated with your story that he would allow you to get away with an NDA that is completely devoid of any specificity as to what the confidential information actually is.

TIPS AND TRICKS

There are a number of tips and tricks to ensure that your trade secrets will remain secret and be recognized by the courts as such.

KEEP IT SECRET

This should be pretty obvious. If you have something that you don't want other people to have access to, to disclose, or to use, take measures to restrict access to your secrets, and make sure that whoever has access to your secrets "knows their limit and plays within it."

Of course, the best way to protect your secret is to not share it with anybody at all, but this may not be practical if you want to implement the secret and make money.

MAKE YOUR EMPLOYEES KEEP IT SECRET

You need to ensure that your employees and independent contractors all sign agreements stating that they won't disclose your (well-defined) secrets to anybody.

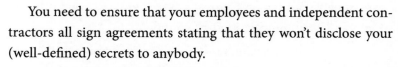

You should have policies that govern what can and cannot be disclosed and how your confidential information can be used. You should have clear guidelines for employees reflected in your employment agreements and employee manuals.

It is also crucial that you have a social media policy covering anyone who comes in contact with your business. Make sure your employees fully understand that it is inappropriate to tweet certain things that may seem like mundane updates to an employee but are, in fact, trade secrets of the company.

DON'T BITE THE HAND THAT FEEDS YOU

Connor Riley was really happy that she was offered a well-paying job at Cisco, but she was still weighing all the pros and cons of accepting it.

She summoned the wisdom of the internet and tweeted: *"Cisco just offered me a job! Now I have to weigh the utility of a fatty paycheck against the daily commute to San Jose and hating work."*

Twitter really helped her solve this dilemma because guess who didn't get the job?

One of Cisco's high-ranking employees tweeted back: *"Who is the hiring manager? I'm sure they would love to know you will hate the work. We here at Cisco are versed in the web."*

USE NON-DISCLOSURE AGREEMENTS (NDA)

Whenever you can, make sure that whoever you disclose your trade secrets to signs a non-disclosure agreement with you. The general rule is simple: the higher the risk, the more detailed your NDA should be.

For a template of a professionally drafted non-disclosure agreement, check out **http://NiceContracts.com** .

Just like with any other type of contracts, NDAs are about *"who wants whom more."*

The more valuable the thing you have to offer, the easier it will be for you to convince others to sign whatever you want them to sign.

It's easy to get your employees to sign NDAs. They want the job, so they will sign the contract. If they don't sign the contract, they don't get the job. Easy.

When it comes to talking to investors, you will have to walk a bit of a tightrope. Most investors will not want to sign an NDA until they know enough about the secret to pique their interest. You will have to disclose just enough information to hook them and then bring up signing an NDA if they want to learn more. The trick is figuring out how much is enough and how much is too much.

Investors are now very careful about signing NDAs unless they are 100% sure that the information you disclose to them will not relate in some way to what they have already been working on. Signing the NDA might jeopardize the investor's ability to continue working on something that would have been developed without your trade secrets. The investor surely does not want to let you claim that if not for your secret, the investor would never have gotten the results that he did.

So your goal is to make them want you more than you want them. You need to figure out a way to tell them as little as possible but still have them drooling to learn more about the rest of your secret. This is when you pull out your NDA and say, *"Please sign on the dotted line."*

If all you can tell the investor is, *"I think I came up with a great way for you to make a lot of money, but I can't tell you until you sign this document right here,"* don't expect to walk away with a signed NDA. In fact, it would be a miracle if the investor even deigned to explain to you why he would never, ever, sign such a document.

ACT NOW!

Guess what? More homework!

Here, you need to identify everything that has value because you are keeping it secret from your competition. Then you need to honestly answer whether you have sufficient rights to use it as IP coming IN and if you have taken sufficient steps to protect it as your IP going OUT.

This table will allow you to instantly see your weak spots. Now you can mend these weak spots in the order of importance of such secrets to your business. The more important the secret, the more serious the measures you should take to keep it confidential.

Feel free to download the template for this table (as well as many other goodies) at *http://ipbook.ca/more* .

TRADE SECRETS	
What trade secrets am I using in my business?	
Secret (know-how or confidential information)	**What formal steps did I take to protect it?**

YOUR REFERENCE POINT FOR TRADE SECRETS

	TRADE SECRETS (a.k.a. KNOW-HOW or CONFIDENTIAL INFORMATION)
What's protected	the *HUSH*
Definition of the protected objects	Any information that is confidential and gives a business an advantage because the information is kept secret.
Classes of protected objects	- know-how; - confidential information; - any other information that is valuable because it is secret.
Examples	- Coca-Cola formula; - special method for assembling a patented invention; - new invention for which patent application has not been filed.
What is needed to get protection?	Know-how must be well defined, not publicly known, and protected.
What it does not protect	Information that has become public knowledge through: - voluntary disclosure; - failure to take proper steps to protect it; - general knowledge of the public; - or any other way not related to an unauthorized disclosure such as a breach of an NDA.
Enforceable against	- the person to whom the trade secret is disclosed under the obligation of confidentiality; and - anyone who receives information from a third party, knowing that by disclosing this information such third party is violating its confidentiality obligations.
What constitutes use? **What are others prohibited from doing?**	Using or disseminating confidential information without authorization.

Where is the owner/author/ inventor protected?	Country of origin or in other countries where the contract is enforceable.
Length of protection	As long as information remains confidential and functions as a trade secret.
Can the initial period of protection be extended?	No.
Who owns the right / Who should apply for registration of the right?	Whoever controls the information owns the trade secret. No registration is available.
Do owners / authors / inventors have some rights if they do not apply for protection?	N/A
How is the right established?	Possession of information which is valuable because it is kept in secret.
Defences & limitations	- the plaintiff failed to take reasonable steps to keep the information secret; - the defendant legally obtained the information independently of the plaintiff; - the information was not defined clearly in the NDA, so the defendant cannot be deemed to have used it.
Available remedies	- injunction; - damages (including exemplary and punitive damages).
When can it be registered?	N/A
How long does the registration take?	N/A
Are there mandatory maintenance fees?	N/A

Government fees relating to registration	N/A
Total ballpark cost if a lawyer / trademark agent / patent agent is involved (including government fees)	N/A

CONTRACTUAL RIGHTS: *WHATEVER*

In Part I, you already learned that while IP may provide very strong protection, contracts are even stronger. Contracts create rights that did not exist and destroy rights that did exist.

I could mark each paragraph of this chapter with symbols, but I decided against it because this would only clutter the book. Just assume that they're there.

Unless a certain kind of transaction is prohibited by law (such as a contract where you'd hire somebody to kill your competitor), you are free to enter into *any* agreements and exchange any promises for any values. This is called *freedom of contract*. Essentially, you can voluntarily agree to pretty much *any* change of the status quo between yourself and the other party.

This is why the magic word for contractual rights is *WHATEVER*.

Again, just to make sure we're on the same page—a contract is an exchange of promises to do something that you don't otherwise have an obligation to do or promises not to do something that you otherwise have the right to do.

Some contracts *must* be in writing to be enforceable, while most others can be oral. Of course, nothing beats a properly drafted written agreement. If I had a dollar for every time a client would tell me, "*Oh, I wish we had it in writing…*"

Actually, lawyers get a lot more than a dollar from clients who didn't bother to put their agreements in writing. This is because it's much more expensive to fix the situation if you don't have a coherent document that defines mutual rights and responsibilities of both parties.

JUST FILL IN THE BLANKS

There is one thing you should realize about contracts and lawyers. You should never, never, ever, rely on a lawyer to tell you what the terms of your contract should be! Lawyers think in terms of templates. We know that we should address certain issues, but we will not decide for you how to address these issues.

A lawyer will tell you that you can expect to be paid royalties if you decide to license out your IP, but we have no idea how much you should be paid, or how often.

A lawyer must explain to you the difference between non-exclusive, sole, and exclusive licenses, but don't expect a lawyer to decide for you if you should insist on retaining the right to license out the same IP to others.

It is a lawyer's duty to point out that a trademark license should contain provisions regarding the licensor's right to control the quality of products and services offered by the licensee, but the lawyer will not know if you should request the right to inspect the licensee's plant weekly or whether the licensee's annual report should suffice.

The lawyer can help you create a customized template that will cover your particular situation, but it will still be just a template with blanks for you to fill in.

This is why it is crucial for you to have a viable IP strategy that fits your business strategy. If you approach every contract you sign from the perspective of whether or not it gets you closer to your objectives, it will be much easier for you to deal not only with the other side, but also with your own lawyer.

IMPORTANT FEATURES OF CONTRACTS

There are a number of important features to contracts that you should be familiar with.

LIMITED SCOPE

Only the persons who entered into a contract with you are bound by its terms. As you may remember from the previous chapter, this is called *privity of contract*.

For example, let's say you have a product that does not have any IP protection. You can still enter into an agreement with a manufacturer stating that the manufacturer will only produce the product for you and for nobody else. But the contract will be of little help to you if somebody else figures out how to make that product. Nothing in your agreement with your manufacturer will stop your competitor from hiring another manufacturer to make the same product.

VALID AND ENFORCEABLE

Your contract must be valid and enforceable in the country where you want the contract to be used. There are a lot of specifics in the national laws of every country that deal with contracts. You have to look at how contracts are supposed to be formed, what they are supposed to contain, and what they are not supposed to contain. You can't rely on the laws of one country when drafting an agreement in another country because these laws may be different.

In many cases, it's possible to create an agreement that will be valid and enforceable pretty much everywhere.

The general rule of thumb is, be as straightforward and detailed about your contracts as possible. The more detailed your contract is in describing the relationship that both parties agree to maintain, the easier it will be to enforce it throughout its intended territory.

The purpose of a good contract is never to trick the other party into signing something they don't want to be a party to. The purpose is to make it abundantly clear for both parties that they are about to give up something of lesser value (to them) in exchange for something of greater value. For example, when you go and buy an iPhone, Apple values the phone less than your money, while you value your money less than the phone. Otherwise, neither of you would be exchanging one for the other.

MUTUAL BENEFIT

A contract presupposes that there was a voluntary meeting of the minds between the parties (called *offer* and *acceptance*) and that both parties got something out of the deal (called *consideration*). This is why you see so many contracts where one party is paid a dollar in exchange for something that seems very valuable. It's easier to prove that you got something out of the contract if you receive money (even just a dollar) than if you receive some non-monetary benefit.

Let me be clear, this issue of proper contract formation is really too complicated for someone who does not know all the ins and outs of contract law, and I promised you that we will keep it digestible for those who have no aspirations to become lawyers. So for the purposes of this book, let's leave it at that.

Just keep in mind that not every piece of paper you sign is a contract, and that sometimes, you may have entered into a contract without signing anything.

MUTUAL UNDERSTANDING

The language of the agreement must not be ambiguous. If one party thinks that the agreement means one thing and the other party thinks that the agreement means something else, the court may find that there is no contract, and if there is no contract, we're back to the status quo.

Now this doesn't mean that the other person has to *read* the agreement for it to be enforceable. If the person didn't read it but still signed it, it's fine—the contract is still valid and enforceable. What is important is to give all parties a reasonable *opportunity* to read the agreement. If the other side chose not to read it, it's not your problem.

What matters is that the contract should not contain language that is open for different interpretations.

Of course, virtually *every* contract will have some provisions that can be interpreted in a number of ways. Whenever lawyers need to attack the validity of a contract, they will try to figure out ways to interpret the contract to mean something that matches their line of logic. As long as we use words in agreements, there will always be *some* degree of ambiguity. The lawyer's job is to minimize the inherent risks of the contract being misinterpreted.

What sets a good contract apart from a not-so-good one is that the good contract will be as clear as humanly possible and, more importantly, it will provide enough benefits to all parties so that they will not want to question its validity.

WHAT YOU NEED TO KNOW ABOUT SOME TYPES OF CONTRACTS

Even though contracts can cover an almost infinite scope of issues, we will only focus on contracts that deal with your ability to create or retain a competitive advantage derived from products of the human mind, whether or not they are intellectual property. Out of the myriad of things you can agree on, these are the most important when it comes to *Protecting Your*

Ideas and Covering Your Assets:

- you acquiring a license from someone to use their IP;
- you buying someone's IP outright;
- you granting someone a license to use your IP;
- you selling your IP outright;
- you agreeing to jointly use IP with somebody else;
- you agreeing with somebody else as to who owns what IP;
- you agreeing to keep someone's information confidential in exchange for learning and using it in your business;
- you sharing your trade secret with someone else in exchange for a fat cheque;
- you getting someone's promise not to compete with you;
- you getting someone's promise not to poach your employees or customers; and
- you getting someone's promise not to use your stuff in a particular way, even if it's not otherwise enforceable.

Most agreements contain a combination of these various promises. In fact, mixing and matching elements from an assortment of single-issue templates is how lawyers create customized agreements for their clients. We use them as building blocks.

The purpose of this section is to highlight a few important issues about different types of agreements that have to do with IP. The list is certainly not exhaustive, and this chapter is not meant to serve as an instruction manual for do-it-yourself contracts.

As with the rest of the book, the purpose is not to overload you with information but to draw your attention to a couple of things, here and there, in order to let you make timely decisions as to *when* you should see your lawyer and have him address the arrangements that best reflect your IP strategy.

SHAREHOLDER/PARTNERSHIP AGREEMENTS

These agreements are the foundation of your business. Even though they usually cover a lot of ground, one issue commonly left out is who owns what IP and what happens to the IP on the dissolution of the company.

Let's say you are a typical software startup. There's just two of you—a biz person and a tech person. The tech person will code night and day, and the biz person will set up a system to convince the masses to buy your company's product. At some point, you decide to incorporate the business and become equal founding shareholders. Question: who owns the code?

Another question: what happens if you find an investor and the investor also gets shares in the company—will the investor get a stake in the IP after the company is dissolved?

One thing to consider: just because you own shares in a company does not mean that you own the company's assets. You don't. The company owns the assets. All you have is a stake in the capital of the company entitling you to a share of the company's profits while the company is still functioning and to a part of the company's worth upon its liquidation.

If a company owns the IP and is dissolved, then the IP does not revert to the previous owners. It gets distributed among all creditors of the company.

So the usual dilemma is, "*Do we dump the IP into the company or do we own the IP as individuals and license it to the company?"* Both options have their pros and cons.

The big advantage of licensing is that it is easy to control the ownership of the IP on dissolution. The default rules are that once the licensee ceases to exist, the license terminates, and all rights revert back to the licensor.

The disadvantage of licensing is that a license is just a permission to use something. The company doesn't own it. This means two things: the company's valuation is lower and there is less certainty that the license will remain in force in case of a dispute between the co-founders.

The advantage of the company owning the IP outright is that you no longer need to deal with individuals and their whims. Once the company owns it, it owns it. It's a lot easier to lure an investor by giving him a share in the company that owns the IP which makes the company special, rather than by giving him a share in the company that owns nothing but a license from a bunch of people who have never experienced what it means to grow a business from 5 to 8 figures. Remember, the worst disputes *always* start with the best friendships.

The disadvantage of the company owning the IP is that individuals no longer control their IP. It becomes an asset of the company, just like office chairs and bank accounts. When the company is sold or is dissolved, you don't get your IP back. You only get the remaining value of what the company owns after all the creditors have been paid.

Every case is different, but this is certainly something that you should consider when you are starting a company that will have more than just you involved in it.

AGREEMENTS WITH EMPLOYEES AND INDEPENDENT CONTRACTORS

You learned this in Part I—just because you pay someone to create IP for you, does not make it yours.

It is important to make sure that everything you pay others to create for your business becomes the asset of your business.

If someone had already created something for you but you don't have anything in writing that confirms your ownership in the IP, do your best to go back to them and secure such ownership by having them sign an *after-the-fact assignment*. This may cost you something, but if the IP is crucial to your business, it will cost you a lot more if you don't have the document.

LICENSE AGREEMENTS

A license is simply a permission to do something that you wouldn't normally have the right to do without it.

You may remember the example we discussed in the chapter related to copyright about a guest you have over to your house whom you allow to stay overnight. Essentially you've granting her a license to do something which without the license would have been considered trespassing. You don't have to have an agreement in writing even though staying at your house is something she would not be allowed to do without your permission.

In the world of IP, a license does the same thing—it allows someone to use IP in ways that without the license would constitute an infringement.

There are three types of licenses depending on the freedom of the licensor to grant further licenses to others: non-exclusive, sole and exclusive.

A *non-exclusive license* permits the licensee to use the IP as set out in the agreement, but the licensor is free to use the IP himself and to give out licenses to anyone else, including your competitors. Every time you pay someone to create IP for you and *don't* have a written agreement that confirms your ownership in it, the courts will usually imply that you have a license to use what was created for you.

The license will be limited to the purposes which were apparent to the person who created the IP for you at the time they delivered the work. In all cases, this implied license will be *non-exclusive*, meaning that the website design you paid for without a written agreement may be resold to your competitor, effectively destroying the purpose of creating your distinctive online presence.

A *sole license* permits the licensee to use the IP as set out in the agreement, while the licensor remains free to use the IP himself. However, the licensor cannot give any more licenses to others, thus making the licensee the only person other than the licensor who can use the IP. When entering into such licenses, it is important to establish whether the licensor had already granted non-exclusive licenses to others. In other words, if the licensor had granted non-exclusive licenses to 10 other people before he granted you the sole license, you would not be able to prevent the other 10 people from using the IP. All it means is that the licensor would not be able to grant *further* licenses.

An *exclusive license* permits the licensee to use the IP as set out in the agreement, and the licensor cannot give any more licenses to others or to use the IP himself, thus making the licensee the only person who can use the IP. Again, same as with sole licenses, the exclusivity only works going forward, so if you are looking for true exclusivity, make sure you get the licensor to guarantee that the IP had never been licensed to anyone but you.

Another important aspect of licenses is whether they can be sublicensed further. Unless the license states that the licensee can grant further sublicenses, the license is only meant for the particular licensee named in the license agreement. What this means is that if a non-transferrable license was granted to you and you want to sell the business, then the buyer of your business will not have the right to use the IP. All of this will certainly be discovered during a due diligence and may not only reduce the value of your company, but even prevent the deal from going forward at all.

Just like with any written agreement, you should try to be as detailed as possible in describing how the licensee can and cannot use the IP. The laws of some jurisdictions contain certain requirements as to what can and cannot be contained in the license agreement, but the more detailed you are in explaining what the relationship is supposed to be, the better off you will be.

Other important aspects of license agreements are the territory for which the license is granted and the term. Typically, if you don't mention the territory, courts will assume that the territory of the grant is limited to the territory of the country where the licensee resides. But don't count on it—make sure to explicitly specify which countries (or even parts of the countries) are covered by the license.

As for the term, the licensee will no longer have the right to use the licensed IP after the termination of the license. In order to avoid disputes, make sure to state that term explicitly, even if it's "forever". Also, if it's not "forever" (or, as lawyers say, *in perpetuity*), make sure to address the issue of whether the licensee can finish selling the products made using your IP after the expiration of the license or whether the expiration of the license also cuts off the right of the licensee to distribute what's left in stock.

ASSIGNMENT AGREEMENTS

Assignment agreements are different from license agreements because you're not simply giving (or getting) permission to use your IP; you are selling it to (or buying it from) a third party. Once you assign your IP, it's no longer yours. The buyer (assignee) owns it outright.

Usually, assignment is forever, but some countries allow the assignment to be for a specified term. Either way, during the term of the assignment, the assignee can do whatever he wants with the IP unless the assignment agreement contains some limitations.

It's not that unusual to have an assignment agreement with a reverse license where you assign something to a third party but then that third party licenses it back to you. This way you continue to have the right to use your IP, but you no longer own it.

CONFIDENTIALITY/NON-DISCLOSURE AGREEMENTS

We have discussed these in the chapter that dealt with trade secrets. You enter into this agreement to ensure that those to whom you choose to disclose your trade secrets don't use or disclose such confidential information other than on certain conditions.

As noted earlier, you need to ensure that these agreements are as detailed as possible.

NON-COMPETE AGREEMENTS

This type of contract helps to ensure that your employees and independent contractors do not quit and open their own business that will compete with you.

Courts are very cautious about this type of agreement because they want to make sure that your non-compete agreement does not impose unreasonable limitations on the ability of your counterpart to make a living.

For example, if you hire a photographer to take photographs of all 3 employees in your business, you can't reasonably expect a court to enforce an agreement stating the photographer, whom you paid a whopping $500, cannot take any photographs for five years anywhere in the world. The enforceability of the non-compete agreement generally depends upon the extent to which you limit the other party's ability to make a living.

If your non-compete clause contains reasonable limitations as to the duration, geographical area, and specific areas of the business, courts will be more likely to uphold it.

An important function of non-compete clauses is deterrence. Someone who has signed one will be less likely to violate it even if you could not enforce it in court.

You may find it strange coming from a lawyer, but I understand that nobody likes to go to court. It takes away from your ability to do something productive. So unless your non-compete clause is absolutely outrageous, most likely your former employee or independent contractor will abide by it.

Granted, there is no guarantee that this clause will always work as planned (so don't rely on it as a magic potion), but one thing I can say for sure: if you don't have this clause in your agreement, you will definitely not be able to enforce it.

WEBSITE TERMS OF USE

These agreements are important when your website has a lot of interaction between your company, your employees, and visitors. This is especially important if you allow your visitors to upload things like images, photographs, videos, links, comments, or music to your website, and becomes absolutely crucial if these things become available to the public.

It's easy to find free Terms of Use and Privacy Policy generators on the web. While they are great for simple non-interactive websites, you need to look elsewhere if you are building a business with your website.

There are two reasons to have proper Terms of Use on your website. First of all, they allow you to establish who owns what and who can use what on your website. Secondly, they allow you to limit your liability in case something goes wrong. If someone posts an image about how delicious rat poison is, and some moron decides to taste it, you don't want to be held responsible for not having removed the image from your website the second it was posted there.

PROMISES, PROMISES

It is possible to use contracts to create *any* positive or negative obligations. A positive obligation is when a party promises to do something, while a negative obligation is when a party promises not to do something.

One smart way of using contracts to cement your competitive advantage is by limiting those who make something for you promise that they won't be making similar things for others.

For example, if you have an invention that is not patentable and is easy to figure out, you can still gain some protection by entering into an agreement with the manufacturer stating that they will not produce whatever you came up with for anyone else.

The contract places an obligation on the manufacturer who would otherwise have the right to do anything they wanted with your unprotected invention. Now they will be in breach of the

contract if they make it for somebody else.

This gives you the head start necessary to build and protect your first-to-market advantage.

Be careful, however. Because of the concept of privity of contract, you will not be able to sue other manufacturers who may figure out how your stuff works on their own. So don't rely on your contract with the manufacturer as a panacea for stopping your competition.

WHERE ARE CONTRACTUAL RIGHTS PROTECTED?

The territory covered is whatever the contract says, provided that it would be enforceable there. You can define the territory to include or exclude any part of the world that you want.

For example, if you enter into a contract to license your copyright to a company and the contract states that the license only extends to Bangladesh and North America with the exception of the Province of Quebec, then the territory covered by the contractual rights is Bangladesh and North America with the exception of the Province of Quebec. The company could not use your copyright in Europe, since the license does not cover it, and you can't use the copyright without a license.

HOW LONG DO CONTRACTUAL RIGHTS LAST?

Similar to the territory covered by contractual rights, the length of protection is whatever term is agreed on in the contract. You could agree that the contract would be in force for one year, five years, ten years, or twenty thousand years. The length of time is completely up to the parties entering into the contract.

An important section of a properly drafted contract is conditions for termination. Make sure your contract contains a list of circumstances which will result in the termination of the contract if they occur. Make sure you fully understand the consequences of such termination.

It is important to understand that the term of the contract may be different from the term of the grant of IP.

For example, you may have made an agreement to get paid a lump sum for granting the license today and are not to receive any royalties in the future. The contract is fully performed when you granted the license and got paid. But the license is still ongoing. Likewise, in case of IP assignments, once you sell your IP, it's gone. Just because there are no more contractual relationships between you and the assignee does not mean that the IP will revert back to you.

Alternatively, an agreement can last longer than the grant of IP. A good example of that would be if you license your intellectual property out for three years, but include a non-disclosure provision for an extra five years.

If all parties agree, then you can always change the term of an agreement by amending the contract.

Finally, agreements often have provisions dealing with renewals and automatic renewals. Make sure that you read those carefully.

REGISTERING CONTRACTUAL RIGHTS

You don't typically need to register contractual rights unless the contract deals with transfer of registered IP. For example, if you are assigning a registered trademark, you would need to record the assignment with the Trademark Office.

If the contract does not deal with registered IP, then all you need to do is make sure you retain your copy of the agreement and that you monitor the other party's performance under the agreement.

WHAT CONSTITUTES A BREACH OF CONTRACT (WHAT CAN YOU SUE OTHERS FOR)?

A breach of contract occurs every time a party does not fulfill its obligations under the contract, whatever they might be.

This is what makes contracts so powerful. An enforceable contract has the power of law for the parties that enter it.

If someone is infringing on your contractual rights, the two main penalties that are imposed are similar to the penalties imposed for all intellectual property violations: ***injunction*** (when the judge orders the losing party to do or not to do something) and ***damages*** (when the judge orders the losing party to pay something to the winning party).

Also, contracts may have some custom remedies built into it, and as long as those remedies are reasonable, the courts will generally enforce them.

DEFENDING AGAINST BREACH OF CONTRACT LAWSUITS

If you are accused of violating the terms of a contract, there are a few possible defences that you can use.

Here they are:

WHAT CONTRACT? THERE WAS NO CONTRACT!

If you can prove that the contract had never been entered into, then there was nothing you could have breached. No new rights have been created and no existing rights have been destroyed.

I already mentioned that the rules of contract formation may seem too convoluted for a non-legal book, so I won't get into it.

Remember that just because the other side says you breached a contract does not mean that there *actually was* a contract. This issue can easily be a deal-breaker.

THE CONTRACT IS INVALID

OK, let's say that there was a contract. The next line of defence is to try and prove that the contract is invalid or unenforceable.

An invalid contract is as good as no contract. Yes, you signed something. But it contains some provisions that cannot legally be contained in an agreement, so the entire thing flies out of the window.

Even if a contract is not invalid, the court may refuse to enforce some of its provisions. This usually happens with non-compete provisions. For example, if you are sued for violating a non-compete provision in your contract, you could argue that the provision in the contract is too broad and restrictive, and as a result, it is not enforceable.

If the judge agrees with you and finds that the provision is invalid or unenforceable, then you're not liable. That's the end of the dispute.

I DIDN'T THINK YOU'D CARE

Another defence is when the plaintiff did something to make you believe that the plaintiff will not enforce its legal right against you.

If you have openly been doing something for a long time and the plaintiff knew about it and chose not to take action, then the plaintiff will no longer be able to go back and claim damages for your violation.

Many contracts have special provisions to address this issue. They are called a *"no-waiver clause"* and their purpose is to state that *any* violation of the contract remains a violation even if the non-breaching party chooses to ignore a particular case of breach by the other party. If your contract contains such a clause, this defence will likely be unavailable to you.

STANDARD IP AGREEMENT TEMPLATES

I have already mentioned the web page where I make available templates for several commonly used agreements dealing with intellectual property: ***http://NiceContracts.com*** .

I created these templates after going through hundreds of agreements I have drafted and revised over my long legal career. Now you can use them at a fraction of the cost of having a lawyer draft a customized agreement just for you. This way, you get a very detailed contract without an intimidating price tag.

At the time of this writing, the page contains templates for:

- **Content Creation Agreement** (covering situations when you are about to hire someone to create some content for you. The contract makes sure that you will end up owning all IP in the content, that whatever confidential information you will disclose to the contractor will remain confidential, and that the contractor will not create something very similar for your competitors);

- **After-the-Fact Copyright Assignment Agreement**
  (covering situations when you paid a contractor to
  create some content for you, and you realize that it
  is the contractor, not you, who owns the IP in the
  content. The contract will confirm that you own all
  rights in such content);

- **One-Way Non-Disclosure Agreement** (covering
  situations when you are about to disclose some
  confidential information to someone else for a
  particular purpose, and need to make sure that this
  information will remain confidential. You are not
  assuming any obligations of confidentiality, just the
  recipient of your confidential information).

I plan to add more templates to this page. So check it out regularly.

ACT NOW!

And finally, more homework.

Here, you need to identify the contracts you entered into or
should have entered into in order to deal with IP coming IN and
IP going OUT.

This table will allow you to instantly see your weak spots. Now
you can mend these weak spots in the order of their importance
to your business.

Feel free to download the template for this table (as well as
many other goodies) at ***http://ipbook.ca/more*** .

CONTRACTS	
Am I using contracts to protect my ideas and cover my assets?	
Contract Type	**Does my contract clearly state in writing who owns what IP? If not, what will I do about it?**
Partnership / shareholder agreement	
Agreements whereby someone creates something for me (web design, logo, marketing materials, etc.)	
Agreements with my employees	
Agreements whereby I allow someone else to use my IP	
Agreements whereby I sell my IP to someone else	
Confidentiality agreements	
Non-compete agreements	
Website terms of use	

YOUR REFERENCE POINT FOR CONTRACTUAL RIGHTS

	CONTRACTUAL RIGHTS
What's protected	the *WHATEVER*
Definition of the protected objects	Permission to do something that one would not otherwise be allowed to do or obligation not to do something that one would otherwise be allowed to do.
Classes of protected objects	- license; - assignment of intellectual property rights; - non-disclosure provisions; - non-competition provisions; - other positive and negative obligations.
Examples	- license to use a song in a game; - permission to use confidential information; - obligation not to make copies of software; - obligation not to work for competitors; - promise not to disclose confidential information.
What is needed to get protection?	The contract must be valid and enforceable.
What it does not protect	No protection against unauthorized acts of unrelated third parties.
Enforceable against	The counterparty to the agreement.
What constitutes use? / What are others prohibited from doing?	Violating the terms of the contract, whatever they are.
Where is the owner/ author/inventor protected?	Depending on enforceability of the contractual provisions in different jurisdictions.
Length of protection	For the term agreed upon in the contract.
Can the initial period of protection be extended?	By amending the contract.

Who owns the right / Who should apply for registration of the right?	Whoever is the beneficiary of the other party's obligation. No registration is generally available.
Do owners / authors / inventors have some rights if they do not apply for protection?	Yes. The parties may rely on the contract.
What are the benefits of applying for protection?	N/A
How is the right established?	Entering into a contract, written or oral.
Defences & limitations	- contract or provision invalid or unenforceable; - acquiescence / estoppel (plaintiff's conduct that leads the defendant to believe that the plaintiff will not enforce its legal right against the defendant).
Available remedies	- injunction; - damages (including exemplary and punitive damages).
When can it be registered?	N/A
How long does the registration take?	N/A
Are there mandatory maintenance fees?	N/A
Government fees relating to registration	N/A
Total ballpark cost if a lawyer / trademark agent / patent agent is involved (including government fees)	N/A

PART III

PUTTING IT ALL TOGETHER

In Parts I and II, I have done my best to provide you with digestible information about intellectual property and the law in general.

Of course, it's not enough for you to go and argue your case in front of a judge, or to draft your own contracts. That was not my goal.

My goal was to equip you with enough knowledge about intellectual property to enable you to timely identify situations when you need to see an IP lawyer and to be able to ask educated questions without intimidation.

In Part III, we will put everything together—not just a summary of what you've learned in the book, but how to apply it to your particular business.

So by now, you know that IP is just an umbrella term that covers several areas of law that are substantially different from each other (the specifics are covered in Part II of the book).

You also know that you should pay attention not only to protecting your own IP from being stolen, but also to ensuring that you don't use a third party's IP without permission if that IP is crucial to your business.

Whenever you plan to ask a lawyer about whether you can do something, remember that the lawyer will probably be answering the question of whether something is legal, not whether you can get away with it. It's all about risk management. If you are not willing to hear the lawyer's typical response of, "*It depends*," make sure you word your question properly.

The first thing you should do is set aside a couple of hours when nobody will disturb you, and go through the questions listed in Part I under the *IP Strategy Review* section. Seriously, take a pen and paper, your laptop, your desktop computer, your tablet—

whatever you want to use. Just do more than simply read the questions—answer them. And be brutally honest with yourself.

Then, make sure to fill out the tables found under the *Act Now!* sections of this book. Again, you can download them, as well as many other goodies, at ***http://ipbook.ca/more*** .

Now, with everything you've learned from the book, you should be able to figure out how to make sure your IP strategy fits your overall business strategy.

First, figure out whether the structure you selected for your business fits your goals. Incorporate your company if necessary.

Second, look at the list of third party IP that is crucial to your business. If you realize that the use of someone's IP is crucial for your business, make sure you get a license that would be broad enough to cover you in good times and in bad times.

Make sure the people you hire to do the work for you sign contracts that would give you ownership over all the IP they create for you.

Finally, look at how you can protect your competitive advantage using intellectual property rights.

Remember the process you went through when we discussed whether you should patent your inventions?

So when you come up with something new and unique, ask yourself:

1. Is it valuable?
2. If it is valuable, can I protect it by any means other than a patent?
3. If I can't protect it other than through a patent, is it patentable?
4. If it's patentable, is it *really-really-really* valuable?

> If it's patentable and really-really-really valuable, find the money and file for the patent. Otherwise, don't bother.

5. If you're not patenting it, can you protect at least some part of it as a trade secret?

> If you can protect it as a trade secret, make sure you institute measures sufficient to keep your confidential information secret.

How important is your brand to you? If it adds to your bottom line or if rebranding would be a serious problem, protect your brand by registering trademarks.

If you are selling a physical product, consider protecting its looks as industrial design and maybe a trademark.

Now you know that the initial protection offered by IP laws is just the beginning. The important play starts with you signing the right contracts and taking the right steps to protect your rights.

Once you know what your goals are—both from the general business perspective and from the IP perspective, it's time to see a lawyer. But don't let the lawyer press you into buying services you don't need.

I cannot emphasize this strongly enough: make sure that the lawyer's advice is in line with your strategy.

Share your vision with the lawyer. Let him see how the services you are ordering fit in with your overall strategy.

And be bold enough to ask the lawyer how his advice gets you closer to your overall goal if you don't readily understand it. Don't buy into the usual *nice-to-have*'s that lawyers are so quick to offer. Don't ask "*Why should I do it?*" Ask "*How will it help me accomplish this particular goal?*" There might be many good reasons to do certain things, but these reasons may not all be relevant to you and your business.

CASE STUDY

Let me illustrate how what you have learned in this book can be applied to a specific example. Just in case I need to make this clear, it is a *made-up* story. All characters appearing in it are fictitious. Any resemblance to real persons or companies is purely coincidental.

Let's say, Tom Techguy comes up with an algorithm to spot good real estate opportunities by looking through ads on Jakelist, a very popular website displaying free classified ads. Tom shares his light bulb moment with Bob Bizhead, who seems genuinely interested in turning this idea into a multi-million dollar business.

Tom and Bob verbally agree that Tom will be writing all the code, and Bob will deal with marketing and promotion. Bob will also deal with the business aspects of the venture. They agree that Bob will invest $10,000 of his own money into this business, and after that the parties will share the costs equally. The profits will also be divided equally between Tom and Bob.

They come up with a name for their startup, "Jakelist Invest", which they both think is a great name because it clearly tells the customers what the startup is about.

While Tom is writing the code, Bob pays $500 to Linda Logogal to develop the logo for Jakelist Invest and $2,500 to Donna Designdiva to create a website. Out of the $2,500, Donna pays $250 to Philip Photodude to take headshots of both Bob and Tom. As an additional expense, Bob pays $2,000 to Vinnie Videographberg, who creates a 2-minute video about Jakelist Invest.

Bob also spends $5,000 to participate in a Las Vegas startup conference where he speaks on stage about Jakelist Invest for five minutes to almost 2,000 people.

The website starts getting traction and attracts the first 50 paying subscribers. The money is not huge, but it's something. Bob projects that the startup will make $90,000 by the end of the year.

Luckily, Bob comes across this book and reads it from cover to cover, taking notes and spending the time necessary to fill out the homework exercises.

He invites Tom to sit down and go over Jakelist Invest's strategy.

He takes out several sheets of paper, draws a huge IPSR Quadrant on each of them, and they start filling out the quadrants.

Here's what they come up with:

WHO

Currently, we have the worst form of business imaginable—a partnership without a written partnership agreement. If something goes wrong, Bob may lose his house and his yacht, so we agree to set up a corporation.

Tom and Bob will be the only two shareholders of the company, and will both own 50% of its voting shares.

The name *Jakelist Invest* is problematic because it uses the *JAKELIST* trademark owned by Jakelist Corporation. Even if we can convince the corporate office to register our company as *Jakelist Invest Inc.*, we will run into problems with Jakelist over this name in the future. We decided to rename the company and the product to *BobTom Invest* and call the company *BobTom Invest Software Inc.* We didn't find similar names when we searched Google,

NUANS, and trademark databases. We got our free trademark search report from Trademark Factory at http://freeTMsearch.com—and it came out clean! Also bobtominvest.com and bobtominvest.ca are both available. We registered bobtom and bobtom invest usernames on Facebook, LinkedIn, YouTube and Yelp.

WHAT

The business will offer subscribers the convenience of being notified of good investment opportunities that we will identify using our unique algorithm.

Our target audience is anyone who has enough money to make real estate investments. They will find out about us through our social media efforts. We will lead them to our website at bobtominvest.com.

Then word of mouth will build up so people will just be searching for "bobtom".

The plan is to build this into a $1M business within 2 years and a $3M business within 5 years. We'll see if we can sell the company to a big fish at that point.

We'll be using information posted by third parties on Jakelist, so we need to protect ourselves by limiting our liability. This way, we have to let people know we're using Jakelist. On the other hand, we think that it would be difficult for people to crack our algorithm, which is really something special.

While all these deals are available to everyone on Jakelist, our service will make it a lot simpler to make correct investment decisions. This is what makes it unique.

IN

This is the IP that came IN:

Object	Who created	Dependency in %
Algorithm	Tom Techguy	100% (If we can't use the algorithm, there is nothing we can sell)
Website	Donna Designdiva	30% (It's a good website, but we could still have a business with a different one)
Jakelist Invest Logo	Linda Logogal	0% (we decided to no longer use the word *Jakelist* in the name, see below)
Photos	Philip Photodude	10% (we can always take new ones)

Videos	Vinnie Videographberg	15% (we need to redo them because of the new name)
Marketing materials and social media posts	Bob Bizhead	35%
Original posts on Jakelist website	Each individual JL user. Also JL owns the engine that makes the posts available.	80% (Maybe we could figure out a way to use the algorithm for other data, but it would be difficult).

Let's see what's copyrightable here:

Works	Do I really have a right to USE?	Do I OWN it?
The actual software based on Tom's algorithm	YES but Tom will need to assign this to the company.	YES, assuming Tom assigns it to the company.

Website	YES. We paid for the website.	NO. Our agreement does not state that we own the design. Will need to talk to Donna.
Logo	Does not matter. Need the new one. Also, we checked TinEye, and it looks like Linda copied our logo from another one. We should not hire her ever again.	Does not matter. Need the new one.
New logo	Will need to make sure to sign proper agreement.	Will need to make sure to sign proper agreement.
Photos	Not sure. We haven't seen the agreement with Philip.	NO. Our agreement with Donna does not mention photos, and we don't have a direct contract with Philip.

Video	YES. We paid Vinnie. If he's reasonable about the contract, we should probably hire him to redo the video for the new name.	NO. We need a written agreement with Vinnie or the new videographer.
Marketing materials and social media posts	YES, but Bob will need to assign this to the company.	YES, assuming Bob assigns it to the company.
Original posts on JL website	NO. Jakelist terms specifically prohibit using scrapers to collect information from Jakelist without a proper license. THIS IS CRITICAL!!! Try to get a license. If can't get a license, see a lawyer to find out if we can get away with not getting a license.	NO. It's their IP. We don't even have the right to use them.

What about trademarks?

Mark	Do I really have a right to USE?	Do I OWN it?
Bobtom Invest	We came up with it. Does not look like it's been used by others.	If we can get a license from Jakelist for the use of their data, we should probably register the trademarks in both Canada and the U.S.
Jakelist Invest	No. We'll run into issues with Jakelist.	No. Because the mark uses the word Jakelist. It's unlikely that we will get their permission

What about patents?

Invention	Do I really have a right to USE?	Do I OWN it?
Tom's algorithm	Need to conduct a proper patent search to confirm that we are not using a patented algorithm.	Probably not a good idea to patent. Costs too much, takes too long, and we'd need to disclose the algorithm.

Industrial designs? Not selling any physical products. Probably irrelevant.

Trade secrets:

Secret	Steps to protect
Tom's algorithm	Maybe Bob should not have made the presentation in Las Vegas, because he might have disclosed too much.

Contracts:

- First of all, need to get Jakelist's permission to use their website and posts;
- Assuming that we can proceed, will need to write an agreement between Bob and Tom to confirm who owns what, who pays for what, and how profits are divided;
- Assuming that we can proceed, we need to have Donna sign an agreement assigning all rights to the website to our corporation. Otherwise, have someone else redesign the website with a proper agreement;
- Assuming that we can proceed, we need to have a designer create a new logo and make sure the designer does not steal stuff from Google Images and that we own the logo design;
- We need detailed Terms of Service for the website.

OUT

Assuming that we can proceed, these are the things we would like to protect:

- Algorithm (institute measures for keeping it secret. Watch the video of Bob's speech in Vegas to make sure the secret has not been disclosed);
- We need to make sure our data cannot be scraped off our website (Terms & Conditions + Tom will write anti-scraper code);
- Trademark our name and logo in Canada and the States. Use TM next to name and logo for now.

After they go through this process, it becomes clear that taking further steps to grow the business without figuring out whether their use of Jakelist's website constitutes an infringement is not a smart idea. If they continue the way things are now, they will be building a business on bad foundations. Businesses built on bad foundations will fail. They realize that as soon as their business starts making serious money, Jakelist will notice and shut them down.

So they send an email to Jakelist's general mailbox requesting a license, but do not get a response.

Realizing that they are going to need some help, Bob and Tom go to see an IP lawyer. They bring their IPSR papers with them to show the lawyer. The lawyer is both stunned and pleasantly surprised to see them so prepared.

Bob asks, *"We understand that as soon as we are in the money, we will attract the wrath of Jakelist. What's the worst thing that can happen if we carry on with what we want to do without a license?*

And what are the odds of it happening?"

The lawyer looks over their business model and tells them that the business will risk all of its profits and maybe even more by implementing their plan. The lawyer also tells them that their risk is substantial.

The lawyer suggests sending a letter to Jakelist on Bob and Tom's behalf seeking a license to use Jakelist's data. The lawyer drafts the letter and sends it to Jakelist. Soon, the lawyer gets a response, but unfortunately, Jakelist is not willing to grant them a license.

Bob decides that he does not wish to take the risk of building a business that can easily be taken away from him.

He thinks about this for several weeks. And he comes up with a new plan. He says, *"The only problem with the original plan was that we have some IP coming IN that we don't own and over which we have no control. The algorithm is still very valuable. Maybe we can release software that will analyze and compare data that users themselves will enter. Where they find it is none of our business. If they find it on Jakelist—fine. If they find it through MLS listings— fine. If they find it elsewhere—fine. This way we don't depend on Jakelist. Yet, we can provide a huge benefit by using the algorithm, because it will be able to suggest which investments are good and which are not. We will still need to have all sorts of disclaimers and limitation of liability clauses, but at least this is something that we can pull off!"*

Tom thinks it's a good idea.

This time, they *start* with setting up a corporation. Tom assigns the algorithm to the company.

Tom and Bob then visit the lawyer again. This time they re- quest that the lawyer conduct a patent search for them. They did one themselves but felt they needed help conducting the search to ensure that there would be no surprises later on. The search by the lawyer confirms that they will not be infringing any patents if they sell their software or operate their website.

Bob and Tom then begin to develop a new logo which takes their new business model into account. They download the standard agreement templates from **http://NiceContracts.com** and, with a few little tweaks, have them signed by the new logo designer. They also ask Donna to redo the website and to sign the proper Content Creation Agreement. Philip agrees to sign the After-the-Fact Copyright Agreement for the photographs he took of Bob and Tom.

They revisit their trademark search report from Trademark Factory® and order All-Inclusive package for the word *BOB-TOM*, their new logo and their tagline *TAKING CARE OF YOUR BOBTOM LINE* as trademarks.

Then they get a law firm to draft detailed terms and conditions and a privacy policy for their website and for their newly released desktop application. The lawyer comes up with the necessary documents to ensure that Bob and Tom are protected.

As their business grows, they realize that most of their customers are actually realtors.

Bob decides that it's time to take the business to a new level and calls the CEO of FW/MIN, a multinational real estate conglomerate. Amazingly, they are interested in licensing the software for all of their realtors. They even want an exclusive! They even prepared their own contract!

Remembering the story about the book writer who sold his book for 30% and got nothing, Bob rushes back to see the lawyer to make sure he is not signing the business away for peanuts. The lawyer goes through the contract with a fine-tooth comb and spots a number of areas that could lead to trouble. Together with the lawyer who acts for FW/MIN, they craft a much better agreement that takes care of both parties.

In exchange for a recurring fat cheque from FW/MIN, BOB-TOM agrees to grant FW/MIN an exclusive subscription and no longer offer the software to others on a subscription basis. However, BOBTOM reserves the right to process one-off requests from anyone.

Tom modifies the software to take care of this.

Surprisingly, the one-off business generates a lot of money on top of the monthly payments from FW/MIN. One day, Tom gets a call from a lawyer acting for ChinaSteal Co. who offers Tom $150,000 if he agrees to disclose the algorithm. Tom is bound by the contract he signed with Bob, and according to it, Tom would lose much more than $150,000. Tom decides not to take the risk.

Ironically, two days later, Bob gets an offer from the CEO of FW/MIN to buy 100% of BOBTOM's shares.

Bob and Tom do the math and decide that it's a good idea. Once again, they head back to the lawyer. After the lawyer goes through the agreement and makes a number of changes, the deal is closed. According to the deal, FW/MIN will acquire 100% of BOBTOM's shares and all of its assets, including the trademarks and the copyright in the software.

And they all live happily ever after.

Of course, this is a simplified story, but it shows you how IP can make a business and how it can break a business. In this example, Bob and Tom started with something that was bound to fail. Bob was quick to recognize the risks and decided to pivot in a new direction. There was no certainty that the new direction would lead to success, but at least the foundations were there. And the investment in proper foundations paid off in spades!

IN CONCLUSION

Today, intellectual property is not just a fancy addition to a business; it *is* the business for millions of people and businesses around the world.

If you are serious about growing your business into a massive success, you owe it to yourself and everyone involved in your business to make sure that you've done everything you can to protect whatever makes you money. Look at intellectual property laws as your toolbox to build a competitive advantage. Hire your lawyers as handymen who are going to use that toolbox to help you build your dream.

I was an insider to the intellectual property industry for most of my life—first as a lawyer, and now as the CEO of Trademark Factory®,— and I can honestly say that the best thing about it has never been the money. It's the ability to deal with brilliant people who come up with amazing ideas that I can help them protect and to become a part of their dream that drives me to do what I do.

I hope you found this book useful and that you will continue using it as your reference point for everything that concerns intellectual property.

And if you need any further help or advice, just send me an email at ***andrei@mincovlaw.com***.

APPENDIX

CONSOLIDATED CHART

YOUR REFERENCE POINT FOR ALL IP

Use the chart below to compare aspects of different areas of IP discussed in this book.

I am sorry for using a microscopic font in this chart. I had to sacrifice legibility to usefulness. The value of the chart is in that it assembles a ton of information in one place. Increasing the font size would make it impossible. Moreover, you can study the same charts for separate areas of IP throughout this book under Your Reference Point sections.

	COPYRIGHT	NEIGHBOURING RIGHTS (a.k.a. RELATED RIGHTS)	TRADEMARKS	PATENTS	INDUSTRIAL DESIGNS (a.k.a. DESIGN PATENTS)	TRADE SECRETS (a.k.a. KNOW-HOW or CONFIDENTIAL INFORMATION)	CONTRACTUAL RIGHTS
What's protected	*the HOW*	*the HOW*	*the WHICH*	*the WHAT*	*the WOW*	*the HUSH*	*the WHATEVER*
Definition of the protected objects	Original literary, dramatic, musical, and artistic works, that is, an original expression (of an idea) fixed in some (usually, tangible) form + Canada also provides limited protection for moral rights: - the right to the integrity of the work; - the right to be associated with the work as its author.	- fixed or unfixed performances of a work by a performer; - sound recordings, including sound recordings of a performance; - broadcasts (communication signals) + Canada also has limited protection for moral rights in respect of live aural performances and performances fixed in a sound recording:	A mark (words, names, symbols, devices, sounds, smells, trade dress) used to distinguish the goods and services of aone business from similar goods and services of all other businesses. + In Canada, it is possible to register the non-functional shape of a product or its packaging (called distinguishing guise, or 'trade dress').	Any new, non-obvious, and useful art, process, machine, manufacture, or composition of matter, or any new, non-obvious, and useful improvement in any art, process, machine, manufacture, or composition of matter.	Non-functional features relating to the shape, configuration, pattern, or ornament and any combination of those features that, in a finished article, appeal to and are judged solely by the eye.	Any information that is confidential and gives a business an advantage because the information is kept secret.	Permission to do something that one would not otherwise be allowed to do or obligation not to do something that one would otherwise be allowed to do.

	COPYRIGHT	NEIGHBOURING RIGHTS	TRADEMARKS	PATENTS	INDUSTRIAL DESIGNS	TRADE SECRETS	CONTRACTUAL RIGHTS
Definition of the protected objects (cont.)		- the right to the integrity of the performance; - the right to be associated with the performance as its performer.	+ In Canada, it is also possible to register certification marks (*i.e.* marks used to demonstrate that goods and services of different companies meet certain criteria set out by the owner of the certification mark).				
Classes of protected objects	- books; - songs; - films; - videos; - photographs; - artistic works; - illustrations; - paintings; - drawings; - maps; - articles; - marketing materials, pamphlets and other writings; - user manuals; - website contents and look & feel; - computer programs, including HTML, javascript and PHP code;	- performances; - sound recordings (phonograms); - broadcasts.	- word; - symbol; - logo; - design; - slogan; - trade dress; - non-functional shape of the product or its packaging.	Functional features of: - tools; - devices; - machines; - processes; - methods; - ingredients.	Ornamental designs for any tangible products (not pure art and not relating to the function).	- know-how; - confidential information; - any other information that is valuable because it is secret.	- license; - assignment of intellectual property rights; - non-disclosure provisions; - non-competition provisions; - other positive and negative obligations.

YOUR REFERENCE POINT FOR ALL IP

The Ultimate Insider's Guide to Intellectual Property

	COPYRIGHT	NEIGHBOURING RIGHTS	TRADEMARKS	PATENTS	INDUSTRIAL DESIGNS	TRADE SECRETS	CONTRACTUAL RIGHTS
Classes of protected objects (cont.)	- tables; - lectures; - operas and other musical works; - dramatic or dramatico-musical works; - plays; - choreography; - compilations; - translations; - charts; - plans; - engravings; - sculptures; - architecture; - works of artistic craftsmanship; - sketches; - etc.						
Examples	- Ayn Rand's novel *Atlas Shrugged*; - *Rambo* the movie; - Salvador Dali's paintings; - architectural plans for the CN Tower; - computer code (but not the underlying idea) for *Microsoft Windows* operating system; - computer code for Facebook; - instructions manual for iPhone;	- any and each live performance of "I Wanna Be Somebody" by W.A.S.P.; - sound recording of Michael Jackson's *"Thriller"*; - broadcasts of the Olympics.	- *iPad* name; - ✓ - "I'm Lovin' It" slogan; - Mickey Mouse character; - *Coca-Cola* bottle; - MGM Roaring Lion sound; - Nokia tune; - magenta color registered by *T-Mobile*.	- Intermittent windshield wiper; - Streaming of audiovisual content over the Internet; - Amazon's 1-click process.	- design of a chair; - design of jewellery; - watch face plate; - pattern of a fabric.	- *Coca-Cola* formula; - special method for assembling a patented invention; - new invention for which patent application has not been filed	- license to use a song in a game; - permission to use confidential information; - obligation not to make copies of software; - obligation not to work for competitors; - promise not to disclose confidential information.

	COPYRIGHT	NEIGHBOURING RIGHTS	TRADEMARKS	PATENTS	INDUSTRIAL DESIGNS	TRADE SECRETS	CONTRACTUAL RIGHTS
Examples (cont.)	- *The Last Command* album by W.A.S.P. (separate copyrights in music, lyrics, songs as a whole, compilation of songs as a whole, cover artwork; video for the songs "*Blind In Texas*" and "*Wild Child*", but does not include performances of the songs, sound recording of the songs, which are neighbouring rights, see column to the right); - photograph of Einstein with his tongue out; - etc.						
What is needed to get protection?	The work must be minimally original and must be expressed in some form capable of being perceived by others.	The performance, sound recording, and broadcast must be minimally original and must be expressed in some form of being perceived by others.	The mark must be distinctive (i.e. it must be used to distinguish the goods and services of one business from similar goods and services of another business), and not confusingly similar to another trademark.	The invention must be new, useful, and not obvious, and the inventor must "teach" the public how to make and use the invention in the patent application.	The design must not be identical or confusingly similar to a design previously used anywhere in the world or registered in Canada by someone else.	Know-how must be well defined, not publicly known, and protected.	The contract must be valid and enforceable.
What it does not protect	- ideas; - plots; - facts; - methods; - most short phrases and slogans;	- underlying works; - general style of performance;	- company names, unless they are used to distinguish goods or services;	- discoveries of the existing natural order; - non-functional elements of an invention;	- functional elements of the product's appearance (can't protect a cup's handle for the function that it performs, but can protect the aesthetics of it);	Information that has become public knowledge through - voluntary disclosure;	No protection against unauthorized acts of unrelated third parties.

YOUR REFERENCE POINT FOR ALL IP

	COPYRIGHT	NEIGHBOURING RIGHTS	TRADEMARKS	PATENTS	INDUSTRIAL DESIGNS	TRADE SECRETS	CONTRACTUAL RIGHTS
What it does not protect (cont.)	- processes; - algorithms; - features of shape, configuration, patterning or ornamentation as they are applied to useful mass-produced articles (manufactured in 50 or more copies).	- professional secrets of sound recording.	- the generic name of goods or services for which the trademark is used (i.e. can't use "apple" as a trademark for apples); - marks that are clearly descriptive or deceptively misdescriptive of the goods or services, unless they have become distinctive; - personal names unless they have become distinctive as trademarks; - functional elements of the product's shape.	- inventions that are impossible to make (for example, the time machine); - inventions that are obvious based on the level of knowledge at the time the patent is applied for.	- features that are invisible at the time of purchase or during normal use; - processes; - principles of construction; - construction materials; - art that is of value independent of the products to which it may be applied.	- failure to take proper steps to protect it; - general knowledge of the public; - or any other way not related to an unauthorized disclose such as a breach of an NDA.	
Enforceable against	Anyone who uses the work without the copyright owner's consent.	Anyone who uses the performance, phonogram, or broadcast without the copyright owner's consent.	Anyone who uses the trademark in association with goods or services for which the trademark is registered or otherwise in a way that causes or is likely to cause confusion with the registered trademark.	- For product patents: anyone making or selling a product that has all the main features covered by the patent; - For process patents: anyone using the process to achieve a result that has all the main features covered by the patent.	Anyone making or selling products to which a registered design has been applied.	The person to whom the trade secret is disclosed under the obligation of confidentiality; Anyone who receives information from a third party, knowing that by disclosing this information such third party is violating its confidentiality obligations.	The counterparty to the agreement.

	COPYRIGHT	NEIGHBOURING RIGHTS	TRADEMARKS	PATENTS	INDUSTRIAL DESIGNS	TRADE SECRETS	CONTRACTUAL RIGHTS
What constitutes use? / What are others prohibited from doing?	Simply put, copyright prohibits others from copying the expression. In greater detail: it prohibits others from doing anything with the work or a substantial part of the work that only the copyright owner has the right to do, unless the copyright owner gives consent. This refers to the exclusive right of the copyright owner to do or authorize others to do the following: - publishing an unpublished work; - producing or reproducing the work in any material form whatever (which includes making a single copy); - performing the work in public; - creating and using any translation of the work; - converting or adapting a work into a different form;	Simply put, neighbouring rights prohibit others from copying the expression. With respect to performances: - recording previously unrecorded performances; - broadcasting previously unrecorded performances; - making copies of unauthorized recordings of the performance; - renting out sound recordings of the performance. With respect to sound recordings: - publishing unpublished sound recordings; - making copies of the sound recording; - renting out of the sound recording. With respect to broadcasts: - recording broadcasts;	With respect to goods (wares), a trademark is deemed to be used if: - the trademark is marked on the goods; - the trademark is otherwise associated with the goods in the mind of the purchaser; - the trademark is marked on the goods' package; - the trademark is marked on the goods or the goods' packaging, if the goods are exported from Canada. With respect to services, a trademark is deemed to be used if the trademark is used or displayed in the performance or advertising of those services. Third parties are prohibited from causing confusion in the minds of consumers between their goods or services and those of a trademark owner.	- making, constructing, using, or selling a product patent; - using a method described in the patent.	Making or selling any product to which an industrial design has been applied.	Using or disseminating confidential information without authorization.	Violating the terms of the contract, whatever they are.

	COPYRIGHT	NEIGHBOURING RIGHTS	TRADEMARKS	PATENTS	INDUSTRIAL DESIGNS	TRADE SECRETS	CONTRACTUAL RIGHTS
What constitutes use? / What are others prohibited from doing? (cont.)	- presenting the work at a public exhibition; - communicating the work to the public by telecommunication (which includes sending it over the internet); - renting out the work (in case of computer programs or recorded musical works); - selling or otherwise distributing an infringing copy of the work (even if the infringing copy was made by someone else).	- making copies of unauthorized recordings of a broadcast; - authorizing simultaneous retransmissions of the broadcast; - demonstrating TV broadcasts in a place open to the public for a fee.	In case of registered trademarks, the confusion is implied if someone uses another's trademark in association with goods or services for which the trademark is registered.				
Where is the owner/ author/ inventor protected?	Each country protects separately, but protection is almost automatically worldwide thanks to international treaties (Berne Convention, WCT, TRIPS).	Each country protects separately, but protection is almost automatically worldwide thanks to international treaties (Rome Convention, WPPT, TRIPS).	Only in those countries where the trademark protection is sought. Unlike Canada and the U.S., most countries do not recognize unregistered trademarks, so the protection only extends to countries where the trademark has been registered, and a small number of countries where the trademark has not been registered but has been used by the trademark owner to distinguish its goods or services.	The countries where the patent is granted.	The countries where the industrial design is registered.	Country of origin or in other countries where the contract is enforceable.	Depending on enforceability of the contractual provisions in different jurisdictions.

	COPYRIGHT	NEIGHBOURING RIGHTS	TRADEMARKS	PATENTS	INDUSTRIAL DESIGNS	TRADE SECRETS	CONTRACTUAL RIGHTS
Length of protection	In Canada, the general term of protection of the copyright is the life of the author (or the last surviving coauthor in case of co-authorship) of a work plus 50 years after his death. In most other countries, the general term of protection of copyright is the life of the last surviving author or coauthor plus 70 years.	In Canada, 50 years after: - unfixed performance takes place; - fixation of the performance; - fixation of the sound recording; - broadcast takes place.	As long as business continuously uses the trademark in connection with the goods or services with which the trademark is associated. For registered trademarks, a renewal is required in Canada every 15 years. The renewal term is 10 years in most other countries.	20 years from the date of filing for the patent application.	In Canada, 10 years after the registration of the industrial design. In the U.S., 14 years after the registration of the design patent.	As long as information remains confidential and functions as a trade secret.	For the term agreed upon in the contract.
Can the initial period of protection be extended?	No.	No.	Trademark protection is indefinite (see above). However, maintenance is required (periodic filings and fees).	No.	No.	No.	By amending the contract.
Who owns the right / Who should apply for registration of the right?	The first owner of copyright in a work is usually the individual who created the work (the author). The most notable exception to this rule pertains to works created during the course of employment, in which case the default rule is that it is the author's employer who is automatically the first owner of copyright.	The first owner of the copyright in a performer's performance is the performer. The first owner of copyright in a sound recording is the maker of the sound recording. The first owner of copyright in a communication signal is the broadcaster that broadcasts it.	Trademark owner: the person or the business entity (e.g., corporation) which uses or controls the use of the trademark. Trademarks can be assigned to another person or company, but the new owner must use the trademark, and the use must not confuse the public as to who is the owner of the trademark.	Inventor. Patents can be transferred to another person or company.	Proprietor of a design. Industrial designs can be transferred to another person or company.	Whoever controls the information owns the trade secret. No registration is available.	Whoever is the beneficiary of the other party's obligation. No registration is generally available.

339

YOUR REFERENCE POINT FOR ALL IP

The Ultimate Insider's Guide to Intellectual Property

	COPYRIGHT	NEIGHBOURING RIGHTS	TRADEMARKS	PATENTS	INDUSTRIAL DESIGNS	TRADE SECRETS	CONTRACTUAL RIGHTS
Who owns the right / Who should apply for registration of the right? (cont.)	Copyright may be transferred to any other person or company. As to moral rights, as in most other countries, they cannot be assigned to third parties in Canada. However, in Canada, it is possible to waive moral rights.	Neighbouring rights may be transferred to any other person or company. As to moral rights, as in most other countries, they cannot be assigned to third parties in Canada. However, in Canada, it is possible to waive moral rights.	Trademarks can also be licensed to another person or company. However the licensor is required to exercise control over the quality of goods and services offered by its licensees under the licensed trademark.				
Do owners / authors / inventors have some rights if they do not apply for protection?	Yes. Generally, copyright is secured when the work is created. However, there are significant benefits obtained by registration (see below).	Yes. Generally, neighbouring rights are secured when the work is created. However, there are significant benefits obtained by registration (see below).	Yes. So long as you are not infringing on another trademark, some rights in a trademark can be acquired by simply using it in commerce. However, a registered trademark provides additional significant benefits (see below).	No.	No.	Yes. Trade secrets cannot be registered at all.	Yes. The parties may rely on the contract.
What are the benefits of applying for protection?	- A registration certificate creates a presumption that the work is protected by copyright; - A registration certificate creates a presumption of ownership of the work; - A registration certificate serves as evidence of ownership of the work;	- A registration certificate creates a presumption that the performance, sound recording, or a broadcast is protected as a neighbouring right; - A registration certificate creates a presumption of ownership of the performance, sound recording, or a broadcast;	- Registration protects your trademark all across Canada, whereas unregistered trademarks can only protect you in geographical areas where you can prove that your brand is known to enough customers;	It is the registration of a patent that creates protection. Without registration, the invention is not protected for what it stands.	It is the registration of an industrial design that creates protection. Without registration, unless other forms of intellectual property (notably, copyright or a trademark) cover the design, anyone can apply the design to their products.	N/A	N/A

	COPYRIGHT	NEIGHBOURING RIGHTS	TRADEMARKS	PATENTS	INDUSTRIAL DESIGNS	TRADE SECRETS	CONTRACTUAL RIGHTS
What are the benefits of applying for protection? (cont.)	- Registration creates a presumption that the infringer was aware that the work is protected by copyright; - A copyright owner may demand damages from an unaware defendant; - In the U.S., a copyright owner may only claim statutory damages (that is, compensation that is not derived from what the plaintiff lost as the result of the infringement) for infringement of copyright, if the copyright has been registered.	- A registration certificate serves as evidence of ownership of the performance, sound recording, or a broadcast; - Registration creates a presumption that the infringer was aware of the subsistence of copyright in the performance, sound recording, or a broadcast; - Copyright owner may demand damages from an unaware defendant; - In the U.S., copyright owner may only claim statutory damages for infringement of copyright, if the copyright had been registered.	- You can apply to register a trademark before you start offering products or services under that brand to the public. Unregistered trademarks are only protected if they are well known to the public; - A registered trademark is presumed valid. A certificate of registration proves ownership of the mark. Often, showing the certificate to the judge is sufficient to establish rights to the trademark. In case of unregistered trademarks, you must prove that your name, logo, and tagline are actually your own them; - Registration serves as public notice that its owner has a claim to exclusivity of that mark; - After 5 years of being registered, a trademark becomes incontestable, unless it was registered with knowledge of the prior rights of third parties;				

	COPYRIGHT	NEIGHBOURING RIGHTS	TRADEMARKS	PATENTS	INDUSTRIAL DESIGNS	TRADE SECRETS	CONTRACTUAL RIGHTS
What are the benefits of applying for protection? (cont.)			- A registered trademark allows non-Canadian owners to register corresponding .CA domain names because it fulfills the "Canadian Presence requirements" of the Canadian Internet Registration Authority (CIRA); - The term of registration is 15 years, renewable an unlimited number of times; - Registration provides additional statutory remedies against trademark infringement, depreciation of the value of goodwill, and losing the rights to the trademark as a result of the adoption of a confusing official mark by a third party; - A registered trademark is a valuable asset and can be more readily sold or licensed. It also increases the value of a company.				

	COPYRIGHT	NEIGHBOURING RIGHTS	TRADEMARKS	PATENTS	INDUSTRIAL DESIGNS	TRADE SECRETS	CONTRACTUAL RIGHTS
How is the right established?	Copyright emerges merely by virtue of a qualifying work being created. Registration of copyright adds certain procedural rights and creates evidentiary presumptions, but is not required to claim that the work is protected by copyright. Copyright exists regardless of whether the work has been registered.	Neighbouring rights emerge merely by virtue of a qualifying performance, sound recording or broadcast being created. Registration of copyright adds certain procedural rights and affords evidentiary presumptions, but is not a legal requirement for subsistence of the right itself.	Common law trademarks: through use in trade. Registered trademarks: through registration with trademark offices in the countries where trademark protection is sought.	Through issuance of the patent by patent offices in the countries where patent protection is sought.	Through registration of the industrial design (issuance of a design patent) by intellectual property offices of the countries where the protection is sought.	Possession of information which is valuable because it is kept in secret.	Entering into a contract, written or oral.
Defences & limitations	- less than a substantial part of the work or other subject matter is used; - work / other subject matter is no longer protected by copyright; - plaintiff is not the copyright owner (wrong plaintiff); - in case of infringement of moral rights, plaintiff is not the author or performer (wrong plaintiff); - plaintiff granted the defendant a license; - expiration of limitation period (3 years). Canada also recognizes certain circumstances, in which unauthorized use of another's work does not constitute an infringement. These circumstances form part of the so called fair dealing doctrine, which provides for the following exceptions from the general rule that protected works may only be used with the consent of the copyright owner:		- the trademark is not "used"; - the plaintiff's trademark is invalid; - the plaintiff's trademark was not registrable at the date of registration; - the plaintiff's trademark is not distinctive; - the plaintiff abandoned the trademark; - the plaintiff was not the person entitled to secure the registration;	- the plaintiff's patent is invalid (prior art, obviousness, improper scope of claims, fraud, non-statutory subject matter); - plaintiff's patent has expired; - defendant's prior commercial use; - plaintiff does not own patent (wrong plaintiff); - antitrust violation;	- denial of infringement; - the plaintiff's design is not proper subject-matter for registration; - design was published more than 1 year prior to the application for registration; - the declaration accompanying the application for registration was false; - the design is not original;	- the plaintiff failed to take reasonable steps to keep the information secret; - the defendant legally obtained the information independently of the plaintiff; - the information was not defined clearly, so the defendant cannot be deemed to have used it.	- contract or provision invalid or unenforceable; - acquiescence / estoppel(plaintiff's conduct that leads the defendant to believe that the plaintiff will not enforce its legal right against the defendant).

YOUR REFERENCE POINT FOR ALL IP

The Ultimate Insider's Guide to Intellectual Property

	COPYRIGHT	NEIGHBOURING RIGHTS	TRADEMARKS	PATENTS	INDUSTRIAL DESIGNS	TRADE SECRETS	CONTRACTUAL RIGHTS
Defences & limitations (cont.)	- use for the purpose of research or private study; - use for the purpose of criticism or review; - use for the purpose of news reporting; - certain uses by educational institutions; - certain uses by libraries, archives, and museums; - incidental use; - certain uses by broadcasters; - certain uses by persons with perceptual disabilities; - use for the purpose of education; - use for the purposes of parody or satire; - creation of non-commercial, user-generated content; - use by reproducing works for private purposes; - use by recording programs for later listening or viewing; - making backup copies; - use to ensure interoperability of computer programs; - and certain other exceptions.		- plaintiff's fraud; - prior concurrent use of the trademark by the defendant in good faith; - good faith use of the defendant's personal name as a trade name; - good faith right to use, other than as a trademark, of the geographical name of the defendant's place of business; - good faith right to use, other than as a trademark, of any accurate description of the character or quality of the defendant's goods or services; - acquiescence + delay (plaintiff's conduct that leads the defendant to believe that the plaintiff will not enforce its legal right against the defendant).	- acquiescence + delay (plaintiff's conduct leads the defendant to believe that the plaintiff will not enforce its legal right against the defendant); - plaintiff granted the defendant a license; - limitation period has expired (6 years).	- defendant's lack of knowledge about registration because of plaintiff's failure to mark the products with D in a circle → injunction only remedy; - plaintiff is not the registered proprietor of the design (wrong plaintiff); - plaintiff granted the defendant a license; - lapse of registration through failure to pay maintenance fees; - registration expired; and - limitation period expired (3 years).		

	COPYRIGHT	NEIGHBOURING RIGHTS	TRADEMARKS	PATENTS	INDUSTRIAL DESIGNS	TRADE SECRETS	CONTRACTUAL RIGHTS
Available remedies	- injunction; - damages (including exemplary and punitive damages); - statutory damages from $500 to $20,000 for each work if infringement is for commercial purposes; - statutory damages from $100 to $5,000 for all works if infringement is for non-commercial purposes; - accounting of profits; - delivery up of infringing materials to the plaintiff.	- injunction; - damages (including exemplary and punitive damages); - statutory damages from $500 to $20,000 for each performance, sound recording or broadcast if infringement is for commercial purposes; - statutory damages from $100 to $5,000 for all performances, sound recordings and broadcasts if infringement is for non-commercial purposes; - accounting of profits; - delivery up of infringing materials to the plaintiff.	- injunction; - damages; - accounting of profits; - destruction, exportation, or other disposition of offending goods.	- injunction; - damages (including exemplary and punitive damages).	- injunction; - damages (including exemplary and punitive damages); - accounting of profits; - disposal of any infringing product.	- injunction; - damages (including exemplary and punitive damages).	- injunction; - damages (including exemplary and punitive damages).
When can it be registered?	Because registration is not a prerequisite for existence of copyright, it can be registered at any time.	Because registration is not a prerequisite for existence of neighbouring rights, they can be registered at any time.	In Canada, a trademark application can be filed on the basis of actual use or an intent to use, but no registration will be issued until the use of the trademark has commenced.	In Canada, an application must be filed no later than 1 year after the first public disclosure of the invention anywhere in the world.	In Canada, an application must be filed no later than 1 year after the first public use of the design.	N/A	N/A

	COPYRIGHT	NEIGHBOURING RIGHTS	TRADEMARKS	PATENTS	INDUSTRIAL DESIGNS	TRADE SECRETS	CONTRACTUAL RIGHTS
When can it be registered? (cont.)	Registration after the infringement will not usually grant the plaintiff the presumptions otherwise made available by the registration.	Registration after the infringement will not usually grant the plaintiff the presumptions otherwise made available by the registration.	Unlike Canada and the U.S., most countries allow registration of trademarks that have not yet been used.	Provisional patent applications in the U.S. normally are not considered public disclosure, but every non-provisional patent application or any other public disclosure of the invention anywhere in the world will trigger the commencement of the 12-month period during which patent applications must be filed in all countries where the patent protection will eventually be sought.			
How long does the registration take?	2–4 weeks in Canada, unless the Copyright Office staff requests that the application be amended. About 6 months in the U.S., unless the Copyright Office staff requests that the application be amended.	2–4 weeks in Canada, unless the Copyright Office staff requests that the application be amended. About 6 months in the U.S., unless the Copyright Office staff requests that the application be amended.	18–24 months in Canada. 9–15 months in the U.S.	4–6 years.	6–12 months.	N/A	N/A
Are there mandatory maintenance fees?	No.	No.	Regular renewals every 15 years. In Canada, the renewal fee is $350.	Yes. Annual maintenance fees are required to keep an application / patent alive. The fees range from $100 to $450.	Yes. To keep a Canadian registration in force for the full 10-year term, a maintenance fee of $350 must be paid before the 5th anniversary of the registration date.	N/A	N/A

	COPYRIGHT	NEIGHBOURING RIGHTS	TRADEMARKS	PATENTS	INDUSTRIAL DESIGNS	TRADE SECRETS	CONTRACTUAL RIGHTS
Are there mandatory maintenance fees? (cont.)			The trademark must continue to be in use by the trademark owner to avoid the risk of it being cancelled at the request of a competitor.		No maintenance fees are payable in the U.S.		
Government fees relating to registration	$50 per work in Canada. $35 per registration in the U.S.	$50 per performance / sound recording / broadcast. $35 per registration in the U.S.	In Canada, for the filing of a trademark application, the government fee is $250. If the trademark is allowed, the registration fee is another $200.	Filing of an application $400. Request for examination fee is $800. Final fee for registration is $300. *Only half of the fees are payable by universities and companies with 50 employees or less.	$400 per design.	N/A	N/A
Total ballpark cost if a lawyer / trademark agent / patent agent is involved (including government fees)	$200–$500 per registration.	$200–$500 per registration.	$1,700–$7,000 per registration.	$5,000–$15,000 per registration.	$1,500–$3,000 per registration.	N/A	N/A

A FEW WORDS ABOUT
ANDREI MINCOV AND THIS BOOK

Andrei Mincov has been passionate about intellectual property ever since he helped his father, a famous Russian composer, defend his rights against a radio station that used his music without permission.

For over 20 years, Andrei was an intellectual property lawyer. He has helped hundreds of clients, big and small, protect their ideas and cover their assets.

*Andrei Mincov is the founder and the CEO of Trademark Factory International Inc. (**http://TrademarkFactory.com**), the only firm in the world where licensed lawyers and trademark agents can help you trademark your brands for a single all-inclusive flat fee with a 100% money-back guarantee.*

His goal is to help business owners maximize their competitive advantage through proper use of intellectual property.

This book is written with non-lawyers in mind and will be particularly useful to business owners and entrepreneurs.